Sarah Reece

The JOY of *Language*

A Christian Framework for Language Arts Instruction

Robert W. Bruinsma

The King's University College
Edmonton, Alberta

The JOY of *Language*

A Christian Framework for Language Arts Instruction

Author: Robert W. Bruinsma
Editor: Mary Endres
Designer: Michael Riester

P.O. Box 35097
Colorado Springs, CO 80935-3509
www.acsi.org

Printed in Canada

ISBN 1-58331-057-6

10 9 8 7 6 5 4 3 2 1 0

Permissions

The section in chapter 4, "An Example: *A Wrinkle in Time* vs. *Big Red,*" appeared previously as part of Robert W. Bruinsma, "Of Dogs and Witches: Dangerous Books in the Christian School Classroom," in *Christian Educators Journal* 33, no. 1 (1993): 15–17, © Christian Educators Journal Association. Used by permission.

Figure 5-1: "The Initial Teaching Alphabet" is from John A. Downing, *How Your Children Are Being Taught to Read with I.T.A.* London: W. & R. Chambers, 1964. No copyright.

The section "The Modern Context" in chapter 5 is adapted from Robert W. Bruinsma, "A Rose by Any Other Name: Response to James Rooks," in *Journal of Research on Christian Education* 4, no. 2 (1995): 271–275. Adapted with permission.

The section "Introduction: An Emergent Literacy Story" in chapter 8 is from Robert W. Bruinsma. "Upside-Down i's and Other Conventions of Print: A Literacy Story," in *Early Childhood Education* 17, no. 1 (1984): 22–25: © The Alberta Teachers Association. Used by permission.

Figure 10-1: "Oral Language Activities for a Grade 6 Social Studies Unit on Ancient Greece" is adapted from box 2.4, pages 47–48, in Joyce Bainbridge and Grace Malicky, *Constructing Meaning: Balancing Elementary Language Arts,* 2nd ed. (Toronto, ON: 2000), © Harcourt Canada. Adapted with permission.

Figure 11-3: "Thirty-Seven High-Frequency Spelling Patterns with Key Words" and figure 11-4: "Key beginning letters and their sounds" are from Patricia M. Cunningham, *Phonics They Use: Words for Reading and Writing,* 3rd ed. (Boston: 2000): pp. 94 and 90, © Addison Wesley/Longman. Used by permission.

The section "Literature Units: Novel Studies" in chapter 11 is adapted from Lloyd Den Boer, ed., *Christian Pathways for Schooling: Language Arts Handbook,* 2nd ed. (Langley, BC: 1996), © Society of Christian Schools in British Columbia. Adapted with permission.

The section "Dyslexia" in chapter 11 is from Patricia Campbell, *Teaching Reading to Adults: A Balanced Approach* (Edmonton, AB: 2003), © Grass Roots Press. Used by permission of the author.

Appendix 1: "Request for Reconsideration of a Book" is from Evelyn Sterenberg and Sharon DeMoor, *Libraries in the 90's: A Handbook for Christian Schools* (Edmonton, AB: 1991), Christian Schools International District 11. Used by permission of Prairie Association of Christian Schools.

Appendix 2: "Readability: Evaluating Text Difficulty" is from Edward B. Fry, "Fry's Readability Graph: Clarifications, Validity, and Extension to Level 17," *Journal of Reading* 21, no. 3 (1977): 242–252. No copyright. Used by permission of the author.

Contents

Acknowledgments

Writing a book must be a little like having a baby (although, as a man, I may be highly presumptuous in saying this). In the final analysis the baby is carried and delivered by its mother, but the entire process, from conception to delivery, is usually aided by a large number of supportive people including the father, siblings, grandparents, family friends, and medical personnel. And, of course, the whole process depends on God's grace for a happy delivery. So it has been with this book.

The year 2001 marked my twentieth anniversary as an education professor at the King's University College. While teaching a variety of courses in language arts, developing an accredited teacher education program, and serving as chair of the education department for six years, I also managed to do some writing and research in the field. In 1989–90, I wrote a small book, *Language Arts in Christian Schools* (Bruinsma 1990a), which is now out of print. In the years since then, extensive research has changed our understanding of how children become literate and how best to support them in this endeavor. Even so, much has remained the same, and I believe that the general orientation of my 1990 book is still largely valid. However, I also have more to say and want to say it to a wider audience of Christian educators.

During the mid- and late 1990s, I became more involved with Christian educators affiliated with the Association of Christian Schools International (ACSI). At the encouragement of Steve Babbitt, ACSI's director of publishing services, I submitted a prospectus for a book to ACSI in early 2000 and applied for a sabbatical from my university. Both ventures proved successful. I began this writing project in July 2001 and delivered a draft of the manuscript in June 2002. The process took a little longer than the usual pregnancy—but then, I took some vacation time as well.

I am especially grateful to the King's University College for the full year away from my regular duties to pursue this project. King's is a small undergraduate Christian liberal arts and sciences college that, despite limited resources, has always encouraged and supported research and scholarship among its faculty. The library staff at King's also deserve thanks for allowing me to borrow more books for longer periods of time than "regulations" generally permit. Jerry Mathis, from the dean's office, took my hand-scribbled figures and used his considerable computer skills to produce the tidy figures that appear in the book.

Three reviewers deserve special mention. I felt it important to have regular feedback on my writing efforts from others in the field so that I wouldn't be working entirely alone. Dr. Gloria Stronks, professor emeritus from Calvin College, and Dr. James Rooks, also from Calvin, were brutally honest in their critiques of various chapters. While we did not see eye to eye on every issue, their insights and reactions have made this a far better book. Debbie Benson, language arts teacher extraordinaire at the Northeast campus of Edmonton Christian School, provided a practitioner's view and made many valuable suggestions that also improved the manuscript immeasurably.

Joel Kleine, a former student of mine who is just concluding his first year of teaching, has a poet's heart and ear, so I asked him to contribute a short section on teaching poetry. Joel cajoled his wife Amanda into helping him, and their work appears in chapter 12. I thank them for taking the time from their demanding schedules to make this contribution.

Cheryl Mahaffy took time out of her own busy professional writing and editing career to greatly improve my prose and to catch the innumerable typos, spelling errors, and grammatical glitches that I generated each writing day without fail. If my comparison of writing a book to having a baby has any merit, then Cheryl is undoubtedly the midwife.

Once a manuscript reaches the publisher, an author's fate is pretty much in the hands of the company editor. In my case, those hands belonged to Mary Endres of *Purposeful Design Publications*, and capable hands they were. Mary and I communicated extensively by email. She was always respectful of my suggestions, and the book, in turn, benefited greatly from her sure editing instincts.

A book manuscript is delivered to the publisher in a format wholly unsuitable for printing. It is the graphic designer who determines how the book will "look" in print. This includes matters such as page layout, fonts, and cover design. Mike Riester deserves special credit for the attractive and user-friendly design of the book you hold in your hands.

My son David, the only one of my three children still living at home and a remarkable writer in his own right, provided good company and cheer throughout my sabbatical year.

My wife Louisa deserves special mention. She faithfully rose early each morning to leave for work without so much as a hint of resentment toward her still-sleeping husband, whose flexible work schedule must have seemed an undeserved luxury. She also provided encouragement during the tough spells that invariably come in a writing project. Her basic advice was to "tell more stories." While I didn't listen to her nearly enough, the classroom vignettes and scenarios found in the book are there largely because of her insistence.

Finally, I thank God for the opportunity that this sabbath provided to recharge my intellectual batteries, and I pray that the result may benefit college students, teachers, and parents, but especially the students who spend so many hours in school "taking language arts." It is my hope that the language arts will take them to places of linguistic joy and service to God and neighbor, and that this book may have helped them in the journey.

Introduction

Language is a great gift from God that allows humans to communicate with Him and with one another. The encoding of oral language into written, symbolic form and the decoding back into oral language has allowed humans to communicate in the present and across time.

God has chosen to communicate with human beings in large measure through words. The Bible speaks to us in words, and it is significant that the apostle John refers to Christ as the incarnate Word of God (John 1). Jesus, our Lord, is God's Word made flesh who came to live among us for a time and whose Spirit still ministers to us daily. It is our joyful duty to serve this Word with the entire business of our lives, much of which we conduct with words. How Christians use language is thus of paramount importance.

The three R's—reading, 'riting, and 'rithmetic—have always constituted the heart of a basic elementary education. The first two, reading and writing, define literacy, which has always been crucial to Protestant education because of the ardent belief that Christians need to be able to read the Holy Bible for themselves. God's revelation also comes to us in creation and in Christ, but it is the written Word, through the working of the Holy Spirit, that testifies of God's dealing with people in history.

Made in the image of God, we humans have been gifted with imagination, and a primary exercise of this gift is in the writing of literature. In fact, the Bible can be seen as God speaking to and through His people in the form of literature.[1] Teaching literacy to each generation is thus an awesome responsibility but also an invitation to joy.

This book explores the teaching of language arts in the context of our primary abilities to listen to and speak language. Together these four areas—listening, speaking, reading, and writing—constitute the language arts. The grade-level focus of this book is on elementary and middle school, or approximately kindergarten through grade 9 in North American schools.

Like all human endeavors in a fallen world, language arts instruction is not without controversy. The teaching of reading especially has been a topic of debate since the beginning of formal schooling in the Western world (Matthews 1966).[2] The battle has been especially heated during the last fifty years in North America, prompting the late Dr. Jeanne Chall of Harvard University to coin the phrase "The Great Debate" to characterize the often acrimonious discussion (Chall 1967, [1996]). The "great debate" has not abated but has in fact escalated to the status of "reading wars" (Goodman 1998). During the 1980s and 1990s, the debate expanded to encompass the language arts in general. The two main camps in this "war" have become identified as **whole language** and **phonics** or **skills-based.**[3] In a survey of Christian school teachers, Mark Thogmartin (1994) found that most respondents identified with the "skills-based" camp, especially regarding the central role of phonics in the teaching of reading. A spirited debate on this issue (to which I contributed [Bruinsma 1994, 1995]) took place in the *Journal of Research on Christian Education*. In part, this book is an attempt to air the debate in a more detailed and accessible manner.

This book ponders what approaches to the teaching of language arts are the most valid in Christian schools on the basis of a Christian view of the learner and the nature of knowledge. It discusses the place for teaching skills such as phonics, grammar, spelling, and oral reading. But it is equally concerned with larger issues, not only the *how* of language arts teaching in Christian schools but also the *why* and *what:*

- Why should children read, anyway?
- What should children read, and when should they read it?
- What constitutes "good literature"? Who decides these matters?
- Who decides what a text means? Is meaning made or found?
- Is learning to read and write essentially the same as or different from learning to speak?
- What about spelling? (Is it really a sin to spell badly, as a teacher acquaintance of mine insists?)
- How is it that some children find learning to read and write difficult while others learn easily?
- What is phonics? Is it different from phonetics and phonemics? Speaking of phonemics, what is all the fuss concerning phonemic awareness really about?

Many questions—the foregoing list highlights only a few. This book attempts to shed Christian light on these and other literacy-related issues. Central to its purpose is the premise that biblically informed Christian faith provides useful insights that break through the language arts teaching impasse.

Part 1, Establishing a Christian Framework, begins by examining some of the big issues in light of the Christian student as God's image bearer, and by exploring a Christian view of knowledge and how we come to know. Chapter 1 begins there because at the heart of all teaching must be an understanding of *who* the students are and *what* it means to say that we *know* something. I believe the "great debate" can be meaningfully addressed only when we acknowledge that, at its root, the debate is about *fundamental beliefs* regarding these matters.

Chapter 2 of part 1 articulates basic principles to be used in designing a language arts curriculum in the light of the orientation sketched in chapter 1.

Because evaluation is such an important aspect of schooling and should always reflect what we believe about learning, chapter 3 introduces this topic. Later chapters revisit evaluation in the context of specific aspects of language arts teaching.

Language arts education is big business in English-speaking countries. A plethora of materials is available, each accompanied by claims about the efficacy of this or that teaching approach. Chapter 4 provides some suggestions for choosing materials to support Christian language arts teaching.

Part 1 concludes in chapter 5 with a fairly detailed historical examination of the roots of the "great debate." Although this term was coined in the 1960s, it is important to see that the question of how best to teach reading stretches back to antiquity. Especially important for English language arts teachers is some understanding of the development of English and how that history has influenced debates about reading pedagogy.

Part 2, The Foundations of Literacy, begins in chapter 6 with a brief recounting of oral language acquisition, crucial to what follows because all other language performance "floats on the sea of oracy" (Britton 1992). This sketch of how children acquire and use oral language prior to formal schooling underlines the fact that most know a great deal about language upon entering school, and language arts teachers must take this prior knowledge into account.

What happens when language goes to school? Many children who learn oral language with little difficulty struggle with the language-learning demands of school. Chapter 7 examines why this may be and suggests ways to minimize the struggle.

Some children gradually develop a basic understanding of literacy before they reach school. Chapter 8 describes what we know about how this **emergent literacy** happens. Those findings suggest approaches for introducing literacy in school, especially to children who do not come from literacy-rich home environments.

Part 3, The Four Language Arts: Principles and Teaching Practice, focuses specifically on the main language arts components. Most attention is given to the teaching and learning of reading (chapter 11) and writing (chapter 12), although listening (chapter 9) and speaking (chapter 10) also receive some attention.[4] The productive language arts of speaking and writing set the stage for performing; thus these chapters also examine the role of drama in the language arts curriculum. While part 3 can justifiably be viewed as the pedagogical heart of the book, it makes sense only in light of the two foregoing parts.

The book concludes with appendixes that provide information about techniques and teaching strategies useful in helping both teachers and students cope with text material of varying difficulty.

The central purpose of this book is to help Christian teachers and future teachers explore what it means for them and their students to love God and neighbor linguistically. While theoretically and theologically grounded, the book intends to provide concrete and practical insights about many of the issues faced by Christian teachers working in Christian and public school classrooms. Overarching everything presented in this book is my fervent belief that we must help children become literate so that they may become discerning users of God's wonderful gift of language.

I do not claim any infallibility for the views put forward here. We live in an imperfect world where understanding will always be limited by our partial insight (1 Corinthians 13:12). Indeed, the Christian teaching community contains room for a variety of viewpoints and methodologies. But there must surely be some commonality of perspective on major issues if the Christian faith is to be seen as relevant to teaching.

Intended Audiences

It may be useful to discuss briefly for whom this book is written. The two main audiences are Christian pre-service education students in both Christian and secular colleges and universities, and language arts teachers in Christian elementary and middle schools in English-speaking nations (primarily the United States, Canada, Great Britain, Australia, and New Zealand). This includes schools represented by the Association of Christian Schools International (ACSI), Christian Schools International (CSI), and Christian Educators Associations International (CEAI), as well as other Christian school organizations.

I believe pre- and in-service elementary and middle school language arts teachers need to understand the roots of the debate about the teaching of language arts. This book intends to provide a *principled and practical Christian framework* for sorting through the many difficult pedagogical issues they face as they attempt to be biblically and professionally informed. Teachers in state schools will also find this book a useful resource as they struggle with how to teach Christianly in their setting.

Principals will find this book an informative primer on the issues they encounter when helping teachers develop curriculum and choose textbooks, and when evaluating instruction. The book will also inform their dialogue with parents about literacy issues. Curriculum writers will find insights here to assist them in building a framework for a literacy curriculum. I hope the book will also support various Christian organizations' curriculum departments as they develop policies about projects related to language arts. Finally, the book will appeal to those Christian parents who wish to be better informed about this important and often controversial area of the school's teaching program.

It is also important to describe briefly what this book is not. It is *not* intended as a complete textbook about or handbook of teaching skills and strategies for elementary and middle school language arts. Most major secular educational publishers carry such books. This book should help college teachers and their students understand the competing pedagogical orientations that their texts represent, however. Further, it provides specifically Christian insights that won't be found in secular sources. Suggestions throughout point to particular works that I have found helpful in my own teaching and that broadly support the pedagogical orientation developed here.[5]

This book seeks to flesh out for language arts teaching the Christian approach to education developed by my dear Christian friend, Albert E. Greene Jr., in *Reclaiming the Future of Christian Education: A Transforming Vision* (1998). While readers would find it useful to peruse Dr. Greene's book, it is not essential to understanding the issues I raise here. I wish to dedicate this book to Dr. Albert E. Greene Jr., whose deep insights into Christian education have been an inspiration to a generation of Christian teachers.

Endnotes

1 By "literature," I mean any writings of importance in prose or verse. The Bible contains many genres or types of literature, such as poetry, parable, proverb, history, letter, prophecy, and narrative.

2 Complete reference citations are found at the end of the book.

3 Terms appearing in boldface throughout the book are especially important to understanding the issues at hand, and identify important vocabulary for instructors and students. These terms are frequently explicitly defined; in other cases, their meaning can be inferred from context. A useful resource is *The Literacy Dictionary: The Vocabulary of Reading and Writing* (Harris and Hodges 1995).

4 Current views of the language arts usually include viewing as another receptive language art. There is little doubt that children in the English-speaking world spend a great deal more time viewing television, movies, videos, and computer screens than reading print. Although this is not my field of expertise, I do believe it is essential that Christian schools provide students with the insights and skills to be discerning users of the visual media. Many of the critical Christian discernment skills and attitudes can be applied to both print and electronic visual media, but the latter require media-specific analytic strategies as well.

5 An excellent Christian handbook for teaching elementary and middle school language arts is the two-volume work: Lloyd Den Boer, ed. *Christian Pathways for Schooling: Language Arts Handbook,* 2nd ed., published by the Society of Christian Schools in British Columbia, Canada, in 1996. It is available from the SCSBC at 7600 Glover Road, Langley, B.C. V2Y 1Y1 Canada.

Part 1

Establishing a Christian Framework

This section of five chapters develops a Christian framework or context for the whole book. In particular, I will set out my philosophy of language arts teaching and learning.

Chapter 1 examines the relevance of one's view of the learner and of knowledge, what philosophers call one's **anthropology** and **epistemology**, to the teaching enterprise. It is important for readers to know that my own theological tradition is broadly Reformed (neo-Calvinist) and that this perspective will undoubtedly color my views. That is not to say that I am unsympathetic to other Christian traditions but simply to admit that we all live consciously or unconsciously out of worldviews that shape our ways of thinking and being. I believe it is best to be consciously and honestly aware of one's shaping tradition and to alert one's readers to that reality.

Chapter 2 looks broadly at the relevance of the perspective described in chapter 1 for the task of shaping a language arts curriculum. A **curriculum** is the courses of study and the teaching practices of a school. It may be of interest to readers to know that the word *curriculum* has a Latin origin related to our word *circus.* (Perhaps teacher readers will smile at this when they think about some of their classroom experiences.) *Curriculum* actually means "a circuit" or "a course for running a race." Therefore, a curriculum is really the course we wish our students to run. In designing a racecourse, it is always important to know what kind of creatures will run on it and what will count as winning the race. That is why chapter 1 is an essential backdrop for chapter 2.

Chapter 3 examines evaluation in schooling in general terms because the topic is so crucial. The specifics of evaluating the various components of the language arts are found in chapters 8 through 12.

Chapter 4 explores the scary world of resources used in teaching the language arts. I use the word *scary* intentionally because materials and resources get us into the business of marketing education and introduce us to some highly contentious issues that divide many Christians. These issues include such matters as the role of certain kinds of literature in the curriculum as well as the use of commercial materials.

Chapter 5 is pivotal because it deals with a long-standing debate about how best to teach the language arts generally and reading in particular. Much of what follows in parts 2 and 3, especially as it relates to pedagogy (teaching practice), is contextualized by my views of what has become known as the "Great Debate."

Chapter 1

Faith and Teaching the Language Arts

This opening chapter explores some central issues related to teaching in Christian schools, with specific reference to the language arts. We begin by sketching two teaching scenarios that highlight some fundamental differences in the teachers' understanding of the nature of children, learning, and teaching. We also ask what it means to know something, and ponder how this question shapes the language arts curriculum. The chapter concludes by arguing that a Christian view of the child, with its focus on redemption in Christ, should lead Christian teachers to deliberately reject reductionist approaches to teaching and learning and embrace views more compatible with a biblical understanding of covenantal hope.

Two Classroom Scenarios[1]

Scenario One—Jenny Thompson's Class

It is Monday at Redeemer Christian Academy. The grade 1 students tumble into Jenny Thompson's classroom on this sunlit spring morning. The room is bright and cheery, sporting several colorful bulletin boards. One board displays posters about Christian character traits, another features simple math facts, and still another is filled with neatly framed student art depicting "Signs of Spring." Ms. Thompson reminds the children to enter quietly, hang their coats on the hooks, and sit in their desks with hands folded until the morning bell. Soon the bell rings, and Ms. Thompson calls out each child's name while marking her attendance sheet. She then calls the children to the carpeted area. Two boys sit in the back and launch an animated conversation. Ms. Thompson says, "I'm pleased with how quietly most of you are sitting, with your bottoms on the carpet and your hands folded in your laps."

The two boys don't respond to this broad hint about desired behavior. Ms. Thompson reaches over to a part of the wall on which are affixed a long row of paired envelopes, one green and one red per pair. Each envelope pair has a student name on it. She calls out, gently but firmly, "Billy and John!" and picks up a couple of slips of paper from her desk, putting one each in Billy's and John's red envelopes. The boys cease talking and look a bit distraught. They know that slips in the red envelope at the end of the day will prevent them from getting the special prizes Ms. Thompson hands out to those students whose slips are all in the green envelope. "Boys, let's see if you can win those slips back to the green envelope today," encourages Ms. Thompson.

Ms. Thompson asks the children for requests to include in her morning prayer. She then has the "special person" of the day come forward to lead the class through its morning routine of Calendar and Weather Watch. The routine ends with the children singing a gospel song to taped musical accompaniment. The children return to their desks, arranged in five neat rows.

Ms. Thompson sets up an easel on which she displays a "big book" version of Pat Hutchins' *Rosie's Walk* (1968). The brightly illustrated book tells the story of a hen taking a farmyard stroll, completely unaware that a fox is trying to catch her. All manner of disasters befall the fox as he tries to catch Rosie, but Rosie just keeps walking—and gets home in time for dinner—while the fox runs off into the distance, chased by a swarm of bees. Pointing to the cover of the book, Ms. Thompson notes that this is a story about a hen that goes for a walk on the farm, but that something interesting may happen to her. Author and illustrator Pat Hutchins has designed this book so that all the action flows clearly from left to right, with wonderfully clear and expressive artwork that hints about Rosie's predicament and the fox's bad luck. Ms. Thompson reads the book in an expressive voice, stopping once to make sure the children realize that Rosie is being chased by the fox as she walks "across the yard, around the pond, past the mill, over the haystack, through the fence, and under the beehives, getting home in time for dinner."

The children thoroughly enjoy the story, and Ms. Thompson allows a few questions about foxes and hens. She then moves the easel aside and focuses the children's attention on the pocket chart fastened to the front board. Taking out a strip of paper, she neatly prints the word *mill* on it and places it in the center of the top pocket of the chart. "Can anyone tell me what this word says?" she asks. Five or six hands shoot up, and she points to Billy, who says "mill."

"Please use a complete sentence in your answers, Billy," she suggests.

"The word on the chart says *mill*."

"Excellent, Billy," replies Ms. Thompson, moving a slip of paper from Billy's red envelope to his green one. Billy is pleased.

Susan raises her hand and asks, "Ms. Thompson, what's a mill?" Ms. Thompson explains that a mill is place where grain is ground into flour for making bread. She then takes out a number of strips of paper on which she has written the spelling pattern (also called *rime*) *-ill.* She places these below the word *mill* and asks if anyone can suggest another letter that could be placed in front of *-ill* to make a new word. Someone suggests the letter *p.* Pleased, Ms. Thompson places a printed *p* in front of *-ill* to make the word *pill.* The lesson continues in this fashion for a short time, and the children use initial consonant substitution to generate the words *bill, fill, hill, jill* (and then *Jill,* when Ms. Thompson points out that this is a proper noun), *kill* (which Ms. Thompson points out is what the sixth commandment prohibits), *pill,* and *will.* Ms. Thompson adds the words *dill, sill,* and *till* with a brief explanation of each.

The children take out their spelling notebooks and are told to use three of the *-ill* words from the pocket chart in a complete sentence. They review the fact that a complete sentence starts with a capital letter and ends with a period. The children write sentences such as "I do not like to eat my pill," "We slid down the hill," "Thou shalt not kill." The bell rings to signal morning recess, and the language arts lesson is over.

Scenario Two—Hilda Smith's Class

It is Monday at Morning Star Christian School. The grade 1 students in Hilda Smith's class tumble into the classroom on this sunlit spring morning. The room is bright and cheery, sporting a number of colorful bulletin boards. Most of the boards display the children's own work: spring art, illustrated stories, life-sized brown paper cutouts of the children with their height indicated in centimeters, an entire wall devoted to maps of the school grounds drawn roughly to scale. There are also commercially produced posters explaining the meanings of common punctuation marks and mathematical symbols.

As the children enter the room, Ms. Smith stands at the door and greets each by name. She reminds a few to enter the room more quietly, in one case actually restraining a boy who hurtles past. "George," she asks, "why shouldn't you run into the room?" George answers something about how it isn't nice to bump into other people and he could get hurt if he fell against a table. Ms. Smith releases George after giving him a hug.

The children go first to the "Name Wall" and move the slip of paper with their name on it from the OUT envelope to the IN envelope. Some children head to the reading corner and select a book to read or browse in. Others gravitate to centers elsewhere in the room. There is a "Math Center" with a variety of math manipulatives, a "Building Center" with bins of Lego® blocks and large cardboard bricks, and a "Drama Center" with a puppet theater and a big box of dress-up clothes. Some children sit at one of the five hexagonal tables in the room to work on unfinished art.

"Three minutes 'til carpet time," warns Ms. Smith. A couple of minutes later she calls out, "One minute, so hurry." Most of the children stop what they are doing, put the materials back where they belong, and move to the carpeted area in the corner of the room. Finally, Ms. Smith counts 10-9-8-7-6-5-4-3-2-1; only one child, Sam, is not in place when the countdown ends. She moves to Sam and gently but firmly takes him to the group, making a mental note to speak with him later, privately.

Ms. Smith asks whether the children had a good weekend and allows three to describe briefly the most interesting thing they did. The other children know they will have their turn to share in due time. She then asks if there are any special prayer requests, and many hands go up. She reminds the children to listen carefully to the requests and then starts the prayer with the request made by the child closest to her. When done, she pauses, and another child prays for her neighbor's request. Another child says "skip," and Ms. Smith prays for his neighbor's request. In the end, all the requests are included in the prayer, mostly by other children.

The "special person" for the day comes forward to help lead the class through the morning Calendar and Weather Watch. To conclude the routine, Ms. Smith allows the special person to pick a song. Taking a guitar from the side of her desk, she joins the class in a lusty version of "This is the day the Lord has made, Let us rejoice and be glad in it."

Next, Ms. Smith leads the children in some quick on-the-spot exercises to shake out their stiffness and ward off fidgeting. When the children sit down again, she brings out a "big book" version of *Rosie's Walk* by Pat Hutchins. She holds the book so the children can see the cover and asks them to speculate about where the story takes place. Some children begin to blurt out responses, and she reminds them to raise their hands to be recognized. She recognizes Jeremy, who says the story takes place on a farm.

"Tell me one reason you think it takes place on a farm," Ms. Smith responds.

"Because there's a barn and a tractor in the picture," replies Jeremy.

"Good, Jeremy. Now as I point to children with their hands up, they can add to Jeremy's reason for believing this story takes place on a farm." In quick succession, children add words such as "haystack," "chicken coop," and "goat." Ms. Smith points to the windmill in the picture and asks if anyone knows what it is. "A windmill," Heather replies. After further probing, Ms. Smith realizes the children don't know the function of a windmill, so she explains how it can be used for grinding grain. Then she reads the book's title to the children and asks them to speculate who Rosie is.

"Rosie's the chicken in the picture," says Clive. All the children seem to accept this.

"How do you know it's not the fox you see hiding in the corner?" asks Ms. Smith.

"Because Rosie is a dumb name for a fox," ventures Kevin.

"And you can see that the chicken is walking in the picture and the fox is just sort of hiding behind the chicken coop," adds Tamika.

"All right, we'll see if you're correct when we read the story," replies Ms. Smith. "Before I read the story with you though, I want to ask you a question. Who would like to write a book this week?"

The children look at Ms. Smith in some bewilderment. A few tentatively raise their hands. Aaron says, "It's too hard to write a book. I don't know enough words." There is some agreement with Aaron on this point.

"Well," says Ms. Smith, "I have confidence in this class, and I know that by the end of the week most of you will have written a wonderful book." The children look at her with both awe and expectation; they know Ms. Smith well enough by now to realize that this marvelous thing will happen even if they are not sure how.

Ms. Smith opens the cover of the book and points out the name of the author and the dedication page. When she turns the page to where the story begins, the children notice pieces of tagboard paper-clipped to the pages. Ms. Smith explains that for the first time through the book, she has covered the words of the story, and they will simply look at the pictures to see what is happening. The children have great fun watching Rosie take her walk and predicting what will happen to the hapless fox.

After this initial viewing and talking about the book at close quarters, Ms. Smith removes the tagboard from the simple text captions and goes through the story again. This time, she carefully reads the text as she points to the prepositional phrases that tell the story. After asking the children to sit at their tables, she puts the "big book" on the easel in front of the room, next to a pocket chart.

Ms. Smith now moves to the flip chart and asks the students to recall the story. She writes the opening line: "Rosie, the hen, went for a walk...." Then she asks the children where Rosie went. As students contribute phrases such as "across the yard" and "around the pond," she adds those words to the flip chart. When all the phrases have been contributed in the correct order, she writes the concluding phrase, "... and got home in time for dinner."

Ms. Smith quickly cuts out these phrases from the chart paper and passes them out, at random, to various children. She then returns to the book and slowly reads the story. As she does so, the children bring up the slips of paper with the appropriate phrases on them and place them in the pocket chart until the entire story has been charted correctly. Ms. Smith draws attention to the prepositions (without using this technical term) by underlining the word at the start of each phrase with a black marker. She calls them "position words" because "they tell you where Rosie went." Asked to provide other position words, students generate such additional prepositions as *above, below, beside,* and *into.* Ms. Smith prints each one on a blank file card and sticks it to the blackboard with a small piece of sticky putty. Before long, more than 30 prepositions are displayed on the cards.

"Now," says Ms. Smith, "I want each of you to think of your favorite animal and where it might go for a walk that is dangerous, just as Rosie did. Does anyone have an idea?"

Rosemelinda's hand shoots up. She says her favorite animal is a squirrel and that a squirrel could go for a walk *in* the forest, *on* a branch, *through* the leaves, and *under* an oak tree. "And there could be an owl chasing her but she doesn't know this and all sorts of things happen to the owl, but Frisky [the squirrel] gets back to his nest full of nuts."

Henry excitedly raises his hand and tells what kind of walk his favorite animal, the tiger, would take and how a hunter would be chasing him. Soon almost everyone wants to suggest an animal and a dangerous walk.

"Well," says Ms. Smith, "I can see you all have lots of good ideas. Tomorrow when we have language arts again, all of the position words will still be up on the board, and then I'll give you a brand new scribbler in which to write your story and illustrate it. [These scribblers have space for illustrations on the top half of the page, with the bottom half lined for writing.] You may work together in pairs if you wish, with one person being the writer and the other the illustrator. In the meantime, *Rosie's Walk* will stay on the easel in the reading corner, and there are also some small versions for you to read during DEAR (Drop Everything And Read) time this afternoon."

"Can't we start now, Ms. Smith?" asks Henry, who can just imagine the fantastic walk he will take his tiger on. Just then the buzzer rings, and the children go outside for recess.

During the rest of the week, Ms. Smith helps the children write their stories, aided by a parent volunteer, who spends extra time with some of the slower children. The children make laminated covers for their books and dedicate them "just like a real author." The completed books will be used for both individual and shared reading in the weeks to come. Ms. Smith will also use *Rosie's Walk* as the basis for brief but direct minilessons on letter sounds and word recognition, and she'll use its vocabulary for spelling and printing lessons.

Views of the Child in Teaching and Learning

Anthropology and Epistemology

It should be evident that both of the teachers in the foregoing scenarios care deeply about children and plan their lessons carefully. Yet they hold significantly different beliefs about the nature of children, about how children learn, and about what is worth knowing.

Central to a search for wise teaching methodology (pedagogy) should be consideration of the nature of the learner as well as the nature of knowledge. The former, philosophers call **anthropology**; the latter, **epistemology**. These are large philosophical and theological issues that neither the brevity of this book nor the depth of my insight can adequately explore. Still, Christian teachers in all disciplines and grade levels must surely consider these matters if they are to be considered responsible professionals.

While the Bible does not serve as a textbook for understanding learning or any other academic endeavor, several fundamental biblical themes can shed light on what it means to be human and to learn. The central narrative motif in the Bible encompasses *creation* by God, the *fall* of humans into sin, *redemption* by and through Christ, and the *restoration* of creation at Christ's return. How should these themes shape our understanding of the learner and the learning process? At a conference for Christian educators, Donovan Graham of Covenant College shared a useful perspective on this question (Graham 1995).[2]

The first principle of creation significant to our understanding of the learner, Graham said, is that human beings bear the image of God. As imaged in Scripture, God is active and purposeful, yet students in Christian classrooms are often treated as passive and aimless. God is creative, yet students mostly reproduce others' knowledge in oral responses to discussion questions or in workbooks and on tests. God lives and works in fellowship with Jesus, the Spirit, and creation, but students are usually expected to work and learn as individuals. God is free and responsible, but students are viewed as irresponsible and in need of control.

While the latter view can be justified by students' fallen nature, Graham argued that the reality of redemption should shift our emphasis to healing, reconciliation, renewal, deliverance, justice, and peace. Rather than assuming that students are controlled by sin, a Christian, redemptive view of the learner (while realistic) must always be hopeful. Rather than seeing students as passive objects for cognitive inculcation or behavioral manipulation, Christian teachers should view them as active, intentional subjects of their King. Ideally, what students learn will equip them to participate in the restoration of creation to God's original design. It follows that our pedagogy must help students not only to *know* but to *do*.

Knowing and Doing

We are quite familiar with the distinction between knowing and doing, and to this day our understanding of these concepts remains heavily influenced by Greek epistemology. With Plato and Aristotle came a radical distinction between **knowing** as cognitive, analytic, rationalistic understanding and **doing** as more-or-less mechanical action unworthy of the ideal philosopher-king. The Western intellectual tradition has made much of the distinction between theory and practice, pure and applied science, fine and practical arts, academics and professionalism. The greater prestige and status usually adheres to the first member of each pair. Certainly the liberal arts tradition, Christian versions included, champions the humanizing (and Christianizing) effect of disinterested, rational inquiry above "mere" vocationalism and professional training.

Yet this distinction between knowing and doing is foreign to a Judeo-Christian conception of knowing and coming to know. The Christian Scriptures pay little heed to the distinction between theory and practice. Instead, the Bible always speaks of knowing in holistic terms. Knowledge is not primarily cognitive understanding (although that is part of it) but heart-centered, committed action. To know God is not primarily to be able to name and describe God's attributes but to do God's will. Knowledge in the Scriptures is not finally something one possesses but something one uses to serve God, neighbor, and creation. The Old Testament prophets constantly upbraided God's people for confusing an abstract, theoretical belief with knowing God. That is also Jesus' central criticism of the Pharisees, who claimed to know the Scriptures but were often woefully lacking in demonstrable love for God and their neighbors.[3]

Graham (1995) nicely summarizes the discussion above: "Learning takes place when the *heart* accepts something as true and it has an impact on subsequent behavior." Unfortunately, most traditional, transmission-style teaching aims primarily at the intellect rather than the heart. Nevertheless, we do have examples of teaching that are more integrative and active, in keeping with the principles of a Christian anthropology and epistemology as implied above.

By its very nature, communal, interactive teaching places the instructor in the role of fellow traveler and guide rather than all-knowing dispenser of "truth." This metaphor of the teacher as a guide traveling a common terrain with students is one that John Van Dyk (1995, 2000) favors to describe distinctively Christian teaching. The journey's common destination, Van Dyk says, is discipleship rooted in hearing and doing the will of God. Following this conception, the teacher helps to equip students for service (Ephesians 4), that is, for the caregiving and stewardship characterized by acts of healing, reconciliation, and peacemaking. Thus, for Van Dyk, teaching Christianly is to *enable* students to function as disciples in our complex world. Again, notice the emphasis on active response as well as on cognitive understanding.

Comparing Our Two Scenarios

It may be helpful to analyze the teaching of Jenny Thompson and Hilda Smith in light of the conception of learning, teaching, and knowing described above. It is not my intention to judge or compare the personal Christian commitment of the two teachers. Also, since teachers' personalities affect the way they teach, there is certainly no *one* acceptable teaching style. Still, it is worthwhile to point out that certain teaching practices may be more or less in keeping with a Christian anthropology and epistemology as characterized above.

Note first that Ms. Thompson appears to view her role more as that of a technician than does Ms. Smith. She is concerned primarily with the children's technical mastery of initial consonant substitution rather than with their overall understanding of the story. Ms.Thompson is more teacher-centered than Ms. Smith is. She does more explicit telling and seems less aware of the need for children to be personally involved in their learning.

Ms. Thompson's discipline plan is based primarily on a behaviorist model of external rewards and punishments, while Ms. Smith is more concerned that children understand and internalize the reasons for their actions.[4]

Ms. Thompson's lesson is not *embedded*, or situated in the real experience of the children and the literature. Instead, it is an abstract skill exercise with little experiential context.[5] For Ms. Thompson, the reading of *Rosie's Walk* serves primarily as a point of departure for a *disembedded* skill lesson on basic spelling patterns and consonant substitution. By contrast, Ms. Smith's lesson clearly flows out of the literature selection and is sensitive to experiences the children bring to the book and to the writing task that follows. Not that Ms. Smith ignores skills in her teaching. She clearly emphasizes them, but she does so in ways that not only help children develop abstract, cognitive knowledge of certain language features but also involve them in the meaningful and developmentally relevant *doing* of a real language task. Furthermore, Ms. Smith, more than Ms. Thompson, gives children choices in their work while providing a flexible structure, or scaffold, that gives direction and guidance.

Thus, while both women are Christians who teach, I would argue that Ms. Smith is a better Christian teacher because she embodies practices that are more in keeping with a scriptural view of the learner and of knowing. Also, her approach is more congruent with what contemporary learning theory tells us about these matters.[6]

Curricular Implications

The two classroom scenarios that open this chapter, and the discussion that follows, aim to show that our views of the nature of the child and the nature of knowledge make a substantial difference in classroom teaching practice. Historically, two main anthropologies have shaped our views on this issue. The first anthropology views the child as inherently evil; the second, as inherently good.

The child as inherently evil Rooted in Christian theology, this view tends to see the child as born into sin and in need of redemption. Although the family and the church are traditionally viewed as the primary institutional agents in this redemption, the Christian school plays a strong supporting role. As a redemptive institution, the Christian school is called upon, especially in more conservative circles, to assist in building careful moral and pedagogic defenses against the child's essentially destructive and ignorant human nature.

How does this view of human nature as depraved affect the organization and curriculum of a school? Generally, the school emphasizes control, imposing institutional restraints as correctives against students' natural inclinations to evil. Such a school often has a "law and order" orientation and a curricular emphasis on mastering facts and skills in an orderly, sequential manner. Often, curriculum and pedagogy manifest a behaviorist bent, behaviorism being preeminently suited to shaping students in desired directions, both cognitively and affectively. In the pedagogy of reading, for example, behaviorism exhibits itself in programs that emphasize "skill and drill" and put students through a careful sequence of learning subskills. Many intensive phonics programs, traditional basal readers, and other published reading schemes embody this approach.

In an illuminating article, Mark Thogmartin (1994) reports that a survey of reading pedagogy in fundamentalist Christian schools in the United States found an overwhelming preference for phonics and the basal reader. [7] This preference was defended on (supposedly) biblical grounds:

> Reading without phonics is like teaching values without the Ten Commandments.
>
> This country was discovered and ordained to exist because of God. From its infancy phonics was the basis of reading. There is a connection. God the Creator knows us and how we work. He used phonics historically.

Regrettably, many Christian educators seem unaware of the behaviorist assumptions underlying the skill-and-drill emphasis of certain intensive phonics approaches.[8] The fact that these behaviorist pedagogies often "work" (cited by Thogmartin as a main reason for fundamentalist support) also demonstrates the unconscious pragmatism behind such curricular choices. This reality is all the more ironic given the vehement criticism these same educators level at John Dewey's pragmatism (also amply demonstrated in Thogmartin's study).

The child as inherently good The view that has shaped much educational practice since the Enlightenment holds that the child is inherently good. This belief in the essential goodness of human nature surfaced as traditional reverence for the foundational texts of Western civilization (e.g., the Bible, Aristotle's writings) seriously eroded. The new age dawning was an optimistic one, characterized by confidence in human reason and natural law. It was accompanied by an increasing indifference to traditional religion and a faith that humanity was finally and visibly freeing itself from the superstitions, prejudices, and blind cruelty of the past. Educated people gradually came to believe they were entering what they described as a *siècle de lumières*, an *Aufklarung*—an "enlightened" era.

Perhaps Jean-Jacques Rousseau represents the quintessence of this view in education. In his tremendously influential work *Emile*, Rousseau describes how a boy should be educated from birth to adulthood. (His views on the education of girls were quite unremarkable, sexist, and traditional.) His foundational presupposition is that human nature is fundamentally good; only external experiences warp the child's inherent goodness. Ever since Rousseau, an optimistic, romantic view of the child has existed in Western educational thought and practice, alongside the traditional pessimistic view.

In curriculum and pedagogy, this optimism leads to a range of positions favoring an absence of constraints and a trust in children's natural instincts. This paradigm assumes that, because children move naturally toward the good, they will choose to learn the things of most value unless prevented by some external condition. Parents or teachers holding this view find no risk or danger in removing constraints and providing children with great freedom. Rigid classroom formats, "traditional" teaching methods, structures, and formalities of all kinds are seen as barriers that prevent children from exercising their naturally good learning instincts. Student-initiated inquiry and divergent project work are preferred to teacher domination and convergent, "correct answer" learning. Reading and language arts emphasize the students' own language experiences, self-selection of reading materials, and individualistic meaning-making. These latter characteristics are clearly identified with whole language approaches to teaching language.

Figure 1-1: Conflicting views of human nature

"Sinner"	"Saint"
• institutional restraint • "tried and true" • restriction • permanence • emphasis on product • subject- (discipline-) centered • focused; convergent • "traditional basics education" • e.g., many schools—especially conservative Christian schools	• lack of restraint • favor innovation • freedom • change • emphasis on process • learner-centered • open-ended; divergent • "open education" • e.g., "progressive" schools—Summerhill

The contrast Figure 1-1 depicts how a sharp distinction between the child as "sinner" or as "saint" influences approaches to schooling. With respect to the way a curriculum is organized, the two differing views often express themselves as sketched in figure 1-2.

Figure 1-2: Curricular implications of the conflicting views of human nature

"Sinner"	"Saint"
• bits 'n' pieces, bottom-up organization of learning experiences	• holistic-interactive organization
• discipline = contingent reinforcement	• discipline = learning from "natural consequences"
• emphasis on learning skills in relative isolation	• emphasis on contextual learning of skills
• product oriented	• process oriented
• non-creative (essentially reproductive)	• essentially creative
• cognitive-memory level of thinking	• divergent/evaluative level of thinking
• focused; convergent	• open-ended; divergent
• teaching seen as transmission of knowledge	• teaching seen as facilitating students' own knowledge making

A Redemptionist View of the Child

Christians who believe in transcendent values and who hold to the doctrine of total human depravity are likely to feel uncomfortable with the view of the child as a "saint," an inherently good creature who can only become a "sinner" through poor social conditioning. Many Christians believe the whole language movement must be opposed precisely because of its humanistic child-centered anthropology. Such Christians gravitate to pedagogies and curricula that reflect a view of the child as "sinner" rather than "saint."

I submit, however, that **Christians ought to feel uncomfortable with both anthropological views.** Neither view is biblically defensible when one regards children (including Christian children) not as isolated individuals but as a corporate entity called to work in the world as part of a redeemed community. Although Christians must take sin seriously, our focus as redeemed sinners is not on our sinfulness. Rather, we focus on the fact that the Redeemer Christ, the Word incarnate, has restored the relationship between God and creation, and renews life through the Holy Spirit. A fundamental presupposition must be that teachers and students in Christian schools are part of a *redeemed community*. Thus, children in a Christian community are to be regarded *realistically* (they fall short of the perfection of Christ) but also *hopefully* (nevertheless they partake in the sanctification that Christ graciously provides). One cannot always make judgments about the salvation of individual children; however, in a Christian school, one does assume the reality of redemption. With such a perspective, children cannot be viewed as essentially "evil little sinners" who must be the *objects* of externally imposed restraint. Rather, as members of God's covenant, children must always be treated with the respect due them as *subjects* of their King whose mission is to help restore that kingdom. A Christian school, then, serves as a cultural instrument whose work is to further the redemptive work of Christ in the world.

What are the curricular and pedagogic implications of a *redemptionist* view of human nature? At a conceptual level, I would suggest that the *freedom versus structure* dichotomy established by the "good versus evil" view of the child dissolves into a *freedom within structure* curriculum design. I believe that a holistic approach to teaching language arts comports better with redemptionist anthropology than does a strongly skills-oriented approach. My earlier book, *Language Arts in Christian Schools* (Bruinsma 1990a, now out of print) provided initial justification for this position. The following chapters recap some of those arguments but also reflect developments in my thinking in the decade since.

I can think of little in Christian education more worthwhile than working out the curricular and pedagogic implications of a redemptionist view of education.[9] The unfortunate trend in much Christian education today, however, is to confess redemption in Christ without thinking through what that redemption should mean for teaching practice. This is especially exemplified when schools embrace pedagogic techniques that use a predominantly transmissional model of teaching like Ms. Thompson's, thus failing to provide scope for children's subjective responses. Much of the current "back-to-the-basics" movement, with its skill-and-drill emphasis, falls into this category. In that context, it is disheartening to know that the sales of fill-in-the-blanks workbooks, especially in the language arts and math, continue to be strong. Such materials do not reflect what we now know about how children learn. On the other hand, many humanistic, child-centered models of learning (including aspects of whole language) underestimate the power of evil in the lives of children (and adults). A view of knowledge often embraced uncritically by these models is **constructivism.**

Constructivism and Literacy Learning

Constructivism is a theory of learning which argues that individual persons use their knowledge to build or make meaning. In this view, texts provide cues to possible meanings rather than containing meaning themselves. Readers are active meaning-makers rather than passive receivers of meaning; because their background knowledge varies, they construct various meanings of the same text.

The theory's most extreme form, known as **radical constructivism**, holds that knowledge is entirely constructed by the person. Radical constructivists do not deny the existence of external sensory inputs of all kinds, including texts, but they argue that the brain processes these inputs in a highly personal manner so that meaning is fundamentally an idiosyncratic construct. An objective world may exist "out there," but because we always filter this world through our senses and our personal experiences, we have no valid way to distinguish between the world "out there" and the world "in here." In fact, the radical constructivist would say that the idea of a world "out there" is meaningless. Ultimately, meaning is what we make of it.

Think about the last time you read a book and discussed it with friends who had also read it. Although you may have discovered many similarities in the meanings constructed by each of you, it's likely you also found some subtle and not-so-subtle differences. You might even have wondered whether you and your friends had read the same book and if so whether they were paying enough attention to understand what it was really all about. In fact, argue the radical constructivists, these differences reflect the constructive nature of all meaning making and the impact of individual experiences on that process.

It is not hard to understand why conservative Christians have great difficulty accepting such ideas. After all, Christians believe faith is based, at least in part, on a creator "God who is there" (Schaeffer 1968). We believe creation has an objective status not wholly dependent on human perception and understanding. Jesus Christ is real, a person who lived in historical time in a particular place, who said and did certain things, who died and rose again. The Bible is God's revelation that provides us with true knowledge about God's dealings with humankind in real space and time. If meaning is a wholly personal construction, the concept of objective truth becomes invalid and all interpretations of a text are equally valid and "good." What role, then, does the teacher play in helping children with reading comprehension or written composition? If the construction of meaning is primarily an individual process, how are shared meanings developed?

Social constructivism, a "softer" form of constructivism, answers these questions by arguing that no one constructs meaning in a vacuum. Instead, we make sense of our experiences within a particular social group, and that group exists within a broader societal and cultural context. The more similar the sociocultural backgrounds of a group's members, the more similar will be the meanings they construct. When discussing a book among friends, then, the similarities and the differences among your constructions of its meaning are equally important.

Social constructivists also accept a common external reality that constrains the meanings we can make. Radical constructivists, by contrast, have difficulty explaining common human experiences wrought by the limits of an apparently external creation. Even if one's personal meaning includes the idea that gravity is insignificant, gravity does not seem to change. It is still personally very painful if not fatal to jump from a ten-story building. Clearly, certain external "laws of nature" (or of creation, as Christians would say) are not open to a great deal of personal interpretation. In fact, the entire enterprise of empirical science depends on this belief in and experience of the regularity and lawfulness of creation.

Even here, however, personal factors are at work. Not all people respond the same way to similar medications. Increasingly, people are embracing alternatives to Western medicine. Even scientifically trained doctors skeptical of religious claims are admitting that prayer does make a difference to healing (Postman 1995). Within Christendom, hundreds of denominations claim allegiance to the same Bible as their rule for doctrine and life but hold substantially different interpretations of this book. Christians cannot ignore the claims of social constructivism, even if those claims do rock certain conceptions of "objective truth."

Educational social constructivism has its origins in the work of Jean Piaget (1971) and especially Lev Vygotsky (1978), who theorized that we learn primarily through social interactions. We learn language, then, by using language in social contexts. According to Vygotsky, children are active in their own development, but other people in their immediate social context also play critical roles. He hypothesized a **zone of proximal development**: "an area of difficulty just beyond the point at which a child can solve problems independently; it is the area in which the child can solve problems in collaboration with others, especially with an adult or more competent peer" (Lindfors 1987, 273). When they work collaboratively, he argues, people negotiate and develop shared meanings.

Of course, not everyone has equal voice in these negotiations. The view of one person or group is often privileged over that of others. To illustrate, we return to the book discussion with your friends. Even within your small group, some people's meanings are given greater credibility. Your gender, race, position in the group, socioeconomic status, education, and language abilities all impact how other people view your ideas. Social constructivists recognize these inequalities and encourage each of us to examine the biases in how we knowingly or unknowingly value the ideas of one gender, race, class, or religion over those of another. Carol Edelsky (1994) posed the following questions to help language arts teachers think through some of the issues social constructivists have raised:

- Who decides what a "good" story is?
- Who decides what children write about?
- Who decides whose turn it is to talk?
- Who decides whose meaning of the text is acceptable?
- Who decides what books are in the classroom?
- Whose view of the world is represented in these books?

In traditional transmission-oriented teaching, the answer to these questions is "the teacher," or sometimes "the curriculum guide," or "the administration." A social constructivist would want to broaden these perspectives to include children as well.

A school does not exist in a social vacuum. Christian schools in particular serve a community of people with a shared faith commitment. In the Bible too, God's dealings are not primarily with isolated individuals but with persons in community. The Old Testament is largely an account of God's dealings with His covenant community of Israel. In the New Testament, all manner of ethnic, racial, and gender barriers are broken as God, in Jesus, deals with the church, the collective fellowship of all who believe the gospel (Galatians 3:26–29). Likewise, a Christian school must make a genuine attempt to hear the many voices of the faith community when setting policy and answering questions such as those posed by Edelsky. Obviously, these voices need to be heard through agreed-upon channels. Considerable charity must be exercised in the conversation because we all see imperfectly (1 Corinthians 13:12). If we approach our conversations in prayerful humility, however, we have the promise that God's Spirit will guide us.

Implications for Language Arts Curriculum and Pedagogy

Skills-Centered and Language-Centered Learning

This book contrasts a narrow transmission approach to language learning, which I term fundamentally **skills-centered**, with a **language-centered** approach that taps into and extends the more natural way children learn oral language. As chapter 5 will demonstrate, children learn oral language in a personally active and socially motivated context. Extrapolating from that fact, the language-centered approach takes a modified social constructivist view of all language learning. I must stress, however, that a language-centered approach, done well, does *not* ignore the skills dimension of language learning. Rather, this approach invites children to learn skills through language that connects with their lives. Chapters 5 and 6 will elaborate more fully on the skills-centered and language-centered distinction.

Skills-centered language teaching is by far the more common approach in both secular and Christian schools today. It has its origin in the long history of Western rationalism from Plato onward, greatly accelerated by the rise of science in the eighteenth century and the psychologizing of education in the twentieth century.

As explained above, until recently the psychology of behaviorism influenced much educational practice, aided and abetted in Christian schools by a faulty anthropology. Behaviorism seeks to reduce learning to a set of predictable external responses to carefully controlled stimuli, mediated by rewards and punishments (reinforcement).[10] In language teaching, such a behaviorist, skills-centered approach puts great emphasis on isolated aspects of language: letters, letter-sound relationships, syllables, words, sentence fragments, single sentences. Often, particularly in workbooks, there is no cohesive, meaningful text and no situational context. This disjointed teaching, in turn, leads learners to put inordinate value on the bits and pieces of language, and not enough value on making sense of stories and complete expository passages. Such instruction often confuses children because it disembeds language from normal, meaningful contexts and uses.

The skills-centered approach tends to view the teacher as an educational technician who has the task of moving children through a set of prescribed exercises and experiences, often carefully scripted by publishers' teacher manuals or prescriptive government curriculum guides. The child is regarded as a trainable organism whose deficits in language skills are to be mitigated through carefully sequenced and contingently reinforced learning experiences. Jargon reflecting this behaviorist bias includes *direct instruction, mastery learning curricula* (complete with *behavioral objectives*), *learning outcomes,* and *input and output variables.*

Unfortunately, many Christian educators who explicitly or implicitly work with a deficit view of the child (on the moral as well as the cognitive plane) gravitate to these methods because they promise control. This search for control often extends to disembedding the components of language arts instruction, devoting separate blocks of time and curricular materials to listening, speaking, and especially reading and writing. In each component, the emphasis is on formal modes. For example, instruction in speaking (if it occurs at all) occurs in a "speech" class, with emphasis on formal rhetoric and forensic debate. In reading, the basal reader is supreme. Careful control of vocabulary and a stress on phonics and other discrete word recognition techniques predominate. Spelling and grammar are viewed separately from "creative" writing.

Language-centered approaches, by contrast, view the teacher as an educated professional. Besides holding specialized knowledge about language and language learning, the teacher has a rich personal involvement with language that she shares with students through modeling and demonstration. She views students as successful language learners and honors their prior language knowledge and experience. Each student continues to enrich and enlarge that experience through interaction with a larger community of language learners (the class), guided by the teacher.

What we are talking about here is **discipline**. The core meaning of the word *discipline* is "to make disciples of." Teachers are leaders and guides; students (as well as teachers) are disciples. For Christians this relationship is modeled by the servant-leader Christ and His followers. Of course, Christian teachers fill Christ's role imperfectly, but it is nevertheless an appropriate role. Ideally, the Christian language arts teacher models what an experienced user and lover of language is like. If this modeling is done well (with all the failures and successes inherent in human endeavors), many students will want to be disciples. They will strive to become members of the club of language lovers represented so engagingly by their teacher. This will be true especially because students' oral language learning has already convinced them that language has the power to make things happen. They may also be convinced of the sheer pleasure of language as they discover it in poetry and story.

Language knowledge is far more than a collection of language facts and discrete language skills. It demonstrates itself primarily in responsible and responsive language use, reflecting an internalized commitment to language as a gift from God—a gift to be used for shared service and personal delight.

Conclusion

In a recent study, Pamela Adams (1997) found that some Christian teachers' literacy beliefs and practices do not always correspond with their stated beliefs about the integration of faith and learning. In this chapter, I have argued that a teacher's *anthropology* and *epistemology*—views of the learner and of knowing—are critical. It is important for Christian teachers to reflect on how they view their students and to assess their teaching carefully to determine whether there is congruence between their anthropology and their pedagogy. Similarly, they must ask themselves whether the way they teach (and evaluate) harmonizes with their epistemology—their belief about what counts as knowledge.

The chapters that follow elaborate the implications of a language-centered, redemptionist view of learning for issues critical to the teaching of the language arts. The next chapter provides a general framework for developing a language arts curriculum for Christian schools.

Questions for Discussion

1. What is your reaction to the two classroom scenarios that open this chapter? In which classroom would you rather be a student? Why? In your opinion, which style of teaching requires more preparation? Why?
2. Do you feel that the *Creation—Fall—Redemption—Restoration* motif captures the essential narrative structure of the Bible? Where do contemporary humans (including you) fit into this schema?
3. What view of the child as learner guides your teaching? Do you think it is important for teachers to think about such matters, or should we leave such thinking to philosophers?
4. How would you describe a *redemptionist* view of the child in your own words?
5. What does it mean for you to know something? How should a school go about determining what students at various levels should come to know, and who should decide—teachers, principals, parents, students, the church, the government?
6. Discuss the implications for a Christian of a social con-

structivist view of knowledge. Does social constructivism necessarily imply that all truth is relative?

7. How would you respond to the questions posed by Carol Edelsky as reported in this chapter?

8. Jesus said, "I am the ... truth" (John 14:6). What does it mean to *be* truth? How can we be truth as teachers?

9. Do children require formal teaching to learn how to talk? If not, what is the role of an adult "teacher" in children's oral language development? How does your response to these two questions relate to the distinction between skills-centered and language-centered approaches to teaching language arts?

10. How would you differentiate between a teacher as a technician and a teacher as a professional? Which do you aspire to be?

For Further Consideration

1. Interview two teachers—a Christian and a non-Christian—about their concept of the child as learner. Determine whether their responses reflect their respective worldviews.

2. Look up the word *discipline* in a good dictionary. How do its various meanings relate to the brief discussion of the word in this chapter?

3. Locate the book by Wolterstorff (1980) mentioned in this chapter, and use it as a basis for discussing differing concepts of the term *discipline*. (You can find the complete citation for this and other works in the References at the back of this book.)

4. To further explore a Christian approach to discipline, read Jack Fennema's *Nurturing Children in the Lord* (1980).

Endnotes

1 These scenarios are based on two actual classrooms recently observed. The names of the schools and teachers have been changed.

2 See Graham's forthcoming book *Teaching Redemptively: Bringing Grace and Truth into Your Classroom* (2003).

3 For further elaboration on the distinction between Greco-Roman and Judeo-Christian epistemologies, see the helpful discussions by Groome (1980, 39–151), Blomberg (1980, 1995), and Van Brummelen (1994, 83–114). A more difficult but worthwhile book on this topic is Boman (1960).

4 See Wolsterstorff (1980) for a helpful discussion on this distinction.

5 See Donaldson (1978) for a detailed exposition of the distinction between *embedded* and *disembedded* learning, which is explored further in chapter 7. Howard Gardner in his book *The Unschooled Mind* (1991), while not using these terms, makes essentially the same distinction.

6 For discussions on the distinction between a teacher who is a Christian and Christian teaching see Van Dyk (2000) and Hull (2003).

7 Thogmartin (1994) uses the designation *fundamentalist* to refer to Christians "who are primarily characterized by a belief that the Protestant Bible was verbally inspired and has been protected by the grace of preservation over the centuries through selected translations and editions" (105).

8 Readers should not interpret my comments to mean that phonics has no place in the teaching of literacy. On the contrary, I strongly believe there is a place for a certain kind of phonics teaching. See chapter 11 for details.

9 The book *A Vision with a Task* (Stronks and Blomberg 1993) raises the same concern and goes a long way toward fleshing out just such a view.

10 Although I strongly believe that, on balance, behaviorism has negatively influenced education, it has taught some valuable lessons: Compliments work better than scolding, and rewards work better than punishments in changing behaviors. For persons with severe cognitive impairment, behavior modification strategies have often been effective in shaping behavior to more socially acceptable and adaptive patterns.

Chapter 2

Instructional Design Principles for a Language Arts Curriculum

This chapter develops some central principles to guide the design and implementation of a language arts curriculum. Pedagogical implications of these principles are alluded to briefly here and are fleshed out in subsequent chapters. As you read this chapter, ask yourself what these principles concretely imply for your teaching of the language arts. Also consider whether the curriculum you use (or propose to use) reflects these principles.

In the beginning was the Word, and the Word was with God, and the Word was God. He was with God in the beginning. Through him all things were made; without him nothing was made that has been made. (John 1:1–3)

These familiar opening words of the Gospel of John identify our Lord Jesus Christ as the co-creator of the universe. The force of God's Word is ultimately creative: God spoke and all things were created. As image bearers, we humans are uniquely gifted among all of God's creatures to use language creatively, for communication. Jesus is identified as God's clearest message, or Word, to us. As God's adopted children, we are called to live our lives (including our linguistic lives) in service to the Word. The language arts curriculum of a Christian school is thus an important element in fostering students' awareness that their ultimate calling is to love God with their whole being and their neighbors as themselves (Matthew 22:37–39). Helping students learn to do this linguistically is the central concern of the Christian school's language arts curriculum.

Components of the Language Arts

Language is used to communicate in all school subjects and thus is a truly interdisciplinary tool. This chapter primarily concerns the English language arts—the elementary and middle school curriculum that focuses on speaking, listening, reading, and writing. Viewing and performing are also part of this list; in fact, language arts components can be grouped as the *receptive* arts of listening, reading, and viewing and the *expressive* arts of speaking, writing, and performing.[1] However we divide them, the language arts form part of an integral whole, a unity, and we must respect that unity as we plan for learning.

Principles of Language Arts Education

The Creation–Fall–Redemption–Restoration Motif

What follows are fundamental principles and beliefs about learning and teaching language arts that are central to developing a language arts curriculum. These specific principles should be seen within the biblical worldview of creation, fall, redemption, and restoration discussed in chapter 1. To recap briefly, Christians confess the following:

- In the beginning, God *created* the world wholly good (Genesis 1).
- Humans *fell* into sin, thus estranging themselves from God and each other (Genesis 3; Romans 3:23).
- Through Christ's sacrificial death, *redemption,* or atonement, is available (Romans 3:24–26).
- We live between the time when God in Jesus came to make all things new (2 Corinthians 5:17) and when Christ will return to fully realize that newness by *restoring* creation to perfection (Revelation 21).

The church (including the Christian school) serves as a signpost to the coming of God's restored kingdom on earth. The church fulfills its task by calling all persons to repentance and inviting them to join in helping God's kingdom "come ... on earth as it is in heaven" (Matthew 6:10). A language arts curriculum contributes to this overall task by seeking to flesh out concretely what it means to love God and neighbor linguistically.

About Language and Language Use

Human language is a unique gift from God to be used in the service of God, neighbor, and self (Psalm 119:91b, Deuteronomy 6:5, Leviticus 19:18, Matthew 22:37–39).

Implication Language is more than a tool for self-expression (although it is that as well). Principally, students must learn how language is meant to be used for communal service; that is, they must learn to communicate effectively with their neighbors.

Key norms for language use are honesty, clarity, economy, and elegance of expression (Proverbs 25:11; Ecclesiastes 5:2; James 5:12).

Implication A Christian use of language is not, first of all, characterized by overtly confessional language, including frequent references to God. Because the intent of language is to communicate clearly, it must not be used to manipulate listeners/readers (honesty), it must not be wasteful and redundant (economy), and it must attempt to be aesthetically pleasing (elegance, or felicity of expression).

Listening, speaking, reading, and writing best serve their purpose when they foster understanding, meaning, problem solving, and learning (both independent and communal).

Implication Fostering understanding or comprehension is the central purpose of the language arts. Comprehension is not simply a set of skills; rather, it involves the marshaling of complex cognitive processes to bridge the gap between what is already known and what remains to be learned. Teachers must resist the temptation to view their role as primarily transmitting discrete skills, for language skills (complex though they may be) are means to enable comprehension, not ends in themselves.

About Learners (and Teachers)

Humans are volitional beings, able to exercise their wills either positively to serve God and neighbor, or negatively to serve some other "god" or "gods." Language is one way people respond (James 3:9–10).

Implication Children are not inherently "good" in any absolute sense, and thus they need guidance from responsible adults to learn how to use language as God desires. Teachers must also realize their own imperfections and sinful tendencies, and must constantly seek better ways of doing God's will pedagogically.

The foundations of literacy are laid in the early preschool years.

Implication Almost all children enter school with a well-developed language system in place (Gleason 2001). It is important for primary teachers to honor and build on that preschool learning rather than assume that children enter school as "blank slates." Thus the preschool acquisition and development of oral language provide insight into the ways children become literate (Britton 1992; Loban 1976). Teachers must know the basic facts and processes of children's language acquisition and understand how preschool children often learn the fundamentals of literacy.[2]

Literacy learning is developmental. Just as children do not all learn how to walk and talk in exactly the same way or at the same rate, so they do not all acquire literacy in the same manner or time frame (Teale and Sulzby 1986).

Implication Most developmental learning proceeds incrementally, with many hesitations and approximations. Children must be supported in their individuality so that they will remain confident learners. Thus, in early literacy teaching, there is a need for teachers to understand and foster **emergent literacy**.[3]

Even though God has given humans both the need and the ability to learn, children will not always rise to the challenge of deepening their understanding of God's world and their place in it (Romans 3:23; Psalm 25:7).

Implication Because children (like adults) are not always predisposed to serve God and neighbor as they should, teaching requires a loving firmness.

About Language Learning and Teaching

Purpose is important in teaching reading and writing (Graves 1983; 1991).

Implication As much as possible, lessons ought to be structured to help students listen, speak, read, and write for authentic purposes. So much of what we teach children seems to have no immediate (or even long-term) purpose. While it is not always possible to make every language arts lesson immediately relevant to students, as teachers we frequently need to ask ourselves: "Why am I teaching this to these students at this time?"

Language should not be contrived so that skills can be learned and used in a predetermined order (Smith 1997).

Implication Although teachers (and instructional materials) must be sensitive to vocabulary and concept level, there is no need for rigid vocabulary control or controlled phonemic spelling patterns in early or later reading materials. Children can read and write using the syntax and vocabulary that they can speak and understand. Thus materials should use natural language appropriate to the subject.

There is evidence that an understanding of the *function* of oracy and literacy is more critical than a detailed understanding of their *forms*. Reading and writing may require an understanding of various forms or components of language, but teaching these in isolation seldom transfers to improvement in the whole task (Tough 1977; Wells 1986).

Implication While grammar (syntax, spelling, punctuation, usage), phonology (including phonics), semantics (meaning), and pragmatics (social conventions) are important aspects of language (Hulit 1997), teachers should not isolate them unduly. Instructions such as "Put away your reading and take out your phonics (or spelling, or grammar)" betray a lack of understanding of the integrality and interrelatedness of these language aspects. (See chapters 6 and 7 for details.)

Language learning should celebrate the wonder of language, the artfulness of literature, and the joy of clear and elegant expression.

Implication Although children need to become literate for practical and career-related purposes, a major value of learning language is the sheer privilege of sharing and participating in its aesthetic dimensions. There is really no excuse for a language arts class to be boring.

At its best, language learning involves students in honestly examining God's world, exploring real issues, recognizing the sinfulness of human life, and pointing toward the redemption promised in Christ.

Implication Christians often try to isolate learners from the "harsher realities of life" by selecting literature that is noncontroversial and "nice" in a middle-class way. Instead, teachers should take a cue from the Bible, which certainly does not shy away from depicting sin and suffering along with hope and joy. Language learning then becomes part of the process of inoculating children against evil, just as weakened forms of a deadly virus build up natural antibodies. (See chapter 4 for details.)

Significant learning, including literacy instruction, is both personal and communal.

Implication Western culture is thoroughly individualistic. While the Bible supports the value of the individual before God, individuality is always contextualized within community. Thus, in the Old Testament God makes a covenant with the *people* of Israel, and in the New Testament the *church* is the covenant community of believers. Our Christian classrooms should function as communities of learners, taking into account both their personal and their social needs.

Students are most likely to internalize affinity for language learning when teachers freely share and demonstrate their own literate lives.

Implication We usually learn the most important things in life from the company we keep. This truth applies to a love of reading and writing as much as it does to learning to fly-fish.

Children need adults in their lives who model all kinds of attitudes and skills. It is not enough for teachers to *tell* their students how important literacy is for them; they must also *demonstrate* love of language by sharing their own reading and writing with students.

Because students approach literacy learning with varying background experiences and different learning styles (Gardner 1999b; McCarthy 1983; Van Brummelen 1998), **instruction should be rich and varied.**

Implication The constraints imposed by mass education make it impossible for one teacher to meet the precise learning needs and dispositions of each child in the classroom. But a teacher can plan and execute literacy lessons that utilize multisensory approaches and call for varied responses.

There is no one way to teach language. Although literacy development exhibits recognizable patterns, there is no hierarchy of subskills or universal sequence in literacy instruction.

Implication North Americans are enamored of technique. We love simplifying complex topics through "ten easy steps" or "seven effective habits" or "four basic principles." Many strategies, approaches, or systems lay claim to being *the* way to teach reading and writing. But language learning is complex, idiosyncratic, and messy. Far better than one-size-fits-all systems are teachers who help students address immediate language needs. Happily, children have a created ability to learn language in its various forms when they are immersed in an environment of rich literacy supplemented by skillful teaching at the point of need.

The real measure of success of any language arts program is whether children actually listen more critically and appreciatively, speak the truth in love, read with increasing discernment, and write with clarity and conviction.

Implication Whether children are good at phonics or grammar or spelling should not be the measure of growth and success in language learning. These skills are simply means toward the end of listening, speaking, reading, and writing with increasing confidence in real-life contexts, in and out of school. Skill acquisition should not be viewed as a literacy goal in itself.

About Language Learning and Community

Language learning is both personal and communal. It is *personal* in that it is developmental. It varies according to individual backgrounds and learning styles, and it may point students toward the need to make a personal commitment to Christ. Language learning is *communal* in that literacy is developed in and through interaction. Obedience to the nature of language learning means building a community where authentic language learning can occur. The classroom becomes a place where students learn about the language of their everyday experience, delve into its history, and explore its intricacies and varied uses. A language learning community should be characterized by:

- unconditional love and acceptance (Hebrews 10:24)
- recognition of the blessings of diversity (1 Corinthians 12)
- desire to remove barriers of judgment and ignorance so that each person can feel accepted, supported, and valued in the context of community (1 Corinthians 12, Ephesians 4, Romans 12)

Curricular and Pedagogical Implications

Following is a brief overview of the key components of an effective language learning community, with emphasis on teaching practices that reflect the community's personal yet communal nature. The success of these components depends on the teacher's commitment to both model the principles enunciated above and provide a secure environment for students. The remainder of this book will discuss these matters in greater detail.

A **personalized reading** program can be both personal and communal. It is *personal* when each student:

- has a wide spectrum of reading choices at an appropriate instructional and interest level
- is challenged to grow in reading ability
- is helped to develop personally useful decoding and comprehension skills
- has the opportunity to interact with a peer or significant adult
- is given tasks that encourage critical, creative, and strategic thinking

A personalized reading program is *communal* when it offers many opportunities for dialogue and when all community members support each other and are held accountable for their own development. Dialogue can take a variety of forms such as "book-talks," minilessons, conferencing, and group sharing.

1. **Writing to learn/learning to write** programs that emphasize process, portfolio assessment, and meaningful contexts are *personal* because they incorporate principles about the way learners learn and they focus on assessment that promotes individual growth. These programs are *communal* in that learners are communicating for a real purpose. "Sharing times," when students share insights about their own and their classmates' writing, further enhance the communal aspect of language. Such times require accountability and promote the learning of skills at the "point of need." The correct use of writing conventions (grammar, spelling, punctuation) is a means of loving one's neighbor linguistically.

2. **Literature-based/integrated themes** are *personal* and *communal* when they provide opportunities for learners to become cognitively and affectively engaged in a topic through activities that require interaction and the sharing of thoughts and insights. Themes provide a way for all

members of the community to contribute their personal knowledge and skills within the context of an open-ended group discussion or task.

3. **Open-ended assignment choices** give teachers the opportunity to align the variables of learning (the learner, the content, the task, and teaching/learning strategies) with *personal* learning strengths and needs. Assignments can be *communal* if they invite answers that go beyond "correct" responses, providing an opportunity for deeper dialogue within the learning community.
4. **Curriculum-based continuous assessment** (e.g., portfolio assessment) is *personal* and *communal* when:
    - it is specific about individual strengths and weaknesses
    - it provides students and parents with useful information about learning needs
    - teachers and students communally set attainable short- and long-term goals
    - it challenges students (and teachers) to respond as disciples of Jesus Christ

Conclusion

In many ways, the language arts curriculum of a Christian school reflects the core beliefs and values of the school community of parents, students, teachers, and staff. Language arts is both a discipline in itself and a service to all the other disciplines in the curriculum. Because of the central role of the language arts, curriculum developers and teachers must shape a curriculum grounded in both scriptural principles and the best of current pedagogy. Our children deserve no less.

Questions for Discussion

1. What do you believe is (are) the main purpose(s) of human language?
2. In your view, what characterizes a *Christian* use of language?
3. Few teachers would disagree that fostering students' comprehension is the goal of teaching in general and language arts teaching specifically. What does comprehension involve?
4. What role does the concept of sin (your students' and your own) play in your teaching?
5. Is it important for a language arts teacher to understand the basic processes and outcomes of children's preschool language acquisition? Why or why not?
6. Are students' mistakes (e.g., oral reading miscues, spelling errors) sins? Why or why not?

7. What do you think about the claim that teachers should frequently ask themselves, *Why am I teaching this to these students at this time?* Isn't it enough for teachers to conscientiously follow the curriculum?
8. What is your position on the role of skills instruction in the language arts?
9. Do you read to and with your students? Do you ever share your personal writing with your students? Do you think these activities are important? Why or why not?
10. Do you agree that there is no one right way to teach literacy? If so, then what's a busy teacher to do?

For Further Consideration

1. Look up the Bible passages this chapter cites in support of a particular principle. Do you feel the passages are used appropriately?
2. There is always a tension between individual and community needs. The argument is made that a language arts class should foster in learners both independence and interdependence. Is that possible? Can you think of children's literature that addresses this struggle in an authentic manner?

Endnotes

1 Performing will be dealt with in chapter 10. Viewing is not explicitly dealt with in this book, although many of the principles related to developing literary discernment are relevant to viewing as well.

2 Chapter 6 deals with language acquisition.

3 Chapter 8 deals with emergent literacy.

Chapter 3

Evaluation and the Language Arts

No topic in schooling raises the emotional temperature quite so quickly as evaluation. Perhaps that is no wonder, for evaluation is related to such contentious educational issues as standards, academic quality, achievement, accountability, and "excellence." Evaluation also influences student ranking, sorting, and selecting in many crucial ways. For example, evaluation may determine a student's current curriculum choices (e.g., vocational or academic), future schooling choices (e.g., technical school or university), and even employment prospects (e.g., laborer or professional). Thus, the topic of evaluation is never trivial. This chapter explores important evaluation issues with particular reference to English language arts teaching. For evaluation strategies appropriate to specific components of language arts, see chapters 9 through 12.

The etymological root of *evaluate* means "to draw value out of" or "to establish the worth of" something. To be human is to evaluate; we are valuing creatures. We constantly compare and contrast (that big Buick is better than that little Volkswagen), measure and weigh (that chocolate bar is thicker and heavier than this one), assess relative worth (Jill's painting is more beautiful than Jack's), and judge levels of performance (our sales figures show that Frank is a better salesperson than Jane). Note that these judgments all imply some implicit or explicit standard or criterion. This fact underlines the critical issue in evaluation: *What standard or reference point do we use to make our evaluative judgments?* A related question is equally important: *Who sets the standard, and on what basis?*

To address these and other questions, it is useful to experience a common form of student evaluation, the test (see figure 3-1). Please write your answers to this test on a clean sheet of lined paper. Read the questions carefully and answer them in complete sentences. Do your own work and be sure to put your name clearly in the upper left corner of your paper. If you complete the test while others are still writing, turn your paper over and take out your silent reading book.

Figure 3-1: Sample Test

1. Who is the president of the United States?
2. Who is the best president that the United States has ever had?
3. $16.00 - $4.00 = ______
4. If you had $12.00 to spend on food, what would you buy to provide a well-balanced diet?
5. How do you spell the word /si-kol-o-jist/?
6. How should a Christian go about selecting a psychologist for counseling about a serious personal problem?
7. How much does Melissa weigh?
8. How much does Melissa love Jesus?
9. Which of the grade 2 stories below is the better written?

I have a cat. Her name is Trouble. Trouble is a nice cat. I love her.

My cat Trouble is a most misceevios raskal! Were their's trouble, theres Trouble. Which is the reson for her name.

10. When was the last time you were tested?

11. When was the last time you were evaluated?

Relax—those instructions are given in jest. But examine the "test" questions carefully and note some of your reactions. Do you feel the urge to give responses other than those asked for? If you are in a class or group, perhaps this would be a good time to jot down some of your reactions and discuss them with someone else for a few minutes.

Chances are, some parts of the test frustrated you. Perhaps you were annoyed that the questions call for quite diverse responses. Questions 1, 3, 5, and 7 require low-level factual or objective responses, for example, while questions 2, 6, and 8 call for higher-level and more subjective responses. Still others (4, 9, 10, 11) required both factual knowledge and more complicated evaluative standards. The point is that even an apparently simple test can raise a host of difficult questions about evaluation. We'll come back to this test as we discuss some of these issues.

Purposes of Evaluation

Evaluation shapes curriculum. To state the matter another way, what gets measured determines what is taught. Given this reality, the way a school chooses to evaluate students and programs should clearly reflect the school's goals. In a Christian school, those goals should grow out of a mission statement that, in turn, reflects a well-thought-out Christian anthropology and epistemology.[1] Chapters 1 and 2 introduced those concepts. In brief, a Christian anthropology views students as created by God with unique abilities and gifts to be developed for service to the community. *Who* the students are is far more important than *what* they can do, or *how much* information they retain. Cognitive understanding, while important, is not true knowledge until it leads to a heartfelt response of committed service. Gaining knowledge is much more than an intellectual acquisition of facts, involving students' whole beings. Therefore, assessment and evaluation procedures in Christian schools should extend well beyond intellectual knowledge. Questions such as 2, 6, and 8 on the preceding "test" are important (although inappropriate in the format presented). The purpose of evaluation in the language arts is primarily twofold:

- *Individual:* to determine a student's growth in language understanding and use, and to identify future learning goals for that student
- *Communal:* to determine whether the language arts program is meeting students' needs and furthering their growth

But evaluation may serve other purposes as well, including:

- sharing information about the development of language competence with students and parents
- reporting to supervisory bodies at various levels, from the local school board to state/provincial or even national bodies

To ensure that evaluation is congruent with a school's beliefs about children and learning, the school must be the primary agent in establishing its evaluation program. This task cannot be blindly delegated to, or appropriated from, publishers or external governmental agencies that may not share the school's central perspectives. By abdicating this crucial responsibility, the school faces the danger of allowing its curriculum to be shaped by external pressures rather than its own vision and framework.

Terminology

Before continuing, we need to understand some terminology associated with evaluation.[2] Below are listed and defined key terms as they will be used in this book:

Assessment refers to the processes used to gather information on student progress. These processes can encompass a wide range of procedures and tools, including (but not limited to) student self evaluation, teacher observation (in the form of written anecdotes or checklists), conferencing, gathering of artifacts (e.g., **portfolios**), and testing. Assessment can be **formative** or **summative.** Formative assessment is continuous, regular monitoring to chart student progress and to guide further instruction. Summative assessment is typically done at the end of a particular unit to determine each student's understanding of the unit's concepts. Obviously, a summative assessment can (and should) serve a formative function as well.

Evaluation refers to the *interpretation* of the information gathered during assessment. Evaluation involves making judgments about *past* student progress and determining the direction *future* instruction should take to assist student growth.

Testing occurs when we measure human performance against explicit, measurable criteria that have been established in advance.

Reporting is the avenue used to communicate student progress to students, parents, and administrators. While typically done through summative report cards, reporting can use formative means as well, including phone calls, newsletters, personal notes, and teacher- and/or student-led conferences. Increasingly, reporting involves students in evaluating and commenting on their own learning growth.

High-stakes assessments refer to single, summative assessments (usually tests) that play a key role in determining a student's educational prospects. For example, an end-of-year test that counts for 50 percent or more of a student's mark and determines promotion to the next grade is a high-stakes assessment. The Scholastic Aptitude Test (SAT) is a high-stakes, external standardized test. Typically, a high-stakes assessment causes students great anxiety and violates the principle of basing student evaluation on multiple modes of response.

Principles of Assessment and Evaluation

Some additional principles concerning assessment and evaluation are the following:

- *How* we evaluate and *what* we evaluate reflect what we value and affect what we teach. Thus assessment and evaluation in language arts should reflect the school's curricular goals and should be based on broad, predetermined standards.
- Because students have unique, God-given learning rates and styles, assessment and evaluation must provide multiple ways for them to demonstrate their knowledge. Language arts assessment and evaluation should thus take place in a variety of contexts, using a variety of tasks.
- Assessment and evaluation should include all aspects of student development.
- Assessment and evaluation must be formative as well as summative. That is, evaluation must be ongoing and concerned as much with the *process* of learning as with *end-point* achievement.
- As the professionals with the most intimate knowledge of their students' learning needs, teachers have primary responsibility for determining how to evaluate their achievement.
- Assessment and evaluation should focus on purposeful student work. It follows that the *form* of an assessment is as important as its content.
- *Individual student* assessment and evaluation must be clearly distinguished in both means and purpose from *program* evaluation.
- High-stakes, summative assessment and evaluation have little place in education, particularly at the elementary and middle school levels.

Four Common Problems

1. Equating Assessment with Objective Testing

Return for a moment to the test presented at the beginning of this chapter. As noted, its questions vary widely. Some are primarily factual, objective, or quantitative, while others demand more subjective or qualitative answers. Certain human abilities can easily be tested, or judged against explicit, predetermined, measurable criteria. For example, we can measure how fast a person runs 100 meters and compare the rate with that of others who are the same age by carefully measuring out a 100-meter course and using a stopwatch to compare performance. Similarly, we can test whether students spell correctly if the criterion for correctness is that each word be spelled exactly as specified in a standard English dictionary. Other human abilities are not so easy to test because only qualitative assessment criteria can be established for them, leaving the results open to interpretation.

Look back at "test" question 9, and ponder which of the grade 2 stories is better written. If the criteria for "good" writing are primarily correct spelling, punctuation, and grammar, then the first story is better because it outshines the second on these relatively objective criteria. But writing well is arguably far more complex than mastering the mechanics of writing; indeed, most of the criteria needed to judge a writing sample are not quantifiable. The best way to assess writing quality is to ask a skilled writer to read a piece and judge whether it is excellent, good, average, or poor. Of course, we can justify that decision by rating specified aspects of the writing (for instance by using a *rubric,* as discussed below). But our analysis should extend far beyond counting the correct (or incorrect) spellings, subject-verb agreements, commas, and so forth. Although these *surface aspects* of the writing inform our assessment, they certainly do not exhaust it.[3]

Much assessment and evaluation in schooling confuses *qualitative assessment* and *quantitative testing.* The problem is further compounded by our preference for *quantitative reporting*. When a student's report card sports a B+ or an 83 percent in language arts, a quantitative scale is being imposed on a kind of learning that requires, to a great extent, a qualitative evaluation. Giving only quantitative grades can be justified only when learning the material means simply mastering discrete, quantifiable bits and pieces of performance. But even the most ardent advocates of skills instruction would not go so far as to argue that we can simply tally performance on discrete skills and then rank students accordingly. Such an approach leads to a "trivial pursuit" conception of what is valuable in education, and in language arts.

2. Confusing Assessment with Instruction

When a school becomes obsessed with quantitative assessment and reporting, teachers frequently fail to distinguish between *assessment* and *instruction*. They come to believe that asking students questions, informally or formally, is the same as teaching. Consider an example from reading instruction:

Teachers typically assign a story for students to read and then, correctly realizing the need to teach comprehension skills, tell them to answer a list of questions (often from a teachers' guide) about the story. But asking questions about a story is comprehension assessment, *not* comprehension instruction. Comprehension instruction would point out differences among literal, inferential, and evaluative questions and suggest strategies for finding answers to each kind. Instruction would help students identify the story's context and uncover why contextual reading is key to understanding more than just surface meaning.[4] In short, assessment is *not* teaching. Having hired *teachers* for our schools, we should expect and encourage them, as professionals, to spend most of their time teaching rather than testing.[5]

3. Lack of Congruence between Evaluation and Instruction

Another problem that bedevils the issue of evaluation is **congruence**, or the appropriate match between teaching and evaluation.

Consider an example from spelling instruction:

Billy's teacher, Ms. Brant, notes (assesses) that Billy's writing contains many spelling errors. She has Billy make a list of his ten most common errors, helps him notice where those errors occur, and gives him suggestions about how to avoid such errors in the future (teaching). At the end of the week, Ms. Brant gives Billy a test on his ten words by reading them to him one by one. Billy scores 100 percent. When looking at Billy's next composition, however, Ms. Brant is dismayed to find that he has misspelled many of the same words again.

Notice what has happened. Ms. Brant's initial and terminal assessments of Billy's spelling took place in the context of his connected writing. The teaching and the subsequent spelling test, however, were isolated from any meaningful connected discourse. Ms. Brant and Billy encountered a typical *transfer of training problem*: the teaching and final assessment were not congruent.[6]

A more serious lack of congruence often occurs when a person other than the one doing the teaching evaluates the student. This frequently happens in high-stakes, government-mandated achievement tests. Unless the school carefully matches its instructional program to the tests (not recommended) or the test just happens to be so matched to the curriculum (not likely), students are penalized by a lack of congruence between instruction and evaluation.

This reality raises essential questions: Do we want government authorities rather than Christian educators to set the agenda for what is important to teach and evaluate? To what extent are government (and other external) tests congruent with the values that undergird a Christian conception of knowledge? Beyond what they tell us about group performance on certain basic skills and other objectively measurable information, such tests deserve very little status in a Christian school. Results certainly should not be used to evaluate individual students, provide significant report card information, or influence marks.

4. Sacrificing Pedagogical Usefulness to Attempted Precision

In our quest to come up with a system of letters or numbers that will give students, teachers, and parents the illusion of precise evaluation, we have lost sight of the very limited usefulness of quantitative designations. A carefully worded report on a student's performance, written by a qualified teacher, is far more valuable and *honest* than the reductionist practice of putting a number or letter grade (with or without pluses, minuses, or decimal points) on an assignment or report card.

Grades reduced to a number or letter are problematic for at least two reasons. First, those discrete marks create a false sense of quantitative precision. Second, they provide very little that is useful, either information about past performance or implications for future instruction.

For example, if Jane gets a B plus in math and John gets a C, what does that communicate? Yes, the teacher assesses Jane to be better at math than John, but how much better? And in what respects? Another example: If two students get 45 percent in reading, what does that communicate? Certainly, neither is reading very well, but are they struggling for the same reasons? Do they lack word recognition skills? decoding skills? practice? cognitive processing ability? The percentage grade provides no answers, whereas a carefully written anecdotal assessment and evaluation could specify those problems clearly. At best, a percentage or letter grade can serve as a proxy for a more detailed evaluation; in reality, such detail is rarely provided.

As educators, administrators, and parents, we should honestly admit that many of our assessment and evaluation schemes are not very accurate—and not very useful, either. We must also remember that our efforts to evaluate significant human activities are always fraught with qualitative subjectivity. Christian schools require teachers who are competent in the areas they teach and who exhibit the fruit of the Spirit (Galatians 5:22–23) in their lives. We must trust those teachers to make informed judgments about what children do at school, and to report those judgments in ways that are informative and helpful for further growth.[7]

Two Key Assessment Tools

1. Portfolios

Portfolio assessment uses a compilation of work done by a student over time. Frequently, the portfolio items are selected by the learner, or by the teacher and the learner together. Items included in a portfolio are deliberately chosen to illustrate what the learner can do. Teachers find portfolios useful in demonstrating a student's learning to parents and administrators and in helping the student understand what learning needs to be accomplished next, including areas requiring particular focus. Portfolios give students an opportunity to see the range of work they have done over time and to assess what they are accomplishing. Portfolios also help teachers reflect on their teaching and on the learning their students are engaged in. Below are a few helpful references offering more detailed information on portfolio assessment in the language arts classroom:

◊ Robert J. Tierney, Mark A. Carter, and Laura E. Desai. 1991. *Portfolio assessment in the reading-writing classroom.* Norwood, MA: Christopher-Gordon Publishers.

◊ Roberta B. Wiener and Judith H. Cohen. 1997. *Literacy portfolios: Using assessment to guide instruction.* Upper Saddle River, NJ: Merrill.

◊ James Barton and Angelo Collins, eds. 1997. *Portfolio assessment: A handbook for educators.* Menlo Park, CA: Innovative Learning Publications.

2. Rubrics

A rubric is a scoring guide that sets specific criteria for quality work. Rather than simply basing a grade on a learning performance or product, the teacher clearly outlines beforehand the criteria he will use in assessing the work and how he will determine quality within each category. For example, it is common for teachers assigning a written research report to indicate that the work will be graded according to the following criteria:

- Comprehension of subject/topic
- Writing effectiveness
  - Idea development
  - Organization
  - Language usage
  - Mechanics

Even if students receive careful explanations for each of those criteria, they still do not know what would count for an excellent, average, or mediocre performance in each. The rubric outlined in figure 3-2, by contrast, gives students far more specific information about how the writing will be evaluated. It also provides a tool that enables the teacher to grade the assignment fairly, applying the same criteria to each piece of work.

Depending on the intention of the teachers and the skills they have taught, they can make a rubric more or less specific, with more or fewer scoring levels. Below are two helpful resources that provide both directions for constructing rubrics and reproducible samples for assessing reading and writing.

◊ Adele Fiderer. 1998. *35 rubrics and checklists to assess reading and writing: Grades K–2.* New York: Scholastic Professional Books.

◊ Adele Fiderer. 1999. *40 rubrics and checklists to assess reading and writing: Grades 3–6.* New York: Scholastic Professional Books.

Figure 3-2: Sample rubric for assessing grade 4 research report writing

Subject/Topic:	Level 3	Level 2	Level 1
COMPREHENSION OF SUBJECT	Writing indicates an excellent understanding of the topic. Reflects use of a range of resources.	Writing indicates a satisfactory understanding of the topic. Reflects the use of one or more resources.	Writing indicates a limited understanding of the topic. Contains factual errors and may be missing critical information.
WRITING EFFECTIVENESS			
Idea Development	Develops relevant ideas clearly and fully. Information focuses on the topic. Details, examples, anecdotes, or personal experiences explain and clarify the information.	Develops ideas satisfactorily with adequate details, examples, anecdotes, or experiences.	Develops ideas incompletely with few or no supporting details. Some information may be unrelated to the topic. Some information may be copied from a source without attribution.
Language Usage	Uses lively and descriptive language. Details, anecdotes, and examples explain and clarify information. Varies sentence structure.	Uses some descriptive language. Demonstrates some sense of sentence variety.	Uses limited vocabulary. Uses repetitive, simple sentences.
Mechanics	Writing shows few errors in basic language conventions.	Limited errors in basic language conventions do not interfere with meaning.	Contains many errors in conventions but still conveys some meaning.

Questions for Discussion

1. Do you agree with the twofold purpose of assessment and evaluation presented in this chapter? What other purposes might there be? For example, do you think it is appropriate to use tests to motivate students to study? to enhance students' self-concept? as a tool for punishment?

2. In your experience as a student, what would you estimate was the ratio of summative to formative evaluation? Do you think that ratio is appropriate?

3. Do you believe it is possible to separate your evaluation of a student's schoolwork from your evaluation of him or her as a person? Discuss this in light of the fact that elementary and middle school students spend a large portion of their waking hours in school and that school may be the only place where they experience formal evaluation.

4. What are some of the "multiple ways" elementary and middle school students can demonstrate their learning in the language arts? Be specific. For example, think of that old standby, the book report. Mention at least ten different ways a student can demonstrate understanding of a book. How many of these ways involve modalities other than writing?

5. Do you feel you have the knowledge and wisdom to evaluate your students in the language arts? Or are teacher manuals and published tests the best assessment tools, since experts have designed them?

6. This chapter paints a scenario in which questions serve primarily as assessment tools and not teaching tools. Can questions be used to teach? If so, how? You may wish to consult chapter 13 of John Van Dyk's *The Craft of Christian Teaching: A Classroom Journey* (2000) for a useful discussion on questioning techniques from a Christian perspective.

For Further Consideration

1. Questions 10 and 11 on the "test" at the beginning of this chapter ask you to distinguish between testing and evaluation in your own life. It struck me as I was writing this chapter that, since my graduate school days more than 20 years ago, I have never written a test. I have been evaluated numerous times, but seldom by answering a prescribed

list of questions in a fixed amount of time. Parents often argue that tests "prepare students for real life." How realistic are most school tests?

2. What role do high-stakes assessments play in the lives of elementary and middle school students in your state or province? Are you comfortable with that role?

3. Read the wonderful little book *First Grade Takes a Test* by Miriam Cohen (1980). How many of the issues about assessment and evaluation raised in this chapter are addressed in Cohen's book, which has a published reading level of grade 2.5?

Endnotes

1 The reader will recall from chapter 1 that *anthropology* refers to one's view of the nature of the learner while *epistemology* refers to one's theory of knowledge. For more extensive treatments of the development of a Christian anthropology and epistemology, see the helpful chapters in part 2 of Albert Greene's *Reclaiming the Future of Christian Education: A Transforming Vision* (1998), also published by ACSI.

2 This section does *not* discuss all the technical terms related to the area of study generally referred to as *testing and measurement.* This is not to say that teachers can ignore this terminology and the concepts it represents. On the contrary, since there is so much emphasis on external accountability and standardized testing in the language arts, it is important that teachers understand both the uses and misuses of these and other assessment measures. That, in turn, will require at least a basic familiarity with assessment terminology and elementary statistics. Most general educational psychology textbooks have a section on basic statistics for teachers.

3 In my judgment, the second story of question 9 is by far the "better" written of the two. My criteria would include vocabulary choice, willingness to risk, and creativity relative to the age of the student. In these samples from actual grade 2 students, the writing of the first is conventionally perfect and "safe," but unremarkable in every other respect. The second piece is quite mature in its sophisticated play with the word "trouble" as well as its vocabulary. It is easier to teach correct mechanics than writing "sense," which the second young writer obviously has in spades.

4 Dolores Durkin (1978–1979) conducted a now classic study about the critical distinction between comprehension assessment and comprehension instruction. Although now more than twenty years old, this study is still

eminently worth reading. It would be revealing to compare Durkin's findings, based in part on then current basal reading series, with what is presented as comprehension instruction in today's basal series.

5 The foregoing example is not meant to suggest that there is no place for question-asking in teaching or even that questions can't be used for instructional purposes. The point is that teachers must carefully think through their questioning behavior.

6 The lack of congruence between instruction and evaluation is a common problem that is not always easy to solve. Sometimes it is necessary to focus on a particular skill dimension of a complex task (e.g., spelling as part of composition). The acid test for spelling competence is how a learner spells in a real writing task rather than on isolated lists or during spelling bees. Teachers must help students develop a spelling conscience and emphasize correct spelling as part of the editing phase of the writing process. See chapter 12 for details.

7 An excellent further discussion of evaluating student learning in Christian schools is provided in chapter 6 of Van Brummelen (1998). For specific plans and strategies for evaluating student achievement in different aspects of the language arts, see the appropriate sections of chapters 9 through 12 of this book. Another excellent resource is the *Language Arts Handbook,* 2nd ed., edited by Den Boer (1996, 665–709).

Chapter 4

Materials for Language Arts Instruction: Basals, Literature, the Library, and the Classroom

Education is big business in North America and most other English-speaking countries, so perhaps it's no surprise that educational publishers vie for a share of the lucrative textbook market. With the possible exception of mathematics, their largest market is language arts, especially basal reading series. Publishers also peddle a plethora of workbooks, blackline masters, overhead transparencies, kits, computer software, and other paraphernalia, as well as literature (both fiction and nonfiction) written especially for children. This chapter provides guidance for the difficult task of selecting from among all those materials for Christian school library and classroom use. It concludes by discussing the use of materials in thematic teaching and by noting how psychological tone and physical arrangement affect the language arts classroom.

Schools are for learning, and literacy is a prerequisite for learning. Helping students to become literate is a major task of schools and the teachers who work in them. Professionals require appropriate tools, and for the language arts teacher the major tool is print. Books in their many forms are still the major repository of print; therefore, schools need first of all to be richly supplied with books of all kinds to support student learning. Students need access to a wide variety of other print materials as well, including magazines, newspapers, and electronic print media. They also need writing tools such as pens, pencils, paper, word processors, photocopiers, printers, paper cutters, and staplers. And they need book-making tools, including art supplies.

Literacy tools cost money, and money is in short supply for many schools, especially Christian schools. However, Christian communities in most English-speaking countries are relatively affluent. Many Christian school families live in attractive homes, drive recent model cars, and take regular family vacations. Christian businesses are equipped with the latest in electronic communication tools, and few Christian farmers forego expensive modern machinery. Yet I am often appalled at the sorry condition of Christian school libraries. Many Christian schools have only a small central library that has limited and often outdated reference materials and even fewer fiction resources. Many classrooms have little more than basic sets of textbooks for the content courses. There are exceptions, but in general the book and print budget for most Christian schools is not nearly adequate for the task at hand. Too many Christian schools rely on sporadic fundraising by auxiliaries and other volunteer groups for what should be a central item in the operational budget. This is a plea to Christian school board members and school principals to encourage their communities to view school and classroom libraries as the heart of their schools' learning enterprise, and to fund them accordingly.

Basal Readers

The **basal reading series** is the dominant tool for teaching reading in English-speaking countries. A typical series consists of a comprehensive, integrated set of student readers, workbooks, teacher manuals, and other materials for teaching reading at increasing levels of difficulty.

An early precursor to today's elaborate basal reading series was the *McGuffey Readers,* the nineteenth century's most popular reading series. Two books in the series were published in 1836, and by 1844 the full set of seven was available. Most previous series assumed that the child had already acquired a basic reading skill, but W. H. McGuffey's readers did not. The first book began by teaching the alphabet. A syllabary soon followed containing stories made with simple words, and later volumes were anthologies of largely moralistic reading selections. The series is still available, in a reprint of the 1844 edition.

Several years ago, a Christian school organization surveyed textbook needs in its schools and found that almost all used commercial reading series and materials for kindergarten through grade 6. The same survey found that the majority of language arts teachers did not perceive an overwhelming need for Christian school publishers to produce a complete reading or literature series. It is probably fair to infer from the survey that many Christian language arts teachers are happy with the basal series they use.

It is not difficult to understand why graduated reading series have such widespread use. Publishing companies invest millions to produce lavishly illustrated readers accompanied by detailed teacher manuals that provide scripted lesson plans and a host of suggested teaching activities. While the basal series seldom have identifiable authors, they do feature the names of reading specialists with impressive academic credentials and thus convey a sense of professionalism and even "scientific" authority. For the busy classroom teacher, the reading series is an impressively packaged, ready-to-use program. For students hampered by the often limited supply of other literacy materials in the school, the readers provide ready access to print.

Yet it is disheartening to know that basals are the primary resource used to teach reading in Christian schools, for they have distinct shortcomings. First, basal readers tend to demean language and literature, especially at the primary levels. Second, they demean the role of both teacher and child in the teaching/learning process. Third, they draw money away from more worthwhile curriculum expenditures. In using these inferior tools, Christian schools are unfortunately no more discerning than their secular counterparts.

Demeaning Language and Literature

As chapter 6 will demonstrate, children acquire language through interaction with more competent users who model whole, functional, meaningful language. No one teaches children to talk by presenting carefully sequenced bits and pieces of English phonology and syntax. Reading and writing are also most easily learned when the environment presents language in whole, functional, and meaningful contexts.[1] Thus even the earliest selections that children are asked to read should exemplify real language, language that is comprehensible and important to them. Most basals do quite the opposite, as Ken Goodman (1986) points out:

> Basals put undue emphasis on isolated aspects of language: letters, letter-sound relationships, words, sentence fragments, or sentences. Often, particularly in workbooks, there is no cohesive, meaningful text and no situational context. That leads learners to put inverted value on the bits and pieces of language, on isolated words and skills, and not enough on making sense of real, comprehensible stories and expository passages. Basals often create artificial language passages or text fragments by controlling vocabulary, building around specific phonic relationships or word-attack skills, and often create artificial texts by applying readability formulas to real texts. Even the use of real children's literature is marred by gearing it to skill development, rewriting it, or using excerpts instead of whole books. (361–362)

A more recent revisiting of basal readers (Shannon and Goodman 1994) found that matters had changed little in the 15 years since Goodman's critique.

A reading/language arts program ought to be based on real literature at all levels rather than on the specially manufactured, often artificial fare of basals. Especially at the primary levels, the series focus almost exclusively on the *how* of teaching to read and very little on the *what,* yet Christian teachers should be as concerned with *what* children are reading as with *how* they are learning to do so. Much that basals present is not worth learning to read. Not only is the language artificial, but the subject matter is often insipid and trivial, a shameful reality given the recent explosion of worthwhile literature for young children. How many selections in the K–3 basal readers have moved you to either genuine laughter or tears?

A related criticism is this: since their subject matter must be inoffensive to everyone, basals often deal with only the most basic of shared Western values. Because society is uncertain what constitutes a family, for example, many publishers shy away from selections having family settings. Similarly, one would not know from examining the readers of any major publisher that religion plays a role in North American lives. Religion is just too hot to handle. Paul Vitz (1986) has found considerable evidence of systematic explicit and implicit bias against religion as well as certain political and economic positions in American school textbooks, especially in basal readers.

Demeaning the Roles of Teacher and Child

Manuals that prescribe detailed scripts for teacher-pupil interaction imply that teachers need to be protected from their own ignorance of how students learn. But teachers are professionals who know best what their particular children require. They are not simply technicians who need outside "experts" to dictate what they should say and how students should respond. Schools and teachers need to make basals curricular servants rather than curricular dictators.

Accompanying most basal readers is a plethora of workbooks, skill sheets, blackline masters, mastery tests, and management systems. Much of this auxiliary material is now finding its way into computer software, giving the programs an aura of technological sophistication and precision. The sad fact is that many reading lessons involve far more underlining, filling in the blanks, circling of answers, and other busywork than actual reading of meaningful connected text. Several widely respected studies estimate that, in a typical forty-minute reading lesson, the average child spends less than five minutes in actual reading. Beyond that, the majority of children in elementary school spend only five to seven minutes a day in reading-related activities, and only about one percent of free time reading from books (Goodlad 1984). Since we get good at what we practice, it is small wonder that many children do not get good at reading.

Basals and Curricular Stewardship

Basals often take money away from more worthwhile curriculum expenditures. The initial cost of outfitting a school with a contemporary K–6 series may well exceed $15,000. Maintaining and purchasing nonreusable components of a series, such as workbooks and tests, may cost as much as $700 per class each year. Of course, costs may vary from area to area, and schools do not always purchase all available support materials, yet by conservative estimates it is fair to say that acquiring and maintaining basals is expensive. Considering the often inadequate condition of many Christian school libraries, it is legitimate to ask whether purchasing a basal reading series is wise curricular stewardship. Children and adolescents do not need more books that teach them how to read; instead, they need more books with material worth reading. Curricular money would be better spent on trade books—poetry, fiction, biography, and content-specific works written for children by children's writers.

To purchase those books wisely, classroom teachers need to become familiar with children's literature, both classic and contemporary. Teachers are also wise to consult librarians, library associations, resource guides, and knowledgeable people in the community who can help identify appropriate works for classroom libraries. The following print resources are also helpful tools in building libraries with a diversity of reading materials at varying levels of difficulty:

◊ Brenda Weaver. 2000. *Leveling books K–6: Matching readers to the text.* Newark, DE: International Reading Association.

◊ Rog and Burton (2002), in a recent issue of *The Reading Teacher*, also describe a useful book-leveling system.

◊ Irene Fountas and Gay Su Pinnell. 1996. *Guided reading: Good first teaching for all children.* Portsmouth, NH: Heinemann.

◊ Irene Fountas and Gay Su Pinnell. 2000. *Guiding readers and writers (Grades 3–6): Teaching comprehension, genre, and content literacy*. Portsmouth, NH: Heinemann.

◊ Mark B. Thogmartin. 1996. *Teach a child to read with children's books: Combining story reading, phonics, and writing to promote reading success.* Bloomington, IN: ERIC Clearinghouse on Reading, English, and Communication. The Family Literacy Center: EDINFO Press.

◊ *Library handbook.* 1997. Langley, BC: Society of Christian Schools in British Columbia.

◊ *Survey of recommended reading lists.* 1998. Colorado Springs, CO: Association of Christian Schools International.

At all times, literacy tools such as pens, pencils, crayons, markers, typewriters, computers (word processors), photocopiers, erasers, rulers, stencils, paper, scissors, and glue must be available. Classrooms need learning centers with materials that involve children in listening, speaking, reading, and writing, both for the activities themselves and to supplement the content of such classes as mathematics, science, social studies, and Bible. In short, the language-centered classroom must be rich in materials that invite children to talk, chant, sing, view, read, and write about the rich diversity of things and ideas in God's creation.[2]

Selecting Literature

Censorship is a dirty word in a democracy dedicated to freedom of expression. Should Christian schools engage in censorship of student reading materials? Is there a difference between censorship and literature selection? How should a Christian school deal with parental challenges to specific literature in the library and classroom?

In *Literature for Children: A Short Introduction* (1997), David L. Russell argues that there is no justification for censorship of any literature, and that includes children's literature. The fact of the matter seems to be that there is absolutely no evidence that essentially good children are turned into bad by reading the wrong kinds of books—just as there is no evidence that reading the "right" books will correct a willful child's behavior (226–227).

This strikes me as a very peculiar view for an educator. It suggests that reading has no impact whatsoever on a child. If that is the case, why bother to teach children to read? Our whole educational enterprise is predicated on the belief that what children hear, read, and see does make a difference to the persons they become. It has always been incumbent on the adult generation to select the influences that will affect children. The Bible says clearly that parents and the community of believers are responsible for nurturing children (see Deuteronomy 6: 4–9 and Ephesians 6:4) and that misleading children can have dire consequences for the adults who do so (see Matthew 18:6, Mark 9:42, and Luke 17:2). Thus absolute freedom to read whatever is available is untenable on both moral and practical grounds. Thousands of titles of children's literature are published every year in English. Even if it were wise to buy them all (which it isn't), such wholesale purchase is fiscally impossible. Schools must make selections, and to do so they must establish some criteria to follow in building classroom and library collections.

Issues in Literature Selection

Isolation vs. Inoculation in Christian Schooling

The criteria we set for what children should or should not read reflect our response to the larger question of how Christians should engage with the surrounding culture.[3] One common view holds that Christians should shun engagement, living apart from the world as much as possible. This response might be called the *isolation* position. The Old Order Amish and other very conservative Anabaptist traditions take this approach. But isolation is not biblical in view of the gospel's call for Christians to be light and salt in the world, nor is it practicable. In this time of mass electronic communication, it is virtually impossible to shelter oneself and one's children from cultural influences.

A metaphor that better characterizes the task of Christian parenting and schooling is *inoculation.* In the health field, we inoculate children against many deadly diseases as a preventive medical strategy because we know it is virtually impossible to isolate them from all potentially harmful bacteria and viruses. An inoculation actually introduces the body to the disease one wishes to combat but in a weakened form and in carefully controlled doses. The strategy prompts the body's immune system to produce antibodies against organisms in the vaccine so that, in the event of serious exposure, antibodies are already there to fight the disease.

Christian nurture can play a similar inoculation role in our children's lives. Christian schools inoculate students by introducing the "spirits of the age" at developmentally appropriate times while honing the ability to discern those spirits. Thus mature, insightful Christian teachers help their students become thoughtful participants in society, equipped to further the redemptive work of Christ on earth.[4]

This is not to say that no literature is out-of-bounds for Christians. Certainly, literature that is blatantly pornographic or that celebrates violence has no place in the Christian life. But one must be careful not to judge a literary work on superficial moralistic grounds. The Bible, for example, includes some graphic accounts containing sex and violence. Many of the heroic figures of the Old Testament are not the sort we would want our children to "hang out" with. Take David, for example. The "man after God's own heart" was also a murderer and adulterer with too much blood on his hands to build God's temple. Yet, despite his many grievous shortcomings, David loved God, confessed his sins, and was used by God as a link in the covenant chain. We must learn to look beyond the surface and probe the moral center of a piece of literature. The following example from my own classroom teaching illustrates this principle.

An Example: *A Wrinkle in Time* vs. *Big Red*

About 25 years ago, when teaching a combination grade 6/7 class in a small Christian elementary school, I experienced my first encounter with a parent adamant about removing a novel from the language arts curriculum. The novel was Madeleine L'Engle's *A Wrinkle in Time* (1962), the 1963 Newbery Medal winner, which remains to this day at the center of controversy in certain Christian school communities.

The parent's reason for asking to have the book removed from study was ostensibly that it "glorifies witchcraft and reduces Jesus to the status of simply one of the great figures of Western civilization." This parent added that she had made some study of the novels on the government's list of approved works for elementary schools, and was pleased to see that I had also assigned *Big Red* by Jim Kjelgaard. In her view, "books like *Big Red* with their sense of adventure and solid values are just what we send our kids to Christian school for," or words to that effect.

I assigned *Big Red* and *A Wrinkle in Time* to my grade 6/7 class for several reasons. Although very different books, they are both "good reads," likely to appeal to a wide cross-section of middle school readers. More importantly, however, I thought (and still think) that grade 6/7 is not too soon to begin teaching something about literary discernment. I hoped I could help them see that *Big Red* is a far more "dangerous" book than *A Wrinkle in Time*.

I must confess that I have never heard a word of criticism from any Christian school community about *Big Red*. First published in 1945, its copyright renewed in 1976, with many subsequent reprintings, *Big Red* is (by all reports) a heartwarming wilderness adventure in which a poor boy makes good through hard work, a bit of luck, and the help of his majestic Irish setter.

Before I am rejected out-of-hand as some high falutin' college professor making simple things complex, it may be best to let these two books speak for themselves. What follows are brief plot summaries, plus a few selected quotations from each book. Listen to the spirits at play:

Big Red in brief

Danny and his widowed father, Ross, are poor trappers living on the vast Wintapi estate of the wealthy but benevolent Mr. Haggin. By a stroke of luck, Danny is allowed to care for Mr. Haggin's prize Irish setter, Champion Sylvester's Boy (Big Red). Together the boy and "his" dog forge a relationship which, as the book's jacket says, leads to Danny's discovery of "what it takes to make a good dog and a good man."

Figure 4-1: Selected quotations from _Big Red_ by Jim Kjelgaard

P. 6: *Throughout his life* [Danny] *had accepted without even thinking about them the hardships and the trials that he lived. It was his, he was the man who could cope with it, he could imagine nothing else.*

P. 24: *Ross had been around long enough to know that people who handled rich men's dogs could make more money in a year than some trappers made in a lifetime. They could be somebody too.*

P. 32: [Mr. Haggin asks Danny] *"What do you think of dog shows?"*

"They seem like a piddlin' waste of time," Danny confessed.

"Danny, you're wrong. You would be entirely right if all a dog show amounted to was a bit of ribbon, or a cup, or a boost in an owner's pride. But there's more to it than that, much more. In one sense you could think of it as part of the story of man, and his constant striving toward something better. A dog show is illustrative of man's achievement, and a blue ribbon is more than a bit of silk. It's a mark, Danny, one that can never be erased. The dog that wins it will not die. If we send Boy to the show, and he comes back as the best of breed, then that's something for all future dog lovers and dog owners to build on. Don't you see? A hundred years from now someone may stand on this very spot with a fine Irish setter, and he'll trace its lineage back to some other fine Irish setter, perhaps to Boy. And he will know that he has built on what competent men have declared to be the very best. He will know also that he, too, can go one step nearer the perfection that man must and will have in all things. It did not start with us, Danny, but with the first man who ever dreamed of an Irish setter. All we're trying to do is advance one step further, and Boy's ribbon, if he wins one, will simply be proof that we've succeeded."

"I see," Danny breathed. "I never thought of it like that before."

"Always think of it that way, Danny," Mr. Haggin urged.

P. 110: *The Picketts could seldom afford a doctor, and even though they now had fifty dollars a month that Mr. Haggin was paying Danny to take care of Red, it never occurred to either of them to pay another man to do what they could do themselves.*

P. 110: *Ross seldom rested, and never wasted time. Ross had always secretly dreamed of having fine things, luxurious things, and from the start was doomed never to get them. But he never seemed to recognize the fact that he was doomed, and always tried to bring as much as he could into the shanty in the beech woods.*

P. 152: [After killing a big buck deer and apprehending an escaped convict] *A warm feeling crept through him. Life in the beech woods might be hard, harsh, and dangerous. But only the strong survived there, and Danny felt a swelling pride as the fact was driven home to him. The dead buck, hung by its antlers and swinging gently in the wind, was more than just another deer. It was another achievement and another victory, an assurance that he was strong.*

Pp. 201–202: *And there in the still of the night it was as though some mysterious vessel poured into him a renewal of an old faith. First, it was faith in himself, and then that in Red.*

P. 215: *Something strong seemed to have grown within him. He was not the Danny Pickett who had been born and lived in poverty all his life. He had cast off the old shackles, the confining bonds that said he and Ross had to struggle along as best they could. If others could do big things so could he.*

A Wrinkle in Time in brief

A group of children must rescue their father from a dark planet that is under the direct influence of a great evil power. They are aided by three strange "ladies" who take them on an interplanetary journey by creating a "wrinkle" in time.

Figure 4-2: Selected quotations from *A Wrinkle in Time* by Madeleine L'Engle

P. 40: [Calvin speaking about his dysfunctional family] "*But I love her. That's the funny part of it. I love them all, and they don't give a hoot about me. Maybe that's why I call when I'm not going to be home. Because I care. Nobody else does. You don't know how lucky you are to be loved.*"

P. 46: [Meg] "*Do you think things always have an explanation?*" [Mrs. Murray] "*Yes, I believe that they do. But I think that with our human limitations we're not always able to understand the explanations. But you see, Meg, just because we don't understand doesn't mean that the explanation doesn't exist."*

P. 63: *Mrs. Who's glasses shone at her gently. "If you want to help your father you must learn patience.* Vitam impendere vero. *'To stake one's life for the truth.' That is what we must do."*

P. 65: [After Mrs. Whatsit transmutes into a glorious centaur-like creature] *Calvin fell to his knees. "No." Mrs. Whatsit said, though her voice was not Mrs. Whatsit's voice. "Not to me, Calvin. Never to me. Stand up."*

P. 67: [Traveling on "Mrs. Whatsit's" back, the children fly over a wonderful garden in which many marvelous creatures are singing.] *Listen then. "Sing unto the Lord a new song...." Throughout her entire body Meg felt a pulse of joy such as she had never known before.*

Pp. 71–73: [The children are brought into a high plateau and look back toward earth only to see a dark shadow that blots out everything.] *What could there be about a shadow that was so terrible that she knew that there had never been before, or ever would be again, anything that would chill her with a fear that was beyond shuddering, beyond crying or screaming, beyond the possibility of comfort? "That dark Thing we saw," she said. "Is that what my father is fighting?"*

"Yes," Mrs. Which said.

P. 84: [Mrs. Whatsit] *"It was really a very great honor for me to be chosen for this mission. It's just because of my verbalizing and materializing so well. But of course we can't take any credit for our talents. It's how we use them that counts."*

Pp. 88–89: [The children visit the "Happy Medium" where they are shown the evil shadow covering their own earth and learn that it is Evil, the Power of Darkness. They are told the shadow has been there a long time but that a battle against evil is being fought, and earth is among the regions that have supplied fighters.] *"All through the universe it's being fought, all through the cosmos, and my, but it's a grand and glorious battle."*

"Who have our fighters been?" Calvin asked.

"Oh, you must know them, dear," Mrs. Whatsit said. Mrs. Who's spectacles shone out at them triumphantly. "And the light shineth in the darkness, and the darkness comprehended it not."

"Jesus," Charles Wallace said.

"Why of course, Jesus! Of course!" Mrs. Whatsit said. "Go on, Charles, love. There were others. All your great artists. They've been lights for us to see by." [Here, in conversation, are mentioned many of the "greats" of civilization: Leonardo da Vinci, Michelangelo, Shakespeare, Bach, Pasteur, Madame Curie, Einstein, Schweitzer, Ghandi, Buddha, Beethoven, Rembrandt, St. Francis, Euclid, Copernicus.]

P. 102: *"Be aware of pride and arrogance, Charles, for they may betray you."*

P. 130: [The Man with the Red Eyes] *"Why don't you trust me, Charles? Why don't you trust me enough to come in and find out what I am? I am peace and utter rest. I am freedom from all responsibility. To come in to me is the last difficult decision you need ever make."*

P. 140: [Charles Wallace captured by IT] *"On Camazotz we are all happy because we are all alike. Differences create problems."*

P. 160: *"But that's exactly what we have on Camazotz. Complete equality. Everybody exactly the same." For a moment her brain reeled with confusion. Then came a moment of blazing truth. "No!" she cried triumphantly. "Like and equal are not the same thing at all."*

P. 172: [Father] *"I am a human being and a very fallible one. But I agree with Calvin. We were sent here for something. And we know that all things work together for good to them that love*

God, to them who are called according to his purpose."

P. 186: *"Are you fighting the Black Thing?" Meg asked. "Oh yes," Aunt Beast replied. "In doing that we can never relax. We are the called according to His purpose, and whom He calls, them He also justifies. Of course we have help, and without help it would be much more difficult."*

P. 191: [Meg is trying to explain the three ladies to the Beasts when Calvin suddenly interjects] *"Angels!" Calvin shouted from across the table. "Guardian angels!" There was a moment's silence, and he shouted again, his face tense with concentration, "Messengers! Messengers from God!"*

P. 201: [Mrs. Who] *"Listen, Meg. Listen well. The foolishness of God is wiser than men; and the weakness of God is stronger than men...."* [1 Corinthians 1:25, 27–28]

P. 207: *And that's where IT made its fatal mistake, for as Meg said automatically, "Mrs. Whatsit loves me; that's what she told me, that she loves me." Suddenly she knew. She knew! Love. That was what she had that IT did not have. She had Mrs. Whatsit's love, and her father's, and her mother's, and the real Charles Wallace's love, and the twins', and Aunt Beast's. And she had love for them.*

As these quotations clearly demonstrate, the fundamental ethos or spirit that informs *Big Red* is one of humanistic, Darwinian self-sufficiency. *Big Red's* **moral center** suggests that humans must rely on their own strength and wits to get ahead in the world, and that getting ahead is largely a matter of acquiring luxurious things. This is, of course, a fundamental heresy—the same heresy of pride in self-sufficiency that led to the Fall.

A Wrinkle in Time, on the other hand, is pervaded by the cosmic struggle between good and evil that can only be won by self-sacrificing love and supernatural grace. Thus *A Wrinkle in Time,* a fantasy, provides a far more realistic (i.e., biblically truthful) account of reality than does the ostensibly "realistic" *Big Red.*

Does that mean *A Wrinkle in Time* has no aspects that invite Christian criticism? Of course not! Does it mean I would endorse banning a book such as *Big Red* from the Christian classroom? Again, of course not! I worry, however, when Christians attack excellent literature for superficial reasons while oblivious of the much more subtle but powerful manifestations of the Lie that often masquerades as "harmless adventure." It is precisely in the Christian classroom that children can be guided to test the spirits expressed in literature.

Fantasy in the Christian Classroom

Of all of the literary genres, fantasy presents the greatest problem to the Christian community and to the Christian language arts/English teacher. This section will explore the roots of this difficulty and suggest a reason why fantasy is in fact a fitting literary vehicle for exploring the truth of the Christian story.

The "problem" with fantasy literature in the Christian classroom is a subspecies of a larger problem, or at least unease, with fiction in any form. After all, many Christians say, doesn't fiction lie? Yes. Fiction lies. But it "lies" to discover the truth. Any Christian who doubts this paradox is unaware that the Bible is filled with fictional "lies." Christ's parables are prime and familiar examples, but others abound. It follows that narration or story should hold an honored place in the Christian life and school. Chapter 6 discusses this topic further; for an extensive exposition, I recommend John Bolt's *The Christian Story and the Christian School* (1993).

As reaction to Madeleine L'Engle's *A Wrinkle in Time* illustrates, fantasy fiction has "special problem" status in the Christian school literary canon. The parent who approached me charged Madeleine L'Engle with glorifying witchcraft and reducing Jesus to less than God. Today I would probably hear that her work is "New Age" as well, a charge also leveled at C. S. Lewis's *Narnia Chronicles* and J.R.R. Tolkien's *The Hobbit* and *The Lord of the Rings* trilogy. Since the Bible enjoins us to eschew witchcraft and the occult, it is argued that Christians should also shun such fiction.

As an aside, the Bible enjoins us to avoid a host of moral dangers, and there is probably no genre of fiction or nonfiction that doesn't deal with at least one such moral danger.

Before addressing the issue of the perceived danger of fantasy as compared with other literature, it may be well to define our terms.

First, what is *fantasy literature?* Very simply, fantasy literature is any literature of the "impossible" where "impossible" means events that contradict the laws of the natural world. In that sense, the oldest fantasy literature is the traditional folk tale with its giants, ogres, witches, wizards, and magic occurrences. Folk tales differ from modern fantasy in that their roots lie in an oral tradition with no definite author. They also tend to be quite formulaic, with stock characters and settings. Such tales have simple, direct plots meant to teach or illustrate a moral truth, or to explain the origins of natural phenomena. Modern fantasy, on the other hand, is crafted by a definite author; is often very complex in structure; and contains deeper character development, more detailed settings, and intricate plots.

Although any classification system is arbitrary, it is helpful to group fantasy fiction into types, as illustrated in figure 4-3.

Figure 4-3: Types of fantasy fiction

ANIMAL FANTASY	
Kenneth Grahame	*The Wind in the Willows*
E. B. White	*Charlotte's Web*
Richard Adams	*Watership Down*
TOY FANTASY	
A. A. Milne	*Winnie the Pooh*
Margery Williams	*The Velveteen Rabbit*
Leo Lionni	*Alexander and the Wind-up Mouse*
ECCENTRIC CHARACTERS	
P. L. Travers	*Mary Poppins*
Astrid Lindgren	*Pippi Longstocking*
Roald Dahl	*Charlie and the Chocolate Factory*

ENCHANTED JOURNEYS AND IMAGINARY LANDS	
Frank Baum	*The Wizard of Oz*
J. M. Barrie	*Peter Pan*
Mary Norton	*The Borrowers*
Carol Kendall	*The Gammage Cup*
Jonathan Swift	*Gulliver's Travels*
SCIENCE FICTION AND SPACE	
Mary Shelley	*Frankenstein*
Monica Hughes	*Isis Trilogy*
Madeleine L'Engle	*A Wrinkle in Time*
John Christopher	*The White Mountains*
Jules Verne	*20,000 Leagues under the Sea*
C. S. Lewis	*Science Fiction Trilogy*
Ray Bradbury	*All Summer in a Day*
SUPERNATURAL AND TIME TRAVEL	
Penelope Lively	*The Ghost of Thomas Kempe*
Phillipa Pearce	*Tom's Midnight Garden*
Alan Garner	*The Owl Service*
R. L. Stine	[Many, many books]
J. K. Rowling	*Harry Potter series [4]*
HEROIC, QUEST, OR HIGH FANTASY	
C. S. Lewis	*Narnia Chronicles [7]*
Lloyd Alexander	*Prydain Chronicles [5]*
Ursula LeQuin	*Earthsea series [6]*
Susan Cooper	*The Dark Is Rising series*
J.R.R. Tolkien	*The Hobbit*
	The Lord of the Rings
Sigmund Brouwer	*Winds of Light series [7]*

Fantasy is often contrasted with *realism*, literature that admits to no transcendent or supernatural influence in life. Realistic fiction takes for granted that the world of empirical reality, that is, of the five senses, is all there is, and that the human condition must be lived largely within this framework. C. S. Lewis argues that realistic fiction might actually be the most dangerous genre for Christians, including Christian children. As he points out, few children really expect to meet a dragon as a result of reading fantasy, but many may come to believe that getting rich through hard work is a primary human value after reading certain "realistic" fiction.

The charges against fantasy literature are numerous. Fantasy, it's said, is escapist, unreal, New Age, and worse. Let's look briefly at those charges:

Escapism can denote a fleeing of legitimate obligations or an unwillingness to confront the harsh realities of life. But it is *not* escapist to want to escape a prison cell if one is unjustly imprisoned. It makes sense to seek escape from dire circumstances. Many times we need to get away from certain places or situations for a while, taking some distance to see life from a new perspective.

The charge that fantasy literature is unreal begs the question, What is reality? which is a question of metaphysics. Although the Bible is not antimaterial (after all, God created matter), it clearly does not support a materialistic naturalism that admits to no reality beyond the empirical. The Apostle Paul tells us that "our struggle is not against flesh and blood, but against the rulers, against the authorities, against the powers of this dark world and against the spiritual forces of evil in the heavenly realms" (Ephesians 6:12). From a Christian perspective, "believing is seeing" just as much as "seeing is believing."

Finally, is fantasy literature New Age? New Age thinking is pantheistic; it blurs the distinction between the Creator and creation. Whereas Christians hold that God is *in* everything, pantheists hold that God *is* everything and that in fact humans can be godlike too. There is such literature and it can be dangerous, as can that which encourages children and adults to treat the occult as entertainment or as a source of real power (which it is). Some fantasy literature falls into this category, especially the supernatural and time fantasy sub-genre. Clearly, though, the great story of God and humankind as told in the Bible is also fantasy, if by fantasy we mean it admits to the reality of the supernatural and the transcendent in human experience.

Heroic or high fantasy is arguably *the* genre of literature best suited to portraying Christian themes in literary fashion. This is the view of J.R.R. Tolkien, the great British Catholic author of *The Hobbit* (1937) and *The Lord of the Rings* (1965) trilogy. Tolkien sets forth his rationale for using high fantasy (or high fairy, as he called it) in a wonderful essay entitled "On Fairy Stories" (1966). Briefly, Tolkien argues that one of the ways humans image God, their creator, is by being subcreators. Only God is a primary creator; only God can fashion something from nothing. But God has created humans with creativity, with the gift of imagining and executing novelty and newness in mind and matter. Writers exercise this gift by creating a setting, characters, and story.

High fantasy, Tolkien suggests, depends by definition on an ability to create (or sub-create) a wholly alternate world in the imagination where all manner of characters (human and otherwise) confront the twin realities of good and evil. This alternate world begins in an idyllic state (Once upon a time ...), into which comes some form of evil. From then on, the forces of Good do battle with the forces of Evil. Usually, there comes a point in the story when it seems Good will be overwhelmed by Evil, but just as all seems hopeless, a heroic figure appears to do battle with Evil. Often, this hero is an unlikely sort such as a lowly hobbit (or babe in a manger), not at all heroic at first glance. At great personal sacrifice, this figure must thwart the Evil that seeks to destroy the world. Tolkien calls this personal sacrifice the *eucatastrophe* of the story: the "good" catastrophe—good for the people, that is, although not for the hero (think "Good" Friday). Finally, through the hero's sacrifice, the kingdom or creation is again restored to its original idyllic state and continues "happily ever after." Figure 4-4 diagrams Tolkien's view of high fantasy and its relation to biblical narrative.

Tolkien asked the academics to whom he presented this essay whether it would not be wonderful if a subcreated fantasy had a parallel in actual reality. He then professed his belief that such a parallel is exactly what we find in the biblical narrative. We are now living in the time of God's great story, between the eucatastrophe of Christ's death and resurrection, and the final consolation of His second coming. Each of us is a character in this story, required in our own way to make a contribution to the plot's final resolution. What a wonderful challenge to set before our students!

Figure 4-4: Tolkien's view of the relation between high fantasy and the Christian story

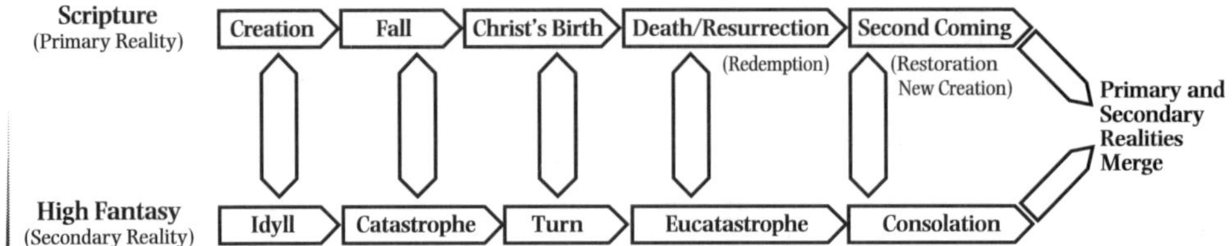

Moralism

Based on a theology of salvation by works, *moralism* (not to be confused with moral value) locates human worth in personal behavior and self-improvement rather than in inherently created value. Moralistic stories are almost always didactic; that is, they teach heavy-handed, transparent "lessons." They are sermons (usually bad ones) disguised as story. The secular version of moralism is little different from the "religious" in that it holds up specific exemplary individuals, although without accompanying "God talk." In fact, religious moralism is secular virtue dressed up in religious language. At the Sunday school level, it takes the "Heroes of the Faith" approach. "Dare to be a Daniel" is an example, and it's revealing that Daniel's virtue rather than God's protecting grace becomes the central focus. Theologically, moralistic stories fail because they give glory to people rather than to God. As literature, they fail because they are transparently false to experience.

Good literature for children is not written out of any self-conscious desire to implant particular moral virtues but evolves from a writer's genuine desire to interact with children through remembered childhood. Its writers speak in an authentically different "voice." Rather than the directive voice of the moralist ("do as I say"), we hear the interactional voice of the fellow traveler, or even co-conspirator ("you and me together"). It is through the writer's obvious delight in the company of young people that instruction happens. Good writing for children, like a truly good pie, is intrinsically flavorful, not simply sweet topping superimposed on a mundane filling. In the end, writing intended to delight has far more power to instruct than writing explicitly calculated to do so.[5]

Balanced vs. Biased Library Collections

Bias is not necessarily a bad thing. I am biased in favor of healthy food and fresh air. A medical library should be biased toward medical resources—one would not expect to find books on flower arranging or space travel in such a library. Similarly, a school's library should be biased in favor of the school's mission, with books and other resources carefully selected to reflect the breadth of its curricular offerings. Thus an elementary school library will have a collection different from its high school equivalent. Administrators and teachers must also ensure an appropriate balance between nonfiction and fiction resources. Finally, the in-school collection should be augmented by any available resources, including public libraries and information centers. The more isolated a school is from external resources, the better its own resources must be.

General Selection Criteria

Nonfiction

Factors to consider in selecting nonfiction resources for both school and classroom libraries include the following:

- **Program relevance** Library resources must support the school's curriculum. It is not enough that students have a single textbook for academic subjects such as science, social studies, Bible, and mathematics. Multiple resources must be available to help students in research projects for reports and presentations. Although good general-purpose encyclopedias and dictionaries are important reference resources, they should not be the sole source of content information.
- **Accuracy and currency** Content resources are of no use if they're out of date. Atlases and almanacs must provide current information. Science resources should similarly reflect current knowledge in diverse fields. A library must develop a weeding policy, regularly reviewing its collection to ensure it remains current.
- **Style and appearance** We live in an age of color and incredibly rich and varied graphic design. No matter how accurate and current a book may be, if its content is presented in a lackluster manner with little attention to layout and design, it will sit unused on the shelf.
- **Diverse viewpoints** A Christian school that seeks to inoculate students needs a library that reflects the diversity of views on controversial issues. Not only do Christians and non-Christians disagree, but Christians hold diverse opinions on many topics: creation and evolution, gender relations, global warming, economics, environmental stewardship, political action, genetic engineering, health care, biblical interpretation. With appropriate sensitivity to the grade levels being served, libraries should contain materials that represent divergent views on those and other crucial issues, encouraging students to exercise their discernment skills. See below, and appendix 1, for some approaches to use when those acquisitions are challenged.
- **Scope and depth** The audience to be served will largely determine the breadth and depth of the materials needed in a library. Obviously, a K–12 school will require a far broader

range of resources at varying levels of difficulty than a school catering only to primary grades. In fact, a K–12 library may wish to distinguish between books available to elementary/middle school students and high school students. Distinctions also may be made between books readily available in open stacks and those available only in classroom libraries, for use under a teacher's supervision. Generally, controversial books may best be limited to the classroom library. For example, I would recommend that books by R. L. Stine not be available for general borrowing in a central elementary library. Because of their overwhelming popularity with middle schoolers, however, I would recommend reading a few Stine books in class as a springboard for discussing the gratuitous violence that drives the plots of this shock fiction.

Fiction

The following questions serve as useful guides to selecting fiction for a school's main and classroom libraries:

- Does the work increase understanding of a culture or way of life?
- Does the work increase reader sensitivity to the human condition?
- Is the work realistic yet hopeful about the human condition?
- Does the work develop worthwhile concepts and themes?
- Does the work offer the potential for worthwhile enjoyment?
- Does the work avoid the gratuitous use of violence, sex, and prejudice?
- Does the work avoid moralism of all kinds?
- Is the work aesthetically pleasing in language, style, vocabulary, illustrations, etc?

Moralism in fiction (including Christian fiction) is such a pervasive problem that it deserves special treatment; however, it is too broad to cover adequately here.

Dealing with Challenges

No matter how thoughtfully a school and its staff select reading resources, no matter how carefully they consult with community representatives, occasional challenges will arise to particular books or media resources. It's far better for a school to have a proactive policy for handling such challenges than to meet them with ad hoc reactions. In all such cases, everyone involved should follow the general principles of dispute resolution as set forth in Matthew18:15–20. One possible protocol for using those principles in response to a resource challenge is briefly outlined below. For a sample form to use when a resource is challenged, see appendix 1.

Suggested Steps for Handling a Challenge

- The complainant first discusses the concern with the teacher or librarian informally.
- If the issue is not resolved, the complaint is brought, in writing, to the library committee. Appointed by the board, the library committee comprises a teacher- librarian (if possible), one educator/parent advisory committee member, two school community members at large, two classroom teachers, and one principal.
- With the complainant, the committee reviews the library's philosophy and goals, and their relationship to the work in question.
- The committee makes a recommendation to the school board.
- The school board makes a final decision.
- Until a final decision is made, no questioned material is removed from the library, either by the library committee or by the board.

Organizing the Classroom for Learning

The Classroom as a Community

Language-centered learning implies not only the availability of many language materials and tools, but also learners who communicate with each other in various ways. If classrooms are to model a community of learners rather than a collection of competing individuals, their very organization needs to facilitate such interaction. That organization has both psychological and physical dimensions.

The stereotypical classroom is a place where students sit quietly in fixed rows while the teacher dispenses information that is dutifully copied into notebooks. Fortunately, this model is becoming less prevalent; unfortunately, it is still common enough to lend credibility to the stereotype. Most of the talk in such classrooms is teacher talk. Most student talk comes in response to teacher-initiated questions, pitched at the level of factual recall.

To alter this stultifying psychological climate, teachers need to share power with their students and enter into genuine dialogue with them. Many of the questions teachers pose must become real questions—to which the teacher doesn't have all the answers but with which the class struggles communally. This means that students' real questions and concerns must be given legitimacy. And it means that classrooms must be communities of trust where both students and teachers are willing to take risks. When functioning as communities of shared talk, classrooms will often be noisy places, full of animated conversation. In this environment, being wrong or unskilled is not a reason for punishment, ridicule, or ostracism but an opportunity for growth and improvement.

Physical Arrangement

Viewing a class as a community of learners has physical implications. The communal classroom must invite a variety of activities. Since every classroom space has its physical limitations as well as its own peculiar human dynamics, it is not possible to prescribe *the* or even *an* ideal arrangement. Yet some common characteristics can be suggested.

Of all K–12 classrooms, kindergartens are most likely to physically reflect a commitment to participatory learning. Typically, you'll find a comfortable open area for group sharing (listening, talking, and oral reading), tables for group work, and carrels for individual work. Learning centers dot the room, each offering a selection of materials designed to accomplish a particular goal or to feature a given theme (more about themes below). Usually, a print-rich resource center contains many books, both fiction and nonfiction. Finally, somewhere off to the side is the teacher's desk.

As we move up the grades, we find ever-greater conformity to the classroom stereotype of fixed rows with the teacher's desk front and center. This happens, I believe, because we tend to think that the learner-focused arrangement, while suitable for young children, is inappropriate for intermediate and middle school students, who must leave childish things behind and get down to "serious" learning.

Unfortunately, serious learning often means adopting an anthropology that views students' minds as more-or-less empty receptacles needing to be filled with the information provided by teachers and textbooks. Couple this view with the Western emphasis on individual achievement and efficiency, and the school is in great danger of being organized along the lines of the traditional factory. Thus students (the raw materials) are shaped into acceptable products (economic producers and consumers) through carefully sequenced input variables (instruction) regularly monitored for efficiency (standardized testing).

Christ's words that we are all to become like little children (Mark 10:13–15) have profound educational implications, modeling how students and teachers should work and play together. The kindergarten classroom arrangement described above is clearly more conducive to interactive communal learning than the rows of desks in the traditional classroom.

Using Themes to Organize Instruction

Integration is today's favored buzzword. Almost every textbook on the market is titled *Something or Other: An Integrated Approach.* Many educators claim to want their students to acquire a sense of the wholeness and interconnectedness of life. They want to avoid learning approaches that treat knowledge as simply the accumulation of masses of random facts and concepts. Despite these efforts, school is still organized around pieces—pieces of knowledge we call subjects or disciplines, pieces of time we call periods, curricular pieces we call lessons and units, and age groupings we call grades.

How do we respond to this business of integrated learning? Do we abandon the way we organize schools, and children's learning within them? These are large and important questions that cannot be fully explored here. But to understand the issue and to suggest at least a preliminary response, let's examine a specific communication challenge.

I once attempted to tell a friend (who is not a hiker) about a recent hike in the mountains at the height of the alpine meadow bloom. I was clearly enthusiastic, and my friend sensed the exhilaration of my experience.

"So, you really enjoyed yourself in the mountains, didn't you?"

"Yes, it was great! I feel refreshed and renewed."

"What's so special about hiking in the mountains?"

Suddenly, I confronted a quandary. How could I explain the joy and exhilaration of my hike to my friend (and in some sense to myself)? How could I describe an essentially holistic experience without trivializing it either with vague generalizations ("I just get a wonderful sense of freedom in the mountains") or with an overly analytic account of its sights, smells, sounds, and emotions? Perhaps I should just say, "You would need to have been there to appreciate what I experienced." To a certain extent that would be true, for the power of language is limited in conveying certain meanings. Yet that approach would severely limit our communication about important matters; it is not always possible to share direct experience. Language can give us vicarious experiences, and sometimes language is the experience itself.

When we design a school curriculum, we face that same challenge. How do we take the seamless whole that is life in all its complexity, and present it to children for their learning? Invariably we take a piece of God's creation out of its context awhile and examine it more closely to enrich our experience of the whole. This challenge recalls our previous mention of embedded and disembedded knowing (about which we will say more in chapter 7). Clearly, hiking in an alpine meadow is an experience embedded in a complex personal, perceptual, psychological, and social matrix. Describing this experience requires us to step back from it and disembed various aspects from the holistic matrix. We may choose to describe what we saw (delicate flowers, azure lakes, snow-clad peaks), and heard (silence), and felt (awe, peace, tranquility).

Similarly, in school we isolate aspects of God's creation and hold them up for closer scrutiny. Our Western intellectual tradition tends to view this analytical enterprise as the defining characteristic of knowing. Thus we have come to believe that the traditional curricular divisions of, for example, mathematics, history, music, and biology have some independent epistemological status. We treat them as if they are self-contained entities or fields of inquiry. In reality, they are primarily arbitrary (although useful) ways of circumscribing certain aspects of our holistic experience in and with the world. They are not hermetically sealed compartments; scholars agree that the boundaries between disciplines are fuzzy and indeterminate. We must take care that students, especially in elementary and middle school, do not experience their studies as a series of fragments that have little to do with each other, or with their holistic experience. Further, since language is the primary medium of discourse for all learning, students need to experience language as a vehicle that serves them in all their traffic with the world.

This sense of the serviceability of language lies at the heart of "language across the curriculum" proposals. It is also a fundamental part of trying to organize learning experiences that are more integrated than the traditional skills-centered and subject-centered approaches. Thus, integrated teaching and learning represents a conscious decision to create a rhythm between more analytic (disembedded) and experiential (embedded) ways of coming to know, with the former always serving the latter. Consciously breaking down unnecessary distinctions between subject areas is the best way to set the rhythm in motion. That is what theme-based teaching is all about.

A **theme** is a major idea or subject, broad enough to cover a wide range of skills and topics within the curriculum. In a sense, a theme is a piece of reality that can reflect the complexity and intricacy of life on a small scale. Themes can range from very concrete (e.g., *bears*) to quite abstract (e.g., *justice*), and must reflect both the developmental abilities of the students and the curricular goals of the school.

As an example, let's briefly consider *bears* as a theme. Although such a theme is appropriate to various elementary grades because of the issues and experiences that can be explored within it, here we will focus on grade 2.

What experiences might grade 2 children have had with bears? I recently asked a grade 2 class what they knew about bears, and discovered the following:

- many children own or have owned teddy bears
- many are familiar with stories, poems, and songs featuring bears
- many have seen bears in zoos
- some have seen wild bears in national and provincial/state parks
- most are aware that there are different kinds of bears
- some know that bears played a significant role in native Indian and Inuit cultures

This grade 2 class had considerable collective experience of and knowledge about bears that would enable them to use the theme of bears to explore, for example:

- security objects (see, e.g., *Ira Sleeps Over* by Bernard Waber [1972])
- literature and song *(Goldilocks and the Three Bears, The Teddy Bears' Picnic, Winnie the Pooh. Paddington Bear, The Berenstein Bears)*
- zoos and issues of animal rights
- conservation/stewardship
- zoology (classification of bears, life histories of different bears)
- social studies (bears in native cultures, economics, religion, mythology)

My list certainly does not exhaust the theme of bears. Most teachers can see possibilities for an integrated unit that allows such activities as these:

- listening to stories, legends, and scientific accounts about bears
- talking about bears both informally and formally
- reading and writing stories, poems, songs, and reports about bears and bear-related topics
- viewing pictures, slides, and films about bears, both literary and scientific

As with almost any theme, the scope of exploration can be as narrow or as wide as student interest and experience allow. Notice that although *bears* might be considered less abstract than *justice*, issues such as bears in captivity and the conservation of bears (as well as other wildlife) bear on concepts of justice (pardon the pun).

Speaking of puns, the word *bear* illustrates other interesting linguistic aspects that can certainly find their way into a thematic unit. There is the animal *bear* (noun), and the action *to bear* (verb). These two words are **homographs**. There is also a **homophone** *(bare)* which can be used as a describing word (adjective), which has a homograph, a verb (I won't *bare* my soul to you). Figure 4-5 is an example of a web incorporating all these ideas.

Figure 4-5: A web about bears

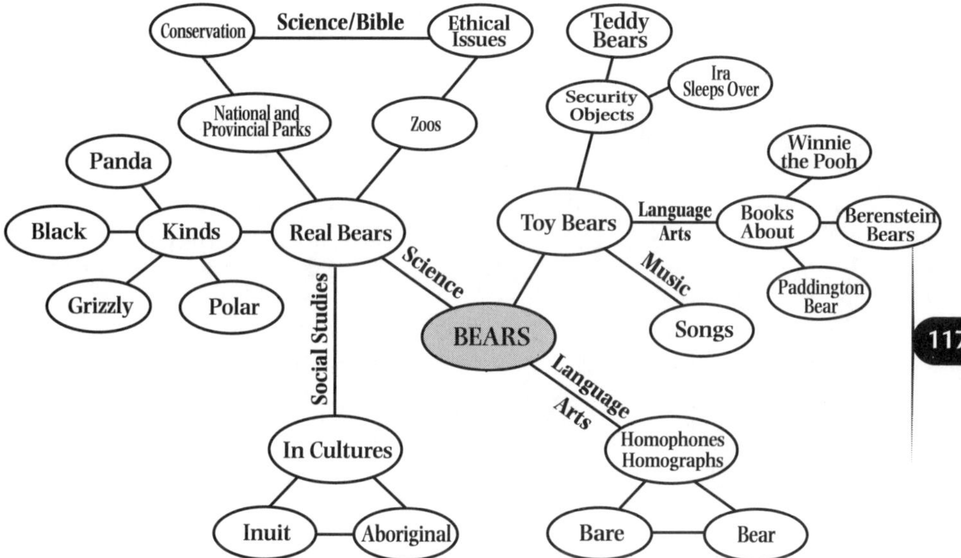

The exciting thing about teaching thematically is discovering the complex and wonderful ways in which everything in God's creation hangs together. As redeemed people, students and teachers in a Christian school have the privilege and pleasure of exploring it all, while knowing Who to thank.

Of course, thematic teaching has its own pitfalls. Sometimes, for example, a piece of literature is abused if used simply to illustrate a theme. Or a theme can be artificially forced beyond useful boundaries. Adding 2 bears + 3 bears = 5 bears is a trivial way to integrate bears into the math curriculum. (Comparing the weights and gestation periods of black, grizzly, and polar bears, by contrast, is not.) The entire school curriculum need not be organized around themes. Thematic teaching is best seen as a vehicle for organizing learning and language experiences around significant and personally relevant topics that cross traditional disciplines and thus invite integrated teaching and learning.

Questions for Discussion

1. Do you remember the reading series you used when learning to read? Do you recall any memorable stories from that series?
2. What do you remember about the libraries in the schools you attended? Did they serve as learning hubs or simply as repositories of books that you could access once or twice a week? Were your classrooms rich with print resources?
3. Do you love to read, or are you *aliterate*? (Aliterate persons are those who *can* read but generally choose not to do so unless they must for some functional reason.) Here's a test: Could you give a credible response if, while interviewing for a teaching job, you were asked, "What three books have been the most influential in your life, and what are you reading now?"
4. What persons and other factors have been most influential in making you into a reader (or not)?
5. What is your perspective on the *isolation vs. inoculation* metaphor used in this chapter to describe two typical reasons for Christian schooling?
6. How do you evaluate the fiction that you read? How would you go about determining the *moral center* of a book or story? Does this concept of moral center apply to nonfiction? If so, how?
7. What would you do if, while teaching in a Christian school, you received a phone call from an irate parent expressing anger about a book you had assigned as reading in your class?

8. Develop an ideal floor plan for a primary classroom and a middle school classroom. Explain why you arranged the room as you did.

9. What suggestions can you provide for changing the imbalance between teacher talk and student talk in most classrooms? Can you distinguish between on-task and off-task talk?

10. Thematic teaching is quite common in primary classrooms but is less common in middle school. What do you think are the reasons? Do you think thematic teaching would work as well in middle school? Explain.

For Further Consideration

1. Find a school that uses a basal reading series as a primary tool for reading instruction. Find out what the school spends to (a) purchase the series and associated materials for all the grades in which it is used, and (b) maintain the series each year (e.g., by purchasing workbooks). At an average cost of $20 per book, how many books for the school or classroom libraries could be purchased for (a) the initial cost of the basal series plus (b) the yearly maintenance costs of the series? Finally, try to discover the school's annual budget for library purchases. Do you think the basal series represents a wise investment for this school?

2. Examine a basal reading series and comment on the nature of the selections featured in its K–3 materials. Is the language natural, or contrived? Are the stories taken from children's literature, or written expressly for the series? Do you think the stories have any literary merit, or are they written primarily to serve some specific instructional purpose?

3. Divide into two groups, one to review the book *Report Card on Basal Readers* (Goodman et al. 1988) and the other to

read the follow-up book, *Basal Readers: A Second Look* (Shannon and Goodman 1994). Report your findings to the class.

4. For a wonderful satire on moralism in storytelling, locate and read the short story "The Storyteller" by Saki (pen name of British writer H. H. Munro). How does this story critique moralism? Is it possible to avoid moralism in teaching young children?

5. Examine the curriculum guide for any subject area and grade in your state or province. Find a prescribed topic, and then brainstorm with a partner or two and create a web to show how other school subjects could be related to this topic. Finally, suggest titles of books that could go with each webbed subject.

Endnotes

1 This is not to imply that teachers should not teach specific skills to students and use reading materials as sources of examples to support specific skill instruction. What should be avoided is regular reading fare that is designed primarily for such skill instruction.

2 More specific information about the teaching of reading and writing in a classroom not dominated by basal reading instruction is provided in chapters 11 and 12.

3 The classic exploration of this question is H. Richard Niebuhr's (1953) *Christ and Culture.*

4 Professor Mark Eckel of the Moody Bible Institute has prepared a very helpful study guide on the Christian's interaction with the pagan world. His 1999 publication *Exposed to or Exposing the Darkness: Christian Interaction with Pagan Thought* is available by contacting him at <mark.eckel@moody.edu>.

5 Although I hesitate to venture into the territory of so-called "character education," much of what I've seen is blatantly moralistic or flirts dangerously with this heresy.

6 These suggestions as well as the form in appendix 1 are adapted, with permission, from Sterenberg and DeMoor (1991).

Chapter 5

Perspectives on the "Great Debate"

In this chapter, we take a brief look at a debate about learning to read that has occupied the professional reading community for most of the past century—and especially for the last 35 years. On the surface, this debate is about how best to teach beginners to read. Its main focus at this level is whether beginners should be introduced to reading with or without specific emphasis on the alphabetic code. At a deeper level, the debate touches on many of the issues discussed in chapters 1 and 2. Beliefs about the learner (anthropology), about knowledge (epistemology), and about what these imply for teaching are at the heart of the "great debate." The chapter begins by discussing the nature and origins of the great debate (including a definition of some critical terms). It then considers the history of learning to read and concludes by describing my position on this debate so that you as reader have a clear sense of my bias concerning this critical issue.

The late Jeanne S. Chall of Harvard University coined the phrase "great debate" in her 1967 book *Learning to Read: The Great Debate,* updated in 1983 and again in 1996. Essentially, the debate contrasts the relative efficacy of two approaches to teaching beginning reading: "decoding" individual sounds and words, or "relating to the meaning of larger units of text from the outset" (Millard 1997, 33). Chall referred to the debate as involving those who argued for "code-emphasis" versus those who argued for "meaning-emphasis" In the three editions of her book, spanning 29 years, Chall was firmly committed to demonstrating that code-emphasis produced superior results. In her words:

> Based on [my] analyses [of research], I found that beginning readers learn better when their instruction emphasizes learning the alphabetic code, one that places first importance at the beginning on learning the relationship between letters and their sounds (that is, learning the alphabetic principle). They learn less well when taught by a meaning-emphasis, that is, one that emphasizes, at the very beginning, how to understand what is read. (Chall 1996, Introduction)[1]

At this early point in the discussion, it may be helpful to define a few key terms. **Alphabetic code** refers to the way the distinctive sounds (or **phonemes**) of the English language are represented by the letters (**graphemes**) of the alphabet. Thus **code-emphasis** teaching explicitly strives to help young children understand the relationship between the speech sounds and the letters representing them. Using more technical language, this is referred to as **phoneme-grapheme correspondence** (or **grapheme-phoneme correspondence**). In the code-emphasis view, a reader must first **decode** the graphemes (letters and letter combinations) into phonemes (sounds) of the language, and then bring meaning to those encoded sounds. Writing is seen as the opposite process: a writer must *encode* the phonemes into graphemes that then combine to make words. For the decoding process, it is posited that a knowledge of **phonics** will be helpful to the reader. Briefly, phonics is "a way of teaching reading and spelling that stresses symbol-sound relationships, used especially in beginning instruction" (Harris and Hodges 1995, 186).[2]

Thus, one of the central themes of the "great debate" hinges on how reading and writing are defined. Proponents of the code-emphasis view hold that reading and writing are made up of hierarchical sets of skills that children must develop in a largely predetermined order, often through practice and drill. Proponents of the meaning-emphasis view hold that reading and writing are skills children learn and develop by engaging in the act of reading itself, in much the same way as they learn to listen and talk—without any apparent direct instruction.

Although these two theoretical orientations may be described in various ways, the former is generally called a basic **skills-centered approach**, while the latter has become known as the **whole language approach** (or the **language-centered approach**, a term I prefer).

Pendulum-like swings in practice have resulted from the "great debate." Especially in the last two decades, language arts education in North America has witnessed two particularly dramatic changes: first, a marked swing toward whole language in the 1980s; then a move back to phonics-based instruction in the mid-1990s, when whole language programs failed to realize promised increases in achievement test scores.

The latter swing was accelerated by the 1990 publication of Marilyn Adams' book *Beginning to Read*. Based on extensive review of research on beginning reading, her conclusion is that direct and systematic phonics instruction is the most effective way to teach beginning reading.[3] Yet other noted writers and researchers (e.g., Kenneth Goodman and Constance Weaver) continue to argue that available evidence favors language-centered, meaning-based approaches to beginning reading instruction (see Weaver 1998).

What are we to make of these competing claims? Who is right, and on what basis? Before we address those questions directly, it may be helpful to ask how people learned to read long before the term "great debate" was coined. After all, people have been reading and writing (and learning to read and write) for thousands of years.

Historical Roots[4]

The Phoenicians and the Greeks

Historians are unsure exactly when the alphabet was invented, but as early as 1000 B.C. the Phoenicians, a Semitic seafaring people, were using a writing system of letters to represent the sounds of their language. Because we are so familiar with this idea from our own written language, we may fail to see what a staggering idea this is. Consider a contemporary parallel: Modern Chinese writing is ideographic rather than alphabetic. That is, the written symbols in Chinese do not stand for the sounds of the Chinese language but for ideas. To be reasonably literate in Chinese, one needs to learn how to decode (read) and encode (write) about 3,000 distinct symbols. An English student, by contrast, needs to know only 26 letters and how they are combined to represent approximately 44 speech sounds (phonemes).[5] Thus alphabetic writing opened the door to systems that are far simpler and more efficient than ideographic or pictographic systems.

The Phoenicians traded with their Greek neighbors, who were intrigued by the power of the Phoenician writing system. Greek traders who learned Phoenician brought this written language home and attempted to use the Phoenician alphabet to represent Greek speech. This was difficult, since Greek and Phoenician differed phonetically. Also, the Phoenician alphabet had no vowels (as is the case with ancient Hebrew, another Semitic derivative of the Phoenician alphabet). Eventually, the Greeks devised an alphabet with vowels and consonants to represent the sounds of their language. The first two letters of the Greek alphabet were named *alpha* and *beta,* from which we derive the word *alphabet.* The wonderful thing about the ancient

Greek alphabet was that it represented an almost perfect grapheme-phoneme correspondence. That is, there was one symbol for each distinct sound in the language.

In early Greek society, learning to read and write was reserved primarily for sons of the elite. Teaching children to read and write was relatively easy because of the regularity of the Greek spelling system. Thus teachers of elementary literacy were held in low esteem, and the monotonous and unimaginative task of teaching children "their letters" was usually assigned to slaves. Calling someone a "schoolmaster" was a distinct insult. Mitford Matthews (1966), a reading historian, relates an old saying in Athens about a man who was missing: Either he was dead, or he had become a teacher of children, in which case he would be too ashamed to appear in polite society. It was thought that persons of high rank who had lived evil lives would be forced, in the next world, to teach reading and writing. Matthews concludes his chapter on the invention of the alphabet by saying:

> There must have been a reason for this universal attitude towards elementary teachers among people as intelligent as the Greeks and the Romans. The most probable explanation of it is that teaching to read was widely recognized as something anybody could do. There was nothing difficult about it. Its acceptable execution called for neither learning nor talent; no distinction could be attained in such a mediocre occupation. (Matthews 1966, 9)

Whatever the truth of this matter, the Greeks achieved everlasting distinction by perfecting the idea that a writing system based on representing *sounds* was ever so much more efficient and flexible than one based on *things* (pictographic writing) or *ideas* (ideographic writing).

The Phoenicians wrote from right to left, and this was the initial Greek pattern as well. Eventually, convention shifted to the left-to-right pattern still used in English and many other written languages. Perhaps the change occurred because most people are right-handed and found it less messy to write away from the line of print rather than across it, particularly with slow-drying ink. The Greeks retained one Phoenician oddity: a lack of breaks between words. Their writing represented the more or less continuous flow of oral speech,[6] requiring readers to segment writing into words through their knowledge of oral language. Itisalittleliketryingtoreadthissentencewithoutanyspacesbetweenthewords. Not easy. But with practice you mightsoongetthehangofit,yes?

Learning to Read Greek

The first task for a boy[7] learning to read was recognizing the forms of the letters and naming them—that is, learning his alphabet. In those days before mechanical printing, this was more difficult than it seems because different teachers tended to make their letters differently. Only capital letters were in use initially, although lower case letters were later introduced to aid rapid writing. Once a boy thought he could recognize a letter visually, he was set the task of pointing out every occurrence of it in a piece of writing. There was an emphasis on learning the letters in order (A, B, C, . . .), aided by various mnemonic devices. The letters might be associated with common names of people (Abe, Bill, Carl,...) or common occupations (Actor, Baker, Carpenter,...). There is even a record of putting the Greek alphabet to simple music, a foretaste of today's alphabet songs. Thus we can see that, from the very beginning, attempts were made to attach meaning to initial literacy learning.

After mastering letter recognition, the student was set the task of learning the syllables used in Greek writing. In ancient Greek, the syllable is the basic unit of writing; each word has exactly as many syllables as vowels. Thus, for example, the student would learn the sounds associated with syllables:

/ba/ /be/ /bē/ /bi/ /bo/ /bu/ /bō/[8]

Often the student would then master syllable building by learning the sound of a common **spelling pattern** (now called a **rime**) such as */ar/* or */er/* and then adding other initial letters (**onsets**) to the rime to demonstrate the construction of common syllables:

bar gar dar or *ber ger der*[9]

Today, we call this **initial consonant substitution,** though the Greeks wouldn't have used this term since their alphabet didn't have two distinct types of letters (consonants and vowels). The Romans made this distinction much later.

Once a Greek boy was adept at recognizing and sounding out syllables, he could progress to combining syllables into words. While learning to decode letters, syllables, and finally words, he was also learning to encode (write) the same forms. As the pupil advanced in writing, he also received moral instruction through the pieces he was asked to copy, which usually recommended virtues such as industry, honesty, and respect for the gods. Thus the association of literacy with morality and religion dates back to the beginnings of learning to read and write.

The Development of English

In the seventh century B.C., Greek traders were interacting with the Etruscans of Italy, early predecessors of what we've come to know as the Romans. The Etruscans borrowed the Greek alphabet letters but did not name them quite the same. The Greeks had been scrupulous in distinguishing between the names of their letters and of their sounds. When the Romans secured Greek letters from the Etruscans, they allowed the sounds of the vowels (Latin *vocalis)* to serve as their names. For the consonants, they used the letter itself accompanied by a distinctly pronounced vowel sound (Matthews 1966, 11). In fact, the word **consonant** means "to sound with." Thus the Romans set the stage for confusion between the *sound* of a letter and its *name.* Even today, many children take a long time to understand that the names of most letters (the consonants) are *not* their sounds.

As every student of elementary Western history knows, the Romans conquered the Greeks and eventually much of what we know as Europe, including England and the rest of Great Britain. Rome ruled England for 350 years, until about A.D. 500. Christian missionaries brought the gospel to the farthest reaches of the Roman Empire, and with them came the Latin alphabet. Some missionaries attempted to develop writing systems for the vernacular languages of the conquered people, but they used existing Latin letters. Since the phonology (sound system) of English was quite different from that of Latin, the Latin letters could not accurately represent all of the sounds of English as it was then spoken. Thus, from the very beginning, the almost purely alphabetic nature of Greek and Latin was not carried over into English writing. As we shall see, this deterioration of the phoneme-grapheme correspondence in English has continued throughout the history of written English, and to this day. It is one of the reasons why teaching reading (and spelling) is not a matter of simply matching sounds and letters.

Another significant event in the development of the English language is the conquest of England by the Norman French in 1066. After the conquest, French became the dominant language of England, at least among the gentry. Of course, commoners continued to use English, and over time the Normans and the English melded into a single group so that French did not become the language of England. But English was never the same after 1066. Middle English at the time of the Norman Conquest was essentially a Celtic language with a much "harder" phonology than Norman French. The influence of the French language tended to "soften" English both in sound and in subsequent spelling.

During the fourteenth and fifteenth centuries, another interesting English phenomenon occurred, which linguists term the **Great Vowel Shift**. Space limitations do not allow a detailed explanation, but essentially the vowel sounds in many English words shifted over the course of perhaps 200 years, especially in London. For example, the Middle English pronunciation of the word *house* is /hūs/, but by Shakespeare's time it was pronounced /haus/, much the same as today.[10] In addition, as England became a great mercantile trading nation, many words from other cultures entered the language with spellings virtually unchanged, but with anglicized pronunciations. Thus the Dutch word *yacht* (meaning a hunting ship) is spelled as it is in Dutch but pronounced /yät/, which is quite different from its harsher Dutch pronunciation. In contrast, the Italian word *cello* (from *violoncello)* retains the Italian pronunciation of the letter *c* as /ch/ (as in *chicken*).

This brief historic and linguistic discussion demonstrates the complex and shifting relationship between spoken English and its written forms. As the phonology of the English language changed over time, so did the way words were spelled. This shift mattered very little, because most people were illiterate. Churchmen and the educated elite read and wrote Latin (and, to a lesser extent, Greek) rather than English in their ecclesiastical and academic lives. But times were changing, and momentous events would soon heighten the interest in learning to read and write English.

Teaching English Reading

Little is known about the teaching of English reading before about 1400. Cathedral schools did attempt to provide elementary literacy instruction in English to boys who would serve the church. This early teaching of English differed very little from the alphabetic and syllabary method described above for Greek and Latin students. As was true for them, there were very few written English texts that could serve as instructional material for young students. In addition, teachers were held in low esteem, were often barely literate, and certainly had no formal training in their craft.

A major tool of instruction from the mid-fifteenth to the mid-eighteenth centuries was the **hornbook**, a wooden device shaped much like a modern table tennis paddle. Attached to the broad surface of the paddle was a single sheet of paper containing a **Christ-cross row** (the alphabet preceded by a cross), part of the **syllabarium** (a list of nonsense syllables, organized alphabetically), and the Lord's Prayer. This sheet of paper was protected, by a hard transparent covering made from animal horn (hence, *hornbook*). The hornbook became known as the

ABC book or the **abecedarium**, for obvious reasons.

After students learned their alphabet and syllables, they were introduced to little booklets that contained primary moral teachings (hence **primers**, a term still used for the beginning books of reading series). Teaching was so poor that few students reached the level of reading actual text. Writing proficiency was even worse: after a few years of (sporadic) school attendance, many students could not write their own names. The best they could produce was the Christ-cross that was prominently displayed on each hornbook. To this day, illiterate persons use a crisscross (or *X*) in place of their signature.

The printing press, developed in Germany, reached England in about 1475, changing everything. The laborious task of producing copies of texts by hand gave way to much more efficient mechanical printing. At the same time, a rising middle class in England wanted their children to have a basic education in literacy and numeracy, realizing the advantage this education would provide in business. Reflecting the shift from academic to business purposes, these merchants were not so much interested in the classical languages of Greek and Latin as in English. Thus the demand for both schooling and printed materials increased dramatically in the sixteenth century. But now printers were faced with a problem: How should English words be spelled, and who should decide? This may seem an odd problem today, when we can simply turn to a dictionary for standard spellings of English words. But no such standards existed in the sixteenth and seventeenth centuries.[11]

Before the printing press, writers of English tended to spell words as they sounded. As shifts in the phonology of the language occurred, spellings changed accordingly.[12] Words were often spelled in various ways, even by highly educated people such as Queen Elizabeth I. This usually caused only a minor problem for readers, since the variant spellings were close enough to the sounds of the words to be decoded. Printers, however, needed some sort of standard when setting their type for the press. Influential printers established their own spelling standards, which tended to have a very conservative influence. While the phonology of the language continued to change, the spelling of printed words did not, or at least not nearly as rapidly. Gradually the letters and the speech sounds for which they stood lost rapport. For example, the words *psalm, knife,* and *subtle* now contain "silent" letters; only a few hundred years ago the *p, k,* and *b* in these words were pronounced, and our spelling still reflects that fact.

Over time, the relationship between the spelling and pronunciation of English words became less and less consistent. Many attempts were made, even as early as the sixteenth and seventeenth centuries, to reform English spelling by dropping letters from words or adding new letters to reflect shifts in pronunciation, but these attempts met great resistance. Matthews (1966, 26) cites evidence that many people thought it sinful to change the number of letters in the alphabet. After all, these letters were derived from Greek and Latin sources, languages in which the New Testament of the Bible was either written or translated, and thus were holy.

Hebrew, as the language of the Old Testament, was also considered holy. Because the Hebrew language tolerated signs or diacritical marks (much like those found in current dictionaries) to indicate how vowels should be pronounced, it was deemed acceptable to print English with such marks. Some books with diacritical markings were produced, but printers strongly resisted this solution because it increased their typesetting labors tremendously. Thus, most attempts to modify the alphabet—and make learning to read English easier—failed miserably.

Figure 5-1: The initial teaching alphabet

æ	b	c	d	ϵϵ	
face	bed	cat	dog	key	
f	g	h	ie	j	k
feet	leg	hat	fly	jug	key
l	m	n	œ	p	ɹ
letter	man	nest	over	pen	girl
r	s	t	ue	v	w
red	spoon	tree	use	voice	window
y	z	ƨ	wh	ch	
yes	zebra	daisy	when	chair	
th	th	ʃh	ʒ	ŋ	
three	the	shop	television	ring	
ɑ	au	a	e	i	o
father	ball	cap	egg	milk	box
u	ω	ω	ou	oi	
up	book	spoon	out	oil	

Even modern times have seen efforts to usher in significant English spelling reform. The British playwright George Bernard Shaw was so appalled by what he considered the "mess of English spelling" that he commissioned the Pittmans (of shorthand fame) to design a modified English alphabet that would restore alphabetic, sound-symbol relationship to the printed language. In the 1960s, British-Canadian linguist and reading specialist John Downing created and promoted the **Initial Teaching Alphabet (ita)** as an aid to early reading acquisition (Downing 1964; 1967). An alphabet of 44 letters that paralleled the 44 phonemes of English, the *ita* was taught to children as they began their reading instruction (see figure 5-1). Instructional materials using the *ita* were produced so that children could practice reading this modified alphabet. Over three years of instruction, *ita* materials were gradually replaced with materials using traditional spellings. Research indicated that children learning to read with the *ita* initially outperformed a control group taught using traditional spellings but that this early advantage tended to disappear after a few years.

A major problem with the *ita* and other modified alphabets was the dearth of available material using them. That remains the case. Libraries are full of books using traditional spellings. Newspapers and magazines use traditional spelling. The environmental print of billboards and signage all use the 26-letter alphabet in more or less traditional ways. As a result, little real reading can be done using a modified alphabet.[13] Although spellings have changed in English over time, the changes lag far behind our changing English phonology; for better or worse, we are stuck with a 26-letter alphabet to represent the 44 phonemes of English, along with all their dialect variations. Likewise, teachers were (and are) stuck with teaching reading with words spelled with our 26-letter alphabet.

For centuries, the teaching of reading strayed little from the ancient methods employed by the Greeks and Romans. Children were taught to recognize the letters of the alphabet (their ABCs) and recite them both forward and backward until they could recognize and name each letter at random. The letters were then grouped into syllables (a vowel and one or two consonants) and these too were learned by rote. Finally, syllables were made into words and words into sentences. Many young scholars had dropped out of school long before they reached this stage.

The central problem with the reading instruction (in addition to the general lack of anything interesting for children to read) was that *teachers failed to distinguish between the names of the letters and the sounds represented by these letters (or combinations of letters)*. For centuries, it was generally believed that saying letter names would help students read the words composed of those letters; that one could learn to read *cat*, for example, by saying "see – ay – tee"—this in spite of the fact that the letter *c* in cat stands for the phoneme /k/, the *a* stands for the phoneme /a/ (often called the *short a*), and *t* stands for the phoneme /t/, all of which have little relationship to the sounds we hear in the *names* of the letters in *cat*.

This failure to recognize the fundamental alphabetic nature of English bedeviled reading instruction in England and in the English-speaking colonies (including the United States and Canada) for centuries. It was the Germans and the French who made the initial breakthroughs to an understanding that the teaching of reading needs to take into account the alphabetic nature of Western languages.

The German and French Solution

The problems with teaching reading and with learning to read were much the same in Germany and France as in English-speaking countries. In Germany, frustration with the ABC method of learning to read surfaced as early as the sixteenth century. Basing his work on a study of ancient languages, including Greek and Latin, educator Valentin Ickelsamer (1501?–1542?) concluded that the **phonology** of a language is primary and precedes its **orthography** (written form). Many cultures have no written language, he noted, but all known human cultures have an oral language. Thus Ickelsamer firmly believed that the way to teach reading was to relate the letters to the sounds of the language and to avoid the confusion of using letter names, which often bore no strong relation to their sounds. He developed a detailed analysis of spoken German and its relationship to written German, coupled with a teaching method that clearly demonstrated for students the sounds that the letters in words stood for.

For example, Ickelsamer might start by writing the common German name *Otto* on the board. He would carefully pronounce the name and have the students do likewise. Next, he would analyze the name (word) into its constituent sounds (/ä/, /t/, and /ō/) and have the students pronounce these carefully in sequence (blending or **synthetic phonics**) before proceeding to other words.

Ickelsamer was quite successful with his method, which we would characterize today as **analytical phonics**. But he took the method to extremes, making it very complex to account for the fact that in German, as in English, letters of the alphabet often have multiple sound values. Unconvinced that Ickelsamer's method offered any advantage, his contemporaries continued to slog away with traditional ABC procedures.

Between 1750 and 1850, there arose in Germany and France the great philosophical concept of **naturalism**, or **sense realism**. This movement posited that one should arrive at truth by using the senses to study nature rather than depending on tradition and rational thought alone. This period ushered in the **child study movement**. Persons such as Jean-Jacques Rousseau, Heinrich Pestalozzi, and Friedrich Froebel[14] viewed children as *developing* through a series of natural stages determined through close observation and stressed the need to teach children in accordance with each stage. In general, they insisted that children must learn the concrete first and then the abstract, rather than the other way around. An early German developmentalist, Friedrich Gedike (1754–1803), argued that only God works synthetically, that is creatively, from part to whole; humans, on the other hand, can only analyze what God has already created, and thus should always work from whole to part. Therefore, he concluded, the teaching of reading should start with whole words rather than letters or syllables.

This idea of teaching from whole to part was echoed by other developmentalists, who argued it was less abstract than going the other way. Eventually the French educator Jean Joseph Jacotot incorporated these ideas into a method of teaching that became know as the *Normal Words Method* or the *Analytic-Synthetic Method.* In brief, the method contains these steps:

1. Show the child a common object or a picture of a common object (like a baby).
2. Write the entire word that names the object *(baby)*.
3. Analyze the word into syllables and then sounds *(ba/by,* then */b/ /ā/ /b/ /ē/)*.
4. Re-synthesize the word *(baby)*.
5. Repeat steps two through four several times, with the children following the teacher in writing the word.

This method made its way over to Germany where, in 1843, the great American educator Horace Mann visited Prussian schools directed by Pestalozzi. Impressed with this teaching method (christened the *Look-Say Method*), Mann brought it back to the United States. It is fair to say that from that day until the present, the debate between whole word (look-say) methods and phonics methods has raged. And that brings us back to the beginning of this chapter, which introduced the controversy by way of Jeanne Chall's writing about this debate, first published in the 1960s.

Of course, this synopsis omits entire chapters in the history of the teaching of reading, in both Europe and America.[15] Some other significant parts of reading history will be related in other parts of this book: for example, the tremendous influence of the Protestant Reformation in encouraging universal literacy, the influence of the McGuffey Readers in the United States, and the shift in emphasis from oral to silent reading. Often, early American reading instruction was an amalgam of various methods: ABC, syllabary, spelling, phonics, and whole word. This is still very much the case.

The Modern Context

Understanding the debate between proponents of phonics and whole word advocates requires a brief extension of that history.

Generally, the look-say or whole word methods won the day in the United States and Canada, under the influence of progressive educators with their emphasis on naturalism, avoidance of drill, and a child-centered pedagogy. All manner of variations of this whole word method were in vogue. In the 1950s and early 1960s, a growing number of voices decried the whole word method as eliminating all trace of connection between phonology and writing, thus reducing English to ideographs, as in Chinese. Chief among these was the linguist Leonard Bloomfield, who teamed with Clarence Barnhart in 1961 to publish *Let's Read: A Linguistic Approach.* This book asserted a need to accentuate the alphabetic nature of the English language in reading instruction, but in a modified form. At a popular level, *Why Johnny Can't Read* (and *Why Johnny Still Can't Read*) by Rudolph Flesch (1955; 1981) argued that, because schools were failing to teach phonics as the basis of learning to read, parents must take the bull by the horns and do it themselves.

The science of psychology, and especially educational psychology, was heavily influenced by the school of **behaviorism**, which sought to make the study of human behavior scientific by limiting such study to observable behaviors (hence its name). Behaviorism promised to develop a scientific approach to education that would in turn lead to more effective and efficient learning in the schools. Given the scare Americans received with the launching of the first Russian satellite in 1957, the appeal of a science of education that might help the United States catch up with the Soviets was strong indeed.

Behaviorist approaches to learning were characterized by analyzing complex tasks into their smallest components and then teaching each bit under conditions of careful reinforcement. A great deal of drill in isolated skills coupled with a rigid synthetic-analytic phonics approach to beginning reading characterized this view of learning. Many reading programs began to adopt such approaches, turning the teacher into an instructional technician. But there were dissenting voices.

In the 1970s, a new field of psychology began to assert itself. Called **cognitive psychology**, it is concerned as much with the inner workings of the mind as with external behavior. Cognitive psychology and its various branches, such as **psycholinguistics** (the psychology of language) and **sociolinguistics** (social and cultural factors in language use), cautioned that reading and learning to read cannot be reduced to the stimulus-response mechanisms of behaviorism. These disciplines, along with others from various literary fields, have helped us view reading and writing as highly complex human activities involving a host of intricate relationships between the written text, the reader, and the reader's community.

Reading educators who appreciate the insights of these latter influences have become identified with a teaching movement often termed **whole language**. Many evangelical Christian educators criticize the whole language orientation to teaching as too child-centered and lacking in skill instruction. They also believe the whole language movement is somehow tied to the epistemology of **constructivism**, which seems to suggest that all truth is constructed by the knower. Such a philosophy of knowing does violence to the Christian view that there are God-given, external truths. For these and other reasons (some outlined in chapter 1), many Christian teachers feel compelled to avoid whole language. Some hold that the best alternative is a highly skills-based approach to teaching the language arts that emphasizes a certain kind of phonics and grammar instruction.

Where Do I Stand?

The "great debate" has often been cast as a simple either-or proposition. Either you are a proponent of phonics teaching for beginning readers, or you are a whole word/meaning first (or whole language) proponent. Of course, the phonics vs. whole language dichotomy captures a sliver of truth about this "great debate," but it is a simplistic characterization. Unfortunately, it is how many have framed the controversy.

My comments in the first chapter of this book may lead some readers to believe that I come down firmly on the whole language side. This is a vast over-simplification of my position, as the rest of this book will make clear. As I said in *Language Arts in Christian Schools* (Bruinsma 1990), while I have learned much from the whole language movement, I believe that the term "whole language" has become a buzzword freighted with a load of conceptual and pedagogical baggage, some of it unhelpful. In addition, whole language purists would reject some of my positions. Thus, to avoid the emotionally tinged reactions associated with pro and anti "camps," I have adopted the more neutral term "language-centered" instruction.

Now, some people may argue that I am really weaseling here, and not clearly distancing myself from whole language. Rather, I am trying to come to grips with the complexity and subtlety of the issues at hand. To some extent, the reading methodology debate is one of the many in education for which one can find empirical support on either side. Much of the research conducted to solve or at least enlighten the "great debate" provides contradictory or inconclusive results. The issue then becomes one of determining which research findings deserve to be trusted. Adjudicating that question is *not* primarily an empirical task but a philosophical one.

As a Christian educator, my main quarrel lies with behaviorism and other forms of positivism that reduce humans to nothing more than complex animals or biological machines. Although initially trained as a biologist, I have always maintained a principled skepticism toward deterministic accounts of human behavior, including the behaviors of listening, speaking, reading, and writing. In my view as a natural scientist and an educator, certain research paradigms in cognitive psychology are as reductionist as is Skinnerian behaviorism. Likewise, some of the leading researchers and writers applying cognitive psychology to literacy are just as reductionist as earlier behaviorists.

Marilyn Jager Adams provides a case in point. Her 1990 book

Beginning to Read: Thinking and Learning about Print came out just as my little book (Bruinsma 1990) was going to print. In a concluding "Resource" section of the book, I was able to include a comment on her book. I wrote:

> This rather formidable book (approximately 500 pages) attempts to mediate the long-standing debate between the phonics versus teaching-for-meaning dilemma. It does so through a review and synthesis of a prodigious amount of empirical research, yet it is clearly and even interestingly written. Whether the book solves the dilemma is a matter that will continue to be debated, but Adams' book will be the source against which progress in the discussion will be measured for some time to come. (133)

Indeed, Adams' book has become a central reference point in the debate and in the reading research agenda for the last dozen years. It contains a great deal that is of value, and I encourage students and teachers who really want to sink their teeth into this pivotal debate to read it. I offer some caution, however, about Adams and others she cites as research sources. It is quite telling, for example, that her prototype for information about the teaching of reading in North American schools is computer modeling, itself a product of a mechanistic mind-set.

The computer models of reading that Adams champions in her book are drawn from **word recognition** models devised by cognitive researchers such as Michael Seidenberg and James McClelland (1989) as well as David Rummelhart (1994). As Sharon Murphy (1991) has ably argued, these word recognition and computer models of the reading process are reductionist on a number of counts. Unable to capture the daunting complexity of the task of reading connected text, typical computer models simply equate reading with word recognition.[16] It is from this research that Adams derives many of her inferences.

Without bogging down in details, suffice it to say that Murphy casts doubt on those assumptions by clearly showing why inferences derived from studies of words with specific properties cannot be applied directly to the reading of connected text.

Murphy raises other questions as well that ought to concern Christian educators. About the use of computer simulations in theorizing about humans, she legitimately asks "whether the manner in which computers 'learn' something is similar to the manner in which humans do" (200). As her work indicates, the theory underlying much current computer modeling of the reading process is connectionism, a form of behaviorism.

Thus we return full circle to the chapter 1 critique of those Christian teachers and administrators (cited in Thogmartin's survey 1994) who insist that using a narrow form of intensive phonics is *the* way to teach beginning reading. Such Christians have bought unwittingly (I hope) into an anthropology and epistemology that does *not* comport well with my understanding of a Christian view on these matters.

To be fair, I owe it to readers to explain why I am more comfortable with the work of psycholinguists such as Yetta and Kenneth Goodman (1997) and Frank Smith (1994), who might well put themselves in the "whole language" rather than the "phonics" camp. This explanation is especially needed because these persons have not made claims (as far as I know) about wanting to be particularly Christian in approach. Yet their work deserves attention because it comes out of a research tradition that has consciously broken with behaviorism and other forms of psychological reductionism.

Following linguist Noam Chomsky's devastating critique of Skinnerian explanations of language acquisition (1959; 1965), meaning and human agency once again became legitimate variables in psychological research.[17] It took a while for Chomsky's critique of behaviorism to impact psychology. But by the 1970s, psycholinguists such as George Miller, Frank Smith, and Ken Goodman reasserted and demonstrated that the drive for making sense of the world plays a key role in human behavior, including such a complex behavior as reading connected text. Furthermore, they paved the way for sociolinguists to demonstrate the complex social dimensions of reading and learning to read. As Doris Entwistle (1971) put it, "the children who learn to read best are those who need to in order to make sense of their lives" (116). Thus, learning to read is as much a matter of family and broader cultural modeling as it is of teaching individuals through specific techniques. Joining the "literacy club" (Smith 1988) is as much a social act as a pedagogical one. Current research and interest in family literacy (for example, Morrow, Tracey, and Maxwell 1995; Morrow 1995) bears out the relevance of this insight. Thus, while it is true that we do not yet know the best way to teach reading, we certainly do know a lot about the social and pedagogic conditions that help children learn to read. The abundant recent research on emergent literacy indicates that such conditions do not emulate the intensive phonics and other skill-and-drill approaches favored by Thogmartin's respondents.

In summary, I have cast my philosophical lot with a certain group of reading cognitivists rather than with behaviorists and some of their cognitive bedfellows. Having said that, I hasten to add that I am aware of the thoroughly humanistic trend represented in the epistemology of constructivism, that offspring of modern cognitive psychology. In radical constructivist terms, the world is made, not found; that is, humans construct their own reality. There is no external, transcendent reality; no God the Creator, who has set out boundaries and norms for human reality. As a Christian, I reject such claims of human autonomy, but I also know that we have been made only "a little lower than the heavenly beings, and crowned ... with glory and honor" (Psalm 8:5). Thus it behooves us as Christian educators to treat our students as responsive subjects of their King, rather than as objects for behavioral or cognitive manipulation. That, for me, is *the* central issue of this "great debate."

Questions for Discussion

1. After reading this chapter, it may be helpful to meet with a classmate or colleague who has also read it and discuss your understanding of the following terms:

   alphabetic language
   phoneme
   grapheme
   phoneme-grapheme correspondence (and vice versa)
   decoding
   encoding
   phonics
   analytic vs. synthetic phonics
   skills-centered vs. language-centered teaching approaches
   consonant
   vowel
   syllable
   hornbook
   primer
   crisscross
   Great Vowel Shift
   whole language
   ita
   traditional orthography
   look-say method
   behaviorism
   cognitive psychology
   constructivism
   the "Great Debate"

2. Why did the invention and development of the printing press have such a *conservative* effect on English spelling?

3. How do you learn best, whole-to-part or part-to-whole? You might think of this question in terms of a specific learning task. For example, if you have acquired a new piece of computer software, do you:

- Carefully read the manual before trying it out?
- Just start "messing around" until you get a feel for how it works?
- Ask a computer-savvy friend to show you how to use the software?
- Use approaches other than *a, b,* or *c* above?
- Use a combination of ways?

4. How much does your previous familiarity (with new software, for example) influence how you approach the learning task?
5. What do these questions have to do with the "Great Debate"?

For Further Consideration

1. Suppose a friendly Martian, Mimi, landed in your neighborhood and interviewed you about some aspects of human behavior that made her curious. Among other things, Mimi mentions that she has observed various humans sitting quietly and looking at an object made up of thin sheets of moveable material with squiggles on it. Mimi asks, "What are these humans doing?" You answer, "They are reading." Then she asks, "What is reading?" What would you tell Mimi? Is reading difficult to describe? What does your response suggest about your beliefs about reading? How do your beliefs relate to the Great Debate?
2. Ask a number of other people "What is reading?" using Mimi the Martian. Choose a couple of elementary students, a couple of teachers, a college professor, and a couple of your peers. How do your respondents view reading—primarily as decoding (sounding out) of letters/words? As taking meaning *from* print? As bringing meaning *to* print? As a combination of these and other concepts? (For an interesting study in which approximately 500 elementary school children were asked this question, see Bruinsma, 1990b.)

3. Talk with someone who learned to read and write a non-alphabetic language before learning English (a Chinese or Japanese person, for example). Ask the person to compare the challenge of becoming literate in the non-alphabetic language with learning to read and write English.

4. Interview three Christian elementary teachers and ask them to describe their approach to reading instruction. Ask them whether they advocate using whole language and/or phonics to teach reading, and why.

Endnotes

1 To be fair, Chall also made it abundantly clear that in reading, "*both* meaning and the use of the alphabetic principle are essential. To read, one needs to be able to use *both* the alphabetic principle and the meaning of words. What distinguished the more effective beginning reading instruction was its early emphasis on learning the code" (Chall 1996: Introduction to the Third Edition).

2 For more details about phonics, see chapter 10.

3 It should be noted, however, that Adams also argued for extensive exposure to books and print before teaching children phonics.

4 This brief historical excursion is based primarily on accounts by Huey (1908), Manguel (1996), Matthews (1966), and Smith (1965).

5 This example should alert the reader to the fact that English writing, while alphabetic, is not perfectly so since there are more phonemes (sounds) in the language then there are graphemes (letters) to represent them. Thus English does not have a one-to-one phoneme-grapheme correspondence. As we will see in chapter 10, this complicates the matter of relying too heavily on phonics as a means of learning to read.

6 The concept of a *word* is actually quite a difficult one. Those of us who are literate derive this concept largely from the fact that modern writing breaks the flow of oral language into distinct groups of letters with white space on either side. Oral language is not nearly so distinct in demarcating words. This is especially noticeable if we listen to a fluent speaker of an unfamiliar foreign language. We tend to hear the undulating intonational pattern of the language and not distinct words.

7 Few girls were taught to read. Even today, literacy learning is often reserved for males. The extreme form of Islam as practiced by the Afghan Taliban is a recent sad example of this sexist bias. A rare exception to this male bias was the recommendation in the mid-seventeenth century by

John Amos Comenius. He argued that "boys and girls should be taught in common, basing his argument on the claims that both are equally created in the image of God, that God has gifted both (girls often more), and that God has not uncommonly called women to lead, rebuke leaders, and prophesy" (David Smith, personal communication).

8 Letters or syllables within slash marks [/] indicate the sound being represented. Thus /p/ should not be decoded as "pee" (the name of the letter), but as the sound made by the small explosion of air that leaves pursed lips just before uttering words containing the letter *p*.

9 Syllable learning as a basis for learning to read continued for more than 2,000 years, including early methods of learning to read English, despite the fact that English is a much more word-oriented than syllable-oriented language. For example, many English syllables contain more than one vowel even though only a single sound is heard for these vowel pairs (for example, beat = /bēt/; make = /māk/).

10 Readers interested in this and other changes in the English language over time will find many books devoted to the development of the English language, including Pyles and Algeo (1993).

11 Even today, dictionaries will contain variant spellings of certain words, and American, Canadian, and British English have different spellings for certain words. Interestingly, other rules or conventions were also not firmly fixed at this time. The use of capital letters was quite erratic, as was punctuation.

12 See Matthews (1966, 20–23) for examples of these changes in English spellings over time.

13 It may be that environmental print will have the greatest effect on spelling change. For example, many of us are quite used to seeing a word such as *night* spelled as *nite* on billboards or in TV commercials. Americans have generally tended to simplify British spellings by dropping "silent" letters. As a Canadian writer, I would normally use British spellings. Because this book is published in the United States, however, I've had to set my computer keyboard to American English so that words such as *color* and *humor* aren't spelled (or spelt) *colour* and *humour,* as they are in Britain and Canada.

14 This book is not the place for a detailed discussion of these men's beliefs concerning education (although Rousseau was mentioned in chapter 1). It is important, however, for future and current teachers to understand the history that shaped current concepts. Again and again, teaching practices hailed as new and revolutionary are just reruns of previously tried and forgotten approaches, with different labels. This is also the case in the current "great debate" about reading instruction. See Lucas (1972) for a fine general history of Western education.

15 The classic work on the history of American reading instruction is by Smith (1965; reissued in 1986 by the International Reading Association with a new prologue, epilogue, and update).

[16] I have no quarrel with those who insist that rapid and accurate word recognition is essential to reading fluently and with comprehension (see Stanovich 1991). While a necessary condition for such reading, it is not, however, sufficient.

[17] The significance of the debate about language acquisition for questions pertaining to learning to read will be elaborated in chapters 6–8. In brief, Chomsky argued that children learn language not primarily through imitation (the behaviorist view) but through creative interaction with a rule-governed linguistic grammar that is innate. This nativist perspective has been challenged, but the fact that children "create" utterances that they have never heard in their linguistic environment is now unquestioned, seriously challenging behaviorist theories of language acquisition.

Part 2

The Foundations of Literacy

In this section of three chapters we leave the philosophical, historical, and curricular contexts of literacy learning and teaching, and direct our attention to the subject of all our teaching efforts—the students. We begin by realizing that the language arts are about language and that children do not come into the world knowing how to speak. Yet the potential for learning to read and write grows out of the primary abilities of listening and speaking. British linguist and educator James Britton has rightly said that "literacy floats on a sea of oracy." Thus, chapter 6 explores the what, how, and why of oral language development in children.

We will see in chapter 6 that oral language learning is a stupendous achievement. In a few short years, most young children learn more about language than linguists can describe in massive volumes of scholarly books. Yet somehow for many children this amazing facility for language learning hits a roadblock when they start school. Chapter 7 explores this phenomenon and attempts to shed some light on why it happens and how we can mitigate the problem.

In the last two decades we have learned much about how young children's understanding of literacy can emerge quite naturally if they are raised in a print-rich environment with supportive caregivers. Preschool and primary teachers in particular need to understand emergent literacy development and their critical role in fostering and supporting it. Emergent literacy is the topic of chapter 8.

Chapter 6

The Roots of Literacy Learning: Oral Language Development

Even before entering school, a child spends five or six years learning a great deal. Amid all that learning, the greatest achievement is acquisition of oral language. The fact that the vast majority of children learn their native language without formal instruction demonstrates that learning is natural to them. This chapter explains what children must learn to be able to speak, and how and why they do so. It emphasizes children's active participation in using language to get things done, and begins to explore what oral language development implies for future literacy learning. As a segue to chapter 7, we conclude by asking why some children struggle with language learning tasks once they enter the classroom.

Beginnings are important, and deserve attention. This is especially so in teaching and learning the language arts. It is crucial to realize that language learning commences not when children begin formal schooling but at birth. This is true not only for oral language but also for literacy.

Most parents are accomplished language models. The children they deliver to school have an extensive, implicitly learned vocabulary containing ninety-five percent of the functional grammar they will ever need. Many children also arrive at school knowing how stories are constructed. This latter competence is especially important; without it, learning to read is very difficult. Because preschool learning has considerable bearing on how children fare during school, teachers need to understand how preschoolers acquire language.

Language Acquisition and Development

The last three decades have seen great advances in our understanding of how children learn, and especially how they learn language. Most research relating to language acquisition and early literacy development is based on observations of infants and children in home settings, but it is now clear that many principles of early language and literacy acquisition in the home also apply to literacy learning in school.[1]

The Content of Language Learning

Because most children learn to speak fluently in just four or five years, we often take the immensity of this feat for granted. We think of it as "natural," meaning ordinary or of no great significance. However, language learning is no mean feat. Even a cursory look at the linguistics section of a university library will demonstrate the complexity of what a person must know and do to communicate with speech. This complexity characterizes not only the formal oral communication of a graduate research seminar but also the routine human speech we use in our daily lives. Just what is it that an ordinary language user must learn about language?

All languages have four major components (see figure 6-1): a **phonology** or sound system, a **syntax** governing acceptable word order, a **semantic** system that specifies acceptable meaning, and a **pragmatic** system that limits what is appropriate in various sociocultural circumstances. When these four systems work together in concert, we consider the speaker/hearer **communicatively competent.** A brief examination of each system will help us appreciate what young children master when they learn to speak English.

Figure 6-1: Four major systems of language

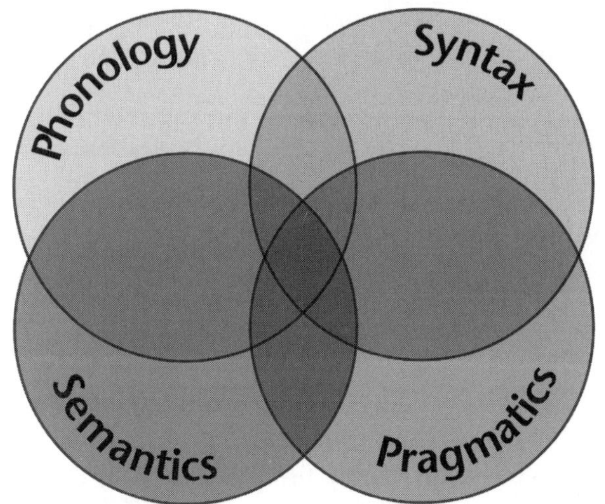

Phonology English contains approximately forty-four distinct sounds **(phonemes)** that affect meaning. For example, the words /pit/ and /bit/ differ in one phoneme (that is, the difference in sound between /p/ and /b/). As an aside, it should be immediately clear that, with only twenty-six letters in the English alphabet, it is impossible to represent each phoneme with a distinct written letter. Thus, English does not have a one-to-one sound-to-letter correspondence. This fact lies at the heart of the considerable difficulty of trying to teach reading solely as a "sounding out" process.

Syntax It is not enough that children learn the sounds of their language; they must learn to organize the sounds into sequences and patterns (words and sentences). Consider the two sentences below:

1. The boy thanked the girl.
2. Boy the girl the thanked.

We readily regard sentence *1* as acceptable but not *2*, even though the phonology of *2* is fine. Its problem involves syntax. English syntax is concerned primarily with word order and inflections (for example, the *ed* ending on *thank* to represent past tense). Syntax contributes powerfully to our understanding language. Thus, although sentence *3* contains a preponderance of nonsense words, its syntax allows us to answer comprehension questions.

3. The argle zoolked the bordiddy in the ershent because the bordiddy larped the argle.
   a. Who zoolked the bordiddy?
   b. What did the bordiddy do to the argle?
   c. Why did the argle zoolk the bordiddy in the ershent?

Semantics At times, both the phonology and the syntax of an utterance are perfectly acceptable in English, yet the meaning is either wrong or vague. Compare sentences *4* and *5*:

4. The dog chased the cows into the barn.
5. The barn chased the cows into the dog.

We readily accept *4* as meaningful but not *5*, even though *5* is phonologically acceptable and has exactly the same syntactic form as *4*. Sentence *5* is semantically unacceptable because it violates what we know from experience to be the properties and actions of dogs, cows, and barns. Semantic ambiguity arises for many reasons. For example, the context may be unclear, as in *6*, or we cannot bring sufficient background information to the utterance, as in *7*.

6. The shooting of the hunters was terrible.

7. Because the seam was split, the notes were sour.

[Does the word *bagpipe* help you bring meaning to 7?]

Pragmatics As children gain linguistic experience in their culture and subculture, they come to understand that there are appropriate and inappropriate ways to speak. A five-year-old announces the arrival of her six-year-old friend with, "Hey, Mom, Elizabeth's here!" A few days later, that same preschooler greets her friend's grade 1 teacher by saying, "Hello, I'll tell my mom that Elizabeth's teacher is here." Clearly, this child understands that a person as important (in her eyes) as Elizabeth's teacher should be greeted with deferential respect. She understands that differences in age and status are important variables in determining the nature of talk. This matter of propriety, that is, the pragmatics of language, reflects cultural and subcultural norms surrounding (among other things) the setting, participants, and purposes of communication.

As indicated by this very brief description of what children must learn about their language, the complexity of the four systems of language (particularly when coupled with their interactions) is staggering. How do children accomplish this learning feat?

The Process of Language Learning

The rate at which normal children learn language is amazing, considering what they must achieve. Again, the following discussion touches on only the most significant milestones in children's language acquisition. More detailed accounts can be found in sources such as Jean Gleason (2001) and Lloyd Hulit (1997), and in many current language arts textbooks, such as Joyce Bainbridge and Grace Malicky (2000).

At birth, most children come equipped with the vocal apparatus and motivation to make a variety of sounds. Early cries and whimpers are related to specific physiological needs, such as food and comfort. Most experienced parents can soon distinguish among cries that mean, "I'm hungry," "I'm wet," and "I'm cold." Before long, babies "discover" that they can make vocal sounds, and they begin to experiment actively with their voices. This is the **babbling stage**. Parents are often delighted by these sounds and babble back; before long, infants begin to imitate those sounds, much to the delight of their parents. Ruth Weir (1962) provides a fascinating account of this early linguistic play, the beginning of phonological development. Linguists can distinguish the babbling of babies as young as six months who are raised in different language environments; Chinese babies, for example, babble differently from English babies.

Adult input is very important at this babbling stage. It may be that such simple language games as "peek-a-boo" provide a rudimentary introduction to the turn-taking behavior that is essential to conversation. Similarly, the reading and reciting of nursery rhymes that occurs in many middle class homes provides infants a model for the rhythm and intonation of their language. This latter understanding is part of the **phonemic awareness** that is an essential precursor to learning to read.

At about twelve months, many children utter their first "words." These words serve many purposes, often signifying entire concepts. Thus "milk" may mean, "I want some milk," "I spilled my milk," or "There's the milkman." This is the **holophrase stage** of language development, so-named to reflect the fact that a single word serves for a whole phrase or idea. Caregivers help children best at this stage by being sensitive to the context of the holophrase, and by interpreting their intent or expanding their meanings. Thus, when a child says, "Milk!" after spilling it, the parent might reply, "Oh, I see you spilled your milk. I guess we'd better clean it up." Besides assuring the child that meaning has been understood, that response provides input for language that is more complex.

From about eighteen to thirty months, children will often use two- and three-word phrases or **telegraphic speech**. An absence of **functors,** or **function words** (such as articles and prepositions) and an emphasis on key nouns and verbs characterize these phrases. Adults sending telegrams take a similar approach, condensing "My car has broken down. Please send me some money for repairs!" into "Car broke, send money." There is a difference between adults and children, however: while adults can choose to abbreviate and concentrate their speech, children at the telegraphic stage cannot. Although they may fully intend "The dog is chasing the cat," they can only say, "Dog cat" or "Dog chase cat." Again, the primary role of adult caregivers is not to "correct" children by instructing them to expand their telegraphic speech. Rather, the wise caregiver simply responds to the child's semantic intent by modeling **expansions** and **elaborations** of the utterances. A child who says, "Milk all gone" can be answered with the expansion, "Yes, I see your milk is all gone," or with the elaboration, "And I see that you ate your cereal too."

The telegraphic stage is a time when children are ripe for linguistic growth. By thirty months, many a child has a vocabulary of fifty to seventy-five words. This is the time for extensive reading to children and for a wide variety of shared experiences accompanied by much talk. It is also the time when children should have access to their own books (Butler & Clay 1987; Butler 1995; Doake 1988) so that they will come to see books as important and normal artifacts of their culture.

While linguistic development has been impressive up to this point, it becomes simply phenomenal around age two and a half. An explosive increase in vocabulary acquisition occurs so that, by age three, many children have more than three thousand words in their functional vocabulary and have learned nearly all the phonemic elements of English. By age four, most children have well-established language in which phonology, syntax, semantics, and pragmatics mesh quite effectively.

During this period, children often produce unique verbal constructions that they have not learned from adults but that reflect their own internal struggle to learn English grammar. Children who discover that English past tense verbs usually add *ed* to present tense verbs may overgeneralize this rule and say "I *runned* home" or "I *wented* to the store." Children are not making errors when they do this, any more than they are making errors when they crawl before they walk. This stage is natural, part of a rule-governed developmental process. Again, adult input and modeling through wide-ranging language use, stimulating conversation, engaging reading, and shared experiences are key to aiding language development at this stage.

From ages five to ten, children polish their language. They learn many of the irregularities of English grammar and develop a greater sensitivity to the pragmatic niceties of language use. At this stage, the influence of schooling is profound, since much formal literacy learning takes place there. Children develop a growing awareness of language as something they can consciously examine and manipulate. That is, they develop **metalinguistic awareness**. It is also at this stage that children become conscious of the power of language to organize their world. Not all children realize this in the same way, however. Size of vocabulary is a rough indicator of a child's linguistic growth during this stage, and studies show that children's vocabularies range from 3,000 to 40,000 words by age ten. Differences in experience such as the amount of conversation and reading in the home and school, and the direct and vicarious activities children have shared in, reflected on, and talked about can account for this large variability.

Theories of Language Acquisition—Why and How Do Children Learn to Talk?

The foregoing sections briefly summarize *what* children need to know to learn to talk and outline the general *sequence* of language acquisition, but they have omitted any reference to *why* and *how* children pick up language. Researchers have proposed various hypotheses, but none solves all the mysteries of early language acquisition, and much remains to be learned. The phenomenon of preschool language learning continues to intrigue teachers—and well it should, because that feat is so very important to later learning, both inside and outside of school.

Behaviorist View of Language Learning

The earliest views of language learning were based on the apparently common-sense notion that children learn language by imitating adult speech. By the 1950s, quite sophisticated behaviorist explanations expanded this imitation theory to include the feedback children receive as caregivers signal whether utterances are appropriate. For example, if a child says "Da-da-da-da" in the presence of her father, she is likely to receive a smile and encouragement that acts as positive reinforcement. Similarly, children experimenting with language will receive and respond to cuddles, frowns, angry retorts, and soft verbal responses. But even this more complex behaviorism views children mostly as *passive* learners who respond to the language of others (Skinner 1957).

As researchers continued to explore children's language development, it became apparent that the behaviorist view of language acquisition could not account for the sheer quantity of language children learn, the unique utterances they make, or all the things they *do* with language.

We now know that children do not learn to talk because someone sits down with them and teaches them, bit by bit, the formal rules of English phonology, syntax, semantics, and pragmatics. We also know that children do not learn to talk only by imitation, although imitation certainly plays a role. Few adults ever say "All gone milk" or "I goed to the store," yet children say such things. Further, we know that children do not learn to talk because adults reward them for correct speech and punish them for incorrect speech. Studies show that most adult caregivers respond to the meaning of children's utterances, not to grammatical structure.

Innatist View of Language Learning

The previous chapter mentioned the American linguist Noam Chomsky, who in 1959 published a devastating critique of Skinner's (1957) *Verbal Behavior.* In the year Skinner's book appeared, Chomsky (1957) published his own major work, *Syntactic Structures*. In it, Chomsky outlined a new view of language learning, now known as the **innatist** view. He argued that children have a natural predisposition to learn language, something built in (he called it a **Language Acquisition Device (LAD)** that enables them to acquire language quickly and easily. This innate language device, he said, generates a deep-seated, universal grammar that is transformed into the surface grammar of the language to which children are exposed. He argued that children are *active* participants in accessing their deep-seated, rule-governed grammar and transforming it into the common surface structures of their own language. In his view, common overgeneralizations of certain grammatical forms (such as *ed* for all past tenses) show that children are actively figuring out and using their grammatical understanding of language and not simply responding to their environment, as behaviorists believe.

Interactionist View of Language Learning

In some ways, the roles assigned to the individual and the culture in the behaviorist and innatist views of language acquisition parallel the old "nature versus nurture" controversy. For behaviorists, imitative learning (nurture) plays the greatest role in language learning, while for the innatist, genetic factors (nature) are paramount. The most recent **interactionist** view of language learning is much more complex than either of those approaches. This view suggests that, before language learning can occur, two interdependent systems must be in place: a fully functioning human being and a fully functioning social system. In other words, language is contextualized, occurring in real situations for real purposes (John-Steiner and P. Tatter 1983). Bainbridge and Malicky (2000) summarize the interactionist perspective as follows:

> If the child is disabled in some way, then normal language learning may not take place. If there is not interaction between the child and the social system, this will create a lack in language learning. Rather than seeing culture, society, and the child's psychological makeup and cognitive abilities as separate entities, the interactionist views all of them as interdependent, much like a woven tapestry. The child is part of the culture as much as the culture is part of the child. Language learning involves both learning *about* the culture and learning about being an individual who is a *part of* the culture. These facets of human life cannot be separated and examined in isolation. They are each part of the other, interacting and contributing to the unique development of all individuals. (37)

The interactionist view thus postulates that children learn language through the interaction of the human being, the social situation, and the culture. Language is contextualized and learned through use. This view of language development has powerful implications for teaching language arts and for using language in learning across the curriculum.

How do children learn to talk? In summary, they do so without undue difficulty by listening as those around them use language in meaningful ways. All children are created with an innate urge to make sense of the world around them. They quickly infer that speech (and not, for example, the hum of the refrigerator or the bark of a dog) allows them to label, sort, classify, and sequence experiences in meaningful ways. Children learn to talk because they need language to make sense of their experiences with other human beings. Failure to learn cuts them off from most meaningful human intercourse. Children need and want to belong to the club of speakers so that they can participate in the multitude of human enterprises that require language.

For children, learning language is not something essentially foreign and distasteful. It is not as if children are born with a huge language deficit that adults must somehow try to overcome by pouring in explicit linguistic knowledge. Rather, children are born with an almost unlimited capacity and an insatiable desire to learn language. Given a supportive linguistic milieu, that is exactly what they do.[2]

Functions of Language—Learning How to Mean

Most early attempts at studying children's language acquisition focused on the structural aspects of language, which we call **grammar**. The influential British linguist Michael Halliday (1973, 1975) took a different approach to studying children's language development. To answer the question "What is language?" Halliday maintained we should look not so much at structure as at the *purpose or intent* behind language events. Children know intuitively what language is because they know what it *does*, Halliday suggested. In other words, children learn about language through using it. They do not learn explicitly what a noun is, but they do learn how to label. They do not understand what grammar is, yet they learn how to string words together into sentences that make sense to them and the people they communicate with. Children thus learn language to express meanings to others and to construct meanings for themselves; that is, children are always busy "learning how to mean." Moreover, the discourse that contributes most to the growth of children's language capabilities and learning is the discourse that *actively involves the child*. Interaction, particularly with significant adults or more mature language users, is necessary for language learning (Wells 1986). Watching television and being talked *at* are no substitutes for genuine involvement and purposeful talk *with* children. These are the most important conditions upon which children's language development rests.

Michael Halliday's Functions of Language

From an initial study of his son Nigel's linguistic development, Halliday suggested a seven-category classification of language functions:

1. **Instrumental** ("I want" or "Gimme!"): Language referring to physical and psychological needs and wants, used as a tool to get something for the speaker
2. **Regulatory** ("Do as I say" or "Stop that!"): Language used to control another's behavior but not for the direct benefit of the speaker
3. **Interactional** ("You and me together" or "How are you feeling?"): Language used for collaborative purposes, to build a "we-ness" betwccn speaker and listener
4. **Personal** ("Here I come" or "I'm scared."): Language used for personal expression and self-revelation
5. **Heuristic** ("Tell me why" or "What's that?"): Language used to find things out—to ask questions, assess answers, and form new questions
6. **Imaginative** ("Let's pretend" or "Knock, knock, who's there?"): Language used purely for the fun of it, for the "feel" of the sounds, and for the fun of combining words and ideas
7. **Representational** ("Let me tell you about ..." or "It's snowing."): Language used to report, to convey information about past and present situations

Joan Tough's Functions of Language

Building on the work of Halliday and others, Joan Tough (1977) conducted research that clearly shows not all children use language for the same purposes—not because they are unable, but because they have been socialized to place different value on various language uses. Upon entering school, most children are quite capable of using language to accomplish the first four of Halliday's functions. However, many children have not grown up in environments that value or encourage the last three functions—precisely the functions the school values most. Note that the first four of Halliday's language functions describe talk that tends to be highly egocentric, useful for accomplishing immediate personal ends, whereas the last three require the child to use language in more impersonal and abstract ways. Margaret Donaldson's (1978) previously introduced terms of *embedded* and *disembedded* language are useful here. Although almost all children come to school adept in embedded language uses, not all children are equally adept at using language for disembedded purposes. Thus, to quote Tough (1977):

> [Some] children are not inclined to reflect on the meaning of their own experiences or to project readily into the experiences of others. They do not give explanations and justifications readily, nor do they reflect readily on past experiences, injecting them into the present to illuminate understanding. Nor do they anticipate the future readily and plan to consider alternative possibilities. (165)

What all of this means for language arts teachers is that they must be less concerned about the *form of language* that children initially bring to school and more concerned about the *functions of language* that children have at their disposal. Not all students are accustomed to using language in the rather abstract and analytic ways valued by the school and the "educated" culture. The considerable linguistic gulf that often exists—between students and teachers, among students, and between in-school and out-of-school culture—can only be bridged if teachers are (1) aware the gulf exists and (2) sensitive to and knowledgeable about ways to close it.

Influenced by Halliday's model of the social uses of language, Tough (1976) developed a simpler classification of language functions to help teachers assess children's language use in the classroom. She then produced guides for fostering communication skills, aimed at preschool through the intermediate grades (1977, 1979). Tough's system collapses Halliday's seven functions into four fundamental language categories:

1. **Directive language** Used in directing others
2. **Interpretive language** Used in reporting or conveying information and in reasoning

3. **Projective language** Used in predicting and anticipating possibilities, in imagining, and in projecting how others feel or why they react in particular ways
4. **Relational language** Used in protecting one's self and expressing needs and wants

As with Halliday's seven functions, it is clear that some of Tough's categories of language use are more highly prized in school than others. Tough's interpretive function is very important, as students are often evaluated according to how well they answer questions, report information, and explain reasoning. Asking questions, making predictions, and identifying how others might feel or react (Tough's projective function) are used less often, but increase in importance after the primary grades. Other language functions are underutilized in schools, perhaps on the assumption that they develop on their own or are more often practiced at home or during play. Thus, school may unwittingly perpetuate uneven language development by encouraging some language uses but ignoring or inhibiting others.

As Tough's (1977) research emphasized, we cannot assume that all families and peer relationships will nurture the full range of functional language growth. The result, as already pointed out, is that many children enter school lacking experiences in some language functions, particularly those that the school values most highly. That is why it is so important to create systematic opportunities for diverse uses of language.

This is not to say that the language used in school, or required of students in school, is always more functionally diverse than that used in children's homes. Gordon Wells' (1986) study of language development in the lived social contexts of children is most instructive here. Wells followed 32 children from ages two to nine, tape-recording several fifteen-minute segments of their oral language interactions every day. Fitting the children with radio microphones, he collected data at various times of the day and in diverse social contexts, then analyzed the talk for grammatical complexity and function. Wells challenged some of Tough's findings by showing that many children from homes of low socioeconomic status did *not* exhibit impoverished language. He did find, however, that the language of all 32 children was suppressed at school: "For no child was the language experience of the classroom richer than that of the home—not even for those believed to be 'linguistically deprived'"(1986). Wells discovered that teachers dominated most conversations and that much of the talk children engaged in at school was inauthentic, lacking the purpose and spontaneity of real talk. Clearly, those findings point to a significant problem with oral language interaction in classrooms.

Studies by Wells and others (e.g., Heath 1983; Tizard and Hughes 1984) underline a need to determine why we are failing to address children's oracy in school and to explore possible ways of expanding this important area of language arts. In our language instruction, we must provide activities that practice and build facility with all language functions. Chapter 10 will provide concrete suggestions for just how to do this.

Evaluating Oral Language Development

Oral language development is difficult to evaluate because it is immediate and transitory. Evaluation can take place by observing the oral language that is a part of everyday learning experiences, and by evaluating the language used in activities specifically designed to focus on oral language. In such evaluation, a distinction must be made between the **structural** and **functional** components of language development. Students who have noticeable speech and language difficulties related to enunciation and fluency (structural concerns) should see a speech-audiology specialist.

Useful resources for the classroom teacher serious about monitoring **structural** aspects of oral language development include the following:

◊ Marie M. Clay, Malcolm Gill, Ted Glynn, Tony McNauton, and Keith Salmon. 1983. *Record of oral language and Biks and Gutches.* Exeter, NH: Heinemann.

◊ Lois A. Bader. 1998b. Oral language. In L. Bader. *Reading and language inventory.* 3rd ed. Columbus, OH: Merrill, 147–150.

◊ For evaluating children's functional uses of language, Joan Tough's (1976) *Listening to children talking* is still an excellent resource. Methods for evaluating various speaking skills are suggested at the end of chapter 10.

Conclusion

In this chapter, we note that God creates children able to learn oral language. Furthermore, children surrounded by supportive adults and other caregivers who respond meaningfully to their efforts achieve this remarkable feat in a relatively short time. We have come to understand that children *actively participate* in their quest for meaningful language. The social milieu in which children are nurtured will greatly affect their understanding of what they can accomplish with language. There have been hints that the school is not always as attuned to the ways of children's preschool learning as it should be. Too many children who have been successful and confident users of language before they start school suddenly find themselves failing and labeled as "at risk" in the classroom. Many others muddle through as best they can but leave school only functionally literate and numerate, with very few fond memories of their elementary and middle school language-learning experiences. Happily, there are also those for whom schooling is the gateway to a rich and lasting experience with language. The next chapter examines in some detail what happens when language "goes to school."

Questions for Discussion

1. What is the difference between phonology and phonics?

2. English grammar is largely a matter of syntax. For example, what part of speech is the word *dog*? You probably answered that it is a noun. But what about the part of speech (or grammatical function) that the word *dog* serves in this sentence: *Why do you dog my every footstep?* Create other sentences in which the grammatical function of a word changes depending on *where* it occurs in the sentence. What do these examples tell you about the usefulness of grammatical labeling of English words independent of a sentence context?

3. Semantics refers to the *meaning* of language. Can you provide some jokes, puns, or idioms to show that meaning is more than just correct phonology and syntax?

4. Pragmatics refers to the *etiquette* of a language. How important is language etiquette? To what extent might some Christians' strong adherence to the King James Version of the Bible be a matter of pragmatic considerations? Write four sentences with substantially the same semantic content that differ pragmatically because they are addressed to the following four recipients:
   - The Queen of England
   - Your close friend
   - Your mother
   - Your dog

5. How might the argument made in this chapter for why children learn to talk be extended to why some children learn to read and write with considerable ease?

6. Why is a behaviorist theory of language acquisition considered inadequate in accounting for children's oral language development?

7. Can you distinguish between the *form* and *function* of children's language development? Why is the latter more indicative of how easily young children will adapt to the demands of formal schooling?

8. What is your experience with language use in school? Does it corroborate or challenge Gordon Wells' findings that schools tend to squelch rich oral language use?

For Further Consideration

1. There are those who argue that children's oral language development has little relevance for literacy learning (Nicholson 1999; Stanovich 2000). These researchers point out that all human cultures have developed oral language, but relatively few have developed a writing system. Thus, they consider speaking to be "natural" whereas reading and writing are not. They use this argument to justify the need for explicit early instruction in phonemic awareness and phonics. What is your reaction to this position?

2. Find a copy of the International Phonetic Alphabet (IPA) in a linguistics textbook to see the forty-four phonemes of standard English as represented by this alphabet. How does this compare with the Initial Teaching Alphabet (*ita*) described in chapter 5?

3. Record a brief conversation with two children—one around two years old and the other three and a half—about a favorite toy or pet. At which stage of language development is each child? Are there syntactic constructions in the children's speech that show evidence of creativity?

4. Suggest some oral language activities that could help children develop a more extensive repertoire of language functions. For example, how might you foster *projective* language use? (See chapter 10 as well.)

5. In small groups, research the work of Michael Halliday, Joan Tough, and Gordon Wells and make brief reports to the class, focusing on educational implications.

Endnotes

1 There are those who disagree that oral language learning is relevant to literacy learning. See the first question in For Further Consideration above for more opportunity to discuss this point.

2 In a broken creation there are, unfortunately, always some exceptions to the norm. Some children do not learn language easily, often because of congenital defects, illness, or severe mistreatment. The discussions in this book are applicable to the large majority of children who fall in the "normal" range of development.

Chapter 7

Language Goes to School

While most children come to school with an impressive record of oral language accomplishments, many soon find themselves struggling with the language learning tasks set by the school. For some, this struggle continues a trend begun in preschool. Others struggle despite seemingly normal oral language development. This brief chapter looks at the challenges facing children as they enter school and provides some suggestions for making the home-to-school transition a positive one for more children.

Children entering school at age five or six have mastered most of the complexities of the language system. They understand the phonology and syntax of English, and they can create a multitude of meanings from what they see and hear. Many are aware of the **environmental print** on cereal boxes, service stations, fast food restaurants, and more. Years ago, when my oldest daughter was about three-and-a-half, she insisted the capital letters *S-H-E-L-L* stood for the word "gas," obviously identifying the Shell logo and words with fueling the car. Most children also come to school knowing how to handle books, and they delight in being read to. They take pleasure in playing with language, and they understand some of the linguistic subtleties that underlie jokes. As we learned in the previous chapter, however, not all children develop such language knowledge equally well.

Walter Loban's Studies of Language Development

Early in the 1950s, Walter Loban studied the language development of a group of children over an extended time. His landmark studies, published in 1963 and 1976, are still worth reading. Loban discovered large differences in the vocabulary children brought to school, and found vocabulary use and knowledge to be a powerful predictor of how children would fare at school. Children with large oral language vocabularies performed better at school from the outset than children with low vocabularies. In addition, the high-vocabulary children retained their advantage throughout their schooling, while the low-vocabulary children tended to fall further and further behind.

Loban also found that direct grammar teaching had little or no impact on the language development of elementary school children.[1] He found that reading and writing abilities are positively related: good readers tend to be good writers as well. Finally, he discovered that more boys than girls are likely to have problems with language, but that more boys also appear in the group with the highest language ability.[2] Overall, Loban showed that children in elementary school learn language more by using it in a variety of contexts than through the explicit teaching of language rules.

Embedded vs. Disembedded Language Learning

British child psychologist Margaret Donaldson (1978) was struck by how many preschoolers go about their language learning happily and successfully, only to falter and fail upon entering school. At that point, difficulty in learning to read and write is often attributed to one or more of a multitude of factors, including perceptual deficits, cognitive limitations, social disadvantages, neurological dysfunction, attention disorders, and dyslexia.[3] For a very small percentage of students, one or more of these factors may play a role. The vast majority of children entering kindergarten and grade 1, however, showed no difficulty in learning the intricacies of oral language. Thus, Donaldson felt there was no good reason to suppose they lacked the capacity to read and write. She proposed that many children find school language learning so difficult because it requires them to think about and use language quite differently from the way they learned before school.

Before school entry, children's language is **embedded** (Donaldson's term) in concrete, lived experiences. Although children learn a great deal about language in a very short time (see previous chapter), they do so intuitively while using language for important purposes. In school, this functional use of language is often replaced by a much more objective, abstract approach. Language now becomes an object for analysis, often **disembedded** from any immediate function. Especially for children who bring little experience with books and formalized language, school instruction can be a foreign and daunting experience with little personal meaning.

A Foreign Language Learning Analogy

Whether we teach language in an embedded or disembedded way depends largely on our view of language learning. An example from foreign language learning may illustrate the distinction between these two teaching styles.

There are two ways of learning a foreign language—one relatively easy, the other very hard. The easy route is similar to the way we learned our native tongue: through immersion. We immerse ourselves in a new culture so that we *need* its language to make sense of our surroundings and get things done. This is how most immigrants learn a new language. Having arrived in their new country, they soon discover they need to know its language to participate meaningfully in the life of their adopted home. Because they need to learn, they do. Not that the learning is always easy, especially for older immigrants beyond the critical age of language acquisition. However, by immersing themselves in the new culture's language, they can function remarkably well in it within about a year.

Having come to Canada from Holland as boy of five, I write about learning a new language from personal experience. My father went to work outside the home and learned English quite quickly. My mother, who worked at home and stayed within the confines of a Dutch immigrant community, found it much harder to learn the language. I had the good fortune of learning English "on the street" for a year before starting school. As a result, I was fluent in English by school entry and have no conscious memory of learning a new language. My older sisters all started school immediately upon their arrival in Canada, however, and had much greater difficulty learning English through formal instruction and disembedded language tests.

My sisters' experience brings us to the second way of learning a foreign language: going to school and having it taught bit by bit. The student learns some vocabulary (*chien* = dog) and some grammar (the plural of *la maison* is *les maisons*), and so builds a piecemeal understanding of the new language. Several of my friends and I studied high school French this way for three years. We discovered that such teaching often transfers nothing more than the ability to speak a few stock phrases and write a simple letter in the new language. Of course, it is possible to combine immersion with formal study of a new language. In fact, that may be the best way to gain a thorough, functional understanding, especially when the goal includes reading and writing. Nevertheless, the question remains: Should we teach English in school to native English speakers as if it is a continuation of their first-language oral acquisition experience, or as a disembedded foreign language?

Unfortunately, most of our schools choose the second option. We often teach children language arts (listening, speaking, reading, and writing) as if they were foreign concepts—but of course they are *not*. While reading and writing are more abstract and less biologically "natural" activities than are listening and speaking, many preschool children in our culture already have a familiarity with the functions, if not the forms, of these skills. Nevertheless, many of our current instructional practices persist in requiring children to *disembed* their language knowledge in developmentally inappropriate ways.

Metalinguistic Awareness

The distinction between embedded and disembedded ways of knowing relates to the concept of **metalinguistic awareness**. Metalinguistic awareness is the "ability to reflect upon language as well as comprehend and produce it" (Cazden 1972), or "the growing ability to use language to talk about language as a formal code" (Lindfors 1987). Normally, we use language as a *vehicle* for communication, not as an *object* for analysis. As James Britton (1970) commented, "In most of our traffic with words we look through the substance to the meaning: the corporeal quality of the spoken word is paid very scant attention in bare, ordinary discourse, and properly so" (78). In other words, during most of our ordinary "traffic with words," we are not very metalinguistically aware. To become more metalinguistically aware requires us to disembed language from its context and consciously examine how it is being used.

This is precisely what Donaldson found to be so difficult for young children, whose thinking is firmly embedded in the context of everyday life and experience. Children relate what they learn to what they know and make sense of new experiences only in the context of what is familiar. A six-year-old child hearing that the family was going to Seattle, for example, said she did not want to go because "I don't even know who Attle is anyway" (reported in Bainbridge and Malicky 2000, 40). Children make sense of tasks they are asked to do in school in similar ways. Thus, they are most likely to understand a new concept when it is introduced in the context of a familiar situation. The sound of the phoneme /p/, for example, will be more likely to "stick" when taught through a familiar alliterative tongue twister rather than a disembedded phonics lesson that isolates /p/ from a familiar context.

In recent years, many investigators have examined a range of metalinguistic abilities that may be related to reading acquisition. Included in these are the ability to segment the stream of speech into language units (words, syllables, phonemes), to comment on the grammaticality of certain utterances, to understand the nature and purposes of literacy, to understand the conventions of written language, and to be aware of what Downing (1976) has termed the "reading instruction register." The latter includes such technical concepts as *word, sentence, story, paragraph, vowel,* and *digraph,* as well as all the phonics generalizations, spelling rules, and terms used in reading instruction. In the primary grades (K–3), emphasis on metalinguistic learning will confuse most students unless such learning is embedded in activities that are part of children's everyday experience. Yet our instructional contexts remain all too disembedded, presuming children to have greater metalinguistic awareness than they do.

Howard Gardner's Intelligences

The fact that not all children learn in the same way further complicates the role of school instruction. American psychologist Howard Gardner (1983, 1999b) has developed a convincing case that human beings do not possess a certain general intelligence, but rather multiple intelligences. Gardner has proposed at least seven basic intelligences: linguistic, logical-mathematical, spatial, musical, bodily-kinesthetic, interpersonal, and intrapersonal.[4] Most people possess all these intelligences in varying degrees, but it is clear that they are seldom distributed equally in any individual. Perhaps the most dramatic example of unbalanced intelligences is the idiot savant, in whom one incredible ability dominates to the exclusion of almost all others. Like Dustin Hoffman's character in the movie *Rain Man,* the idiot savant may be a mathematical wizard or musical prodigy, yet is illiterate and unable to tackle daily chores.

Less extreme but nevertheless real are the exceptional linguistic abilities found in poets, the musical abilities of great composers, and the kinesthetic abilities of Olympic athletes. Throughout Western history, school has particularly prized linguistic and logical-mathematical abilities. Many curricula reflect that emphasis, as evidenced by the long-held view that reading, 'riting, and 'rithmetic, the three Rs, are basic. This bias in the curriculum, which tends to favor children who have strong linguistic and logical-mathematical intelligences, proves a disadvantage for those with strengths in other areas. Gardner (1991) further asserts that the unschooled minds of children (and adults who have not attended school) are powerfully disposed to think in certain ways—ways that are quite different from those of the scholastic mind. School is difficult, he says:

> ... first because much of the material presented in school strikes many students as alien, if not pointless, and the kind of supporting context provided for pupils in earlier generations has become weakened. It is difficult, second, because some of the notational systems, concepts, frameworks, and epistemic forms are not read-

> ily mastered, particularly by students whose intellectual strengths may lie in other areas or approaches. Thus, for example, students with strengths in the spatial, musical, or personal spheres may find school far more demanding than students who happen to possess the text-friendly blend of linguistic and logical intelligences. And it is difficult, in a more profound sense, because these scholastic forms of knowing may actually collide with the earlier, extremely robust forms of sensorimotor and symbolic knowing, which have already evolved to a high degree even before a child enters school. (149)

It seems that Gardner is here expressing in other words what Donaldson implies by distinguishing between embedded and disembedded ways of knowing. Later in his 1991 book, while addressing the particular issue of literacy learning in the United States, Gardner decries the continuing mania for instruction in "basic skills." That mania, he says, is

> ... dramatized by the fact that that young children in the United States are becoming literate in a *literal* sense, that is, they are mastering the rules of reading and writing, even as they are mastering their addition tables. What is missing is not the decoding skills, but two other facets: the capacity to read for understanding and the desire to read at all....
>
> To attain basic skills requires drill and discipline. Yet, the imposition of a strict regime does not suffice. What is missing, in my view, are the contexts in which the deployment of these skills makes sense. Too many students do not see the three Rs being used productively at home, nor do they witness their utility at school.... [U]nless students come to appreciate why the skills and concepts are being inculcated and how to make use of them once they leave school, the entire classroom regimen risks being a waste of time. (186–187)

In a subsequent review of teaching approaches in various disciplines, Gardner mentions "whole-language" approaches. He suggests they are more successful than drill in phonics at providing "a context for literacy activities while at the same time helping students to acquire the basics that will allow them eventually to read and write on their own" (211). He describes such approaches as mimicking apprenticeship models in education, inviting children to master new skills by participating as adults around them read and write for real purposes. Such an atmosphere, he says, "more closely resembles a newspaper or magazine editorial center than an old-fashioned teacher-dominated classroom" (211). From Gardner's perspective, the key to successful whole-language approaches is that children see adults (their teachers) using literacy meaningfully in their own lives. In this way children "read not because they are told—let alone ordered!—to read, but because they see adults around them reading, enjoying their reading, and using that reading productively for their own purposes, ranging from assembling a piece of apparatus to laughing at a tall tale" (211).

I am a bit nervous quoting Gardner's praise for whole language literacy teaching because that approach has fallen out of fashion in the decade since Gardner wrote this book. In addition, many Christians react negatively to whole language for reasons cited in chapters 1 and 5. If we can look past the emotional and political connotations of the term, the idea that children learn best when they can emulate enthusiastic role models should strike a positive chord with Christians. Significant learning is usually a function of the company we keep, and it is telling that Jesus used an apprenticeship model in teaching His own disciples.

Summary and Conclusion

Donaldson refers to the language we use to communicate concrete, experiential knowledge of the world as **embedded language** because it is language we use unconsciously to facilitate our everyday participation in the world. It is the language of personalized, contextualized discourse, embedded in immediate experience. It is the unschooled language that nearly all children learn at home.

Donaldson refers to the language we use to communicate our analytical knowledge of the world as **disembedded language** because it is pulled out of its context and consciously used to label our analytic insights and experiences. It is the language of impersonal, decontextualized discourse. It is the language of much formal schooling.

As both Donaldson and Gardner point out, although in differing terminology, it is the shift from the everyday embedded language of the home and street to the analytic, disembedded language of the school that creates great difficulty for many beginning pupils. Further, children's ability to understand and use disembedded language varies considerably because of differing levels of intelligence and socialization. Teachers of young children need to recognize this variability and minimize the difficulty many children have in moving from an embedded to a disembedded language environment.

It should be evident that Donaldson's use of the contrasting terms **embedded** and **disembedded** is closely linked to the concept of metalinguistic awareness and, by implication, to the contrasting methodologies of skills-based and language-based teaching described in chapter 1. The pedagogical implication of these distinctions is captured by the image of a bridge. Reading instruction must be adapted to bridge the gap that often exists between the linguistic culture of the school and that of most children's homes. This bridging does not imply that the school should simply mimic and indefinitely maintain home-based, embedded language. The school is, after all, an institution created primarily to foster analytical ways of knowing and to communicate those in a more formal and decontextualized (disembedded) discourse than home-based oral language. As Herbert Simons and Sandra Murphy (1986) point out:

> It seems clear that school is both continuous and discontinuous with the knowledge and experiences of children.... Children bring highly developed language skills to the task of learning to read and write, and instruction should build upon the language skills children possess when they enter school. It is equally clear, however, that children will also need to acquire new skills in order to process written language effectively. (229)

At issue, then, is how the home-school language gap is bridged to allow children to acquire what for many are new skills. Differences in metalinguistic awareness and intelligences among children just beginning school argue for a more gradual introduction to disembedded reading/writing methods and materials than is the case in many beginning literacy programs. A more gradual approach does *not* imply that instruction in specific reading skills (including phonics) should be excluded, but it *does* imply that such skill instruction must not be divorced from the central meaning-getting and meaning-making purposes of reading. Specifically, language arts methods should move from the concrete to the abstract, from the whole to the parts, from the familiar to the less familiar, from the oral to the written—all within a framework that is rich in meaning for the child. Such instruction will allow children with different levels of metalinguistic awareness and intellectual abstraction to move confidently into literacy.[5]

Questions for Discussion

1. A number of essential terms were introduced in this chapter. Explain the distinction between **embedded** and **disembedded** views of knowing and learning. How do those terms relate to **metalinguistic awareness**? How does Howard Gardner's concept of **multiple intelligences** bear on this discussion?
2. Why are differences in preschool vocabulary knowledge so influential in both initial literacy learning and long-term scholastic success?
3. In what way does reading this book require a great deal of metalinguistic awareness? Does reading it contribute to your growth in metalinguistic awareness as well?
4. Why do you think the linguistic and logical-mathematical intelligences have been more highly prized in Western schooling than the other five intelligences described by Gardner?

5. Complete the following table by relating school subject areas and jobs/vocations to Gardner's seven intelligences.

Intelligence	Related school subjects	Related jobs/vocations
Linguistic		
Logical-mathematical		
Spatial		
Musical		
Bodily-kinesthetic		
Interpersonal		
Intrapersonal		

For Further Consideration

1. Do you think the foreign language learning analogy used to illustrate the distinction between embedded and disembedded ways of learning is valid? Why or why not?

2. Think about your own interests and gifts. Which of Gardner's seven intelligences are most "natural" to you? Which have your formal schooling experiences helped you to develop?

3. Which intelligences are most helpful in exercising the "fruit of the Spirit" mentioned in Galatians 5:22–23? The gifts mentioned in 1 Peter 4:9–10, Romans 12:6–8, and 1 Corinthians 12:8–11 and 28–31? The intelligence required of the craftsmen mentioned in Exodus 31:1–6, 35:30–35, and 36:1?

4. Think about how you learned to ride a bicycle and answer the following questions:
   - Why did you want to learn to ride a bike?
   - Who taught you how to ride a bike? What was the nature of this "teaching"?
   - What was your role in learning how to ride a bike?
   - Would explicit instruction in the physics of bicycle riding (i.e., metabicycle awareness) have been helpful in learning to ride your bike?[6]

Endnotes

1 We return to this finding in our discussion of grammar teaching in chapter 12.

2 For a fascinating account of gender issues in literacy learning, see Best (1983).

3 Dyslexia is discussed in chapter 11.

4 Recently, Gardner (1999b) has speculated that there may be additional intelligences as well.

5 See Bruinsma (1987) for further details on the proposed relationship between metalinguistic awareness and teaching approaches.

6 See Bruinsma (1990b) for a research study on the comparison between learning to ride a bicycle and learning to read.

Chapter 8

Emergent Literacy

Just as children do not walk before they learn to sit and crawl, so they do not learn to read and write in one giant step. In a developmental process termed *emergent literacy,* children come to associate print with meaning early in life and gradually continue their literacy learning to the stage of conventional reading and writing. This chapter traces the process of emergent literacy from its preschool origins through its continuation in primary school.

Upside-Down i—An Emergent Literacy Story

Ann, who is six years old and a first-grader, has discovered the joys of reading and writing. Almost every day she brings home a page of her illustrated diary to share with her mother and father, who take genuine delight and interest in both the product and the process. In the family's living room is a low table well supplied with paper, pens, pencils, paints, crayons, markers, rulers, erasers—the necessary tools of an artist or writer. Here Ann writes letters and notes, illustrates stories, and just "messes around."

Ann has a sister Kathryn, age three and a half. Kathryn has lived in a world filled as much with reading, writing, and drawing as with talk. For her, it is essential to learn to read and write. She needs to do these things to make sense of the world around her. Kathryn wants "in" on the activities that seem so central to the experiences of her mother and father and, particularly, her big sister. And so, Kathryn wants to read and write—especially to write since, as Carol Chomsky (1971) suggested long ago, writing more than reading satisfies young children's egocentric urge to project themselves into events and activities.

One morning, after Ann has left for school, Kathryn hands a blank sheet of paper to her mother and says, "Fold this, please; I'm going to make a book."

Dutifully her mother folds the paper, and Kathryn places it on her table, turning it this way and that until she is satisfied the folded edge is to her left. She then announces that her story is to be titled *Sandy and the Bee*. She says, "Sandy, S-S-S-andy," prints an *S* and then calls to her mother in the kitchen, "How do you spell *Sandy* after the *S*, Mom?"

Her mother spells *a-n-d-y*. Next, Kathryn prints the phrase *AND THE*, words that she needs no help with. Then she prints a *B*, stops, looks thoughtful for a moment, and asks, "How do you spell *bee*, Mom?" Her mother answers, "Just make a *b*, dear."

"Is that how a buzzing bee is spelled?"

"Oh, that kind of bee. That's spelled *b-e-e.*"

Kathryn writes *BEE,* opens her folded page, and draws a picture of a tree with a hole "where the bees live," and the little girl Sandy, and a blue sky. Next to the picture of Sandy, she writes the letter *B.* "I don't know how to draw a bee," she says. "That *B* means *bee,* OK, Mom? The bee stings Sandy and she yells 'Ow!'"

After showing and telling her mother all this, Kathryn sits down again to do some more writing. Up in the blue sky she writes an *O* and says in progressively louder tones, "Ow, Ow, Ow!" She then adds, in a voice filled with the satisfaction of discovery, "This needs an upside-down *i* so you know she said it loud."

With that, Kathryn adds a large exclamation mark after her *O.* This gesture seems so satisfying to her that she adds another squiggle and, showing the completed creation to her mother, explains that it is a question mark she made "just for fun." Thus ends the writing of Kathryn's story, *Sandy and the Bee.*

What Can We Learn from This Story?

Doris Entwistle has remarked that "the children who learn to read best are those who need to in order to make sense of their lives" (1971, 61). The same is true for reading's companion activities—listening, speaking, and writing. Kathryn has made discoveries about language and print because she is surrounded by people for whom reading and writing are important. These people have modeled literacy activities and provided opportunities for Kathryn to try them out for herself.

What is it that Kathryn, at three and a half, has already learned about written language? In other words, what emergent literacy concepts and skills has she demonstrated in writing her story? At a minimum, Kathryn knows the following about writing and print.

She has considerable understanding of the concept of a *book,* including at least some of the conventions that Marie Clay (1979a) considers precursors to fluent reading and writing: (1) The spine is positioned to the reader's left. (2) The title is on the cover. (3) The story is inside. (4) Writing begins on the left of a page and moves right. (5) Print tells the story and illustrations support it.

- She has beginning notions of sound-symbol relationships, as evidenced by her focus on the initial sound of *Sandy* and her ability to encode that sound as *S.*
- She understands that spelling encodes oral language into written language.
- She has learned to print many of the uppercase letters of the alphabet, and she knows how to encode some entire function words (e.g., *AND* and *THE*) from memory.
- Having begun to realize that writing is "silent language," Kathryn senses that punctuation marks represent the variations in stress, pitch, and juncture that she hears in speech.
- By grappling with the difficulty in distinguishing among the phonemes */b/* and */ē/* and their various representations in print *(B, BEE)* and in the real world (letter, creature), Kathryn is beginning to realize the arbitrary relationships among phonemes, graphemes, and their referents. Lev Vygotsky (1962, 128–130) has suggested that such realization may be crucial to the emergence of literacy in children.

Kathryn's efforts confirm Michael Halliday's (1973) claim that language is learned when it is used to create and mirror personal wants and meanings. Of course, these wants and meanings do not spring up in the child ex nihilo; they have a social context. Parents, siblings, teachers, and the child are members of a team involved in nurturing the dynamic growth of literacy. Primary school teachers must be particularly alert to the literacy behaviors of their young charges and develop skills as "kid watchers." As Margaret Clark (1976) emphasizes:

> Education begins neither at five years of age nor at nine o'clock in the morning! We are too ready to attribute (learning) failures to the home, but to claim the entire success for the school and formal education. (106)

Kathryn's story illustrates many of the emergent literacy understandings that children typically develop early in life. It is crucial for language arts teachers to recognize the preschool conditions that favor such literacy learning and to extend those conditions into the primary classroom. Even for children whose foundations of literacy development have not been laid in the home, it is quite possible—and all the more necessary—for teachers to create and demonstrate a context that fosters emergent literacy.

By paying very close attention as preschoolers gain oral language and literacy, we can discover ways to fill literacy learning with discovery, satisfaction, and joy for both children and teachers. Unfortunately, as we saw in the previous chapter, when language learning goes to school, it often acquires quite a different face.

The Development of the Emergent Literacy Concept

New Zealand literacy educator Marie Clay first used the term *emergent literacy* in 1966. Before that (and continuing well into the 1980s), educators commonly referred to **reading readiness,** by which they meant a developmental stage signaling preparedness to begin reading. As used, the term *reading readiness* reflects a strong **maturationist** view of reading, a belief that children who fail to learn to read are not yet at the appropriate stage of development. Among other factors, it was believed that children need a mental age of at least six and a half to profit from reading instruction. Since maturation rather than instruction was seen as necessary to move children to the next stage of development, the solution to reading problems was to delay instruction until children were "ready."

Others at this time held a more developmentalist perspective and suggested that certain prereading experiences could hasten children's readiness to learn to read. So was born the reading readiness workbook. Often added to the front end of basal reading series, these workbooks focused primarily on language development, visual-motor abilities, and auditory discrimination. Typical reading readiness activities included coloring pictures of rhyming words, choosing objects that faced the same direction, arranging pictures in order, and drawing lines between related pictures (e.g., a baby with a mother, an umbrella and rain). Note that few of these activities involved children with written language; after all, children were deemed unready for reading. Even those who entered grade 1 knowing how to read (a circumstance greatly frowned upon by many schools) were set to work on readiness activities, driven by the prevailing view that those particular skills were essential prerequisites to learning to read![1]

By the 1960s, however, social constructivist views were beginning to influence the field of early literacy. Working in New Zealand, Marie Clay (see Crawford 1995) found many children entering school with considerable knowledge of reading and writing that they could use in meaningful ways, just as Kathryn used her knowledge to write a story. Clay coined the term **emergent literacy** to indicate that reading and writing involve growth along a continuum rather than mastery of specific reading readiness skills. Note that Clay's terminology denotes a broader perspective than *reading* readiness in that it speaks of *literacy,* thus encompassing both reading and writing. An emergent literacy perspective places no sharp distinction between not being literate and being literate. Emergent literacy can begin almost at birth, with the earliest experiences in the home, and can continue to age eight or nine for some children (Sulzby 1991).[2]

Signposts of Emergent Literacy

In truth, emergent literacy is *not* characterized by distinct stages that each child must go through to reach some threshold known as conventional or "real" literacy. Rather, the development of reading and writing is continuous, beginning with a child's earliest attempts to interact with print and progressing to proficient reading and writing. Traveling this continuum at their own pace, children display growing understanding of the purposes of written language, the nature and forms of written language, and speech-print relationships.

Awareness of the Purposes of Written Language

Children's views about the value and function of written language directly reflect experiences in their family and the wider social context. In many families, children are read to from birth, and literacy forms part of the fabric of life. In such literate families, young children may not recognize letters and words as such, but soon come to understand that what they see written in books, or what family members write (e.g., notes, lists, cards, letters) contains meaning. From about age two, many children can grasp a crayon or a pencil and become involved in representing and expressing meaning.

By being read to regularly, children in literate homes develop positive feelings and attitudes toward books and print. Children who hear many narrative stories begin to internalize a sense of narrative structure and the language of books. By watching others read a diversity of print materials for both pleasure and information, and by participating in those pursuits, children come to associate print with worthwhile activities.

Of course, not all children are born into or raised in literate environments. While it is important to avoid stereotyping, there is evidence that children in homes of low socioeconomic families come to school with fewer and less diverse print experiences than children from middle-class homes (Taylor and Dorsey-Gaines 1988; Purcell-Gates 1998). This is not a warrant for the school to view such children as deficient, but rather a reason to expect a wide range of individual differences when planning beginning literacy instruction.

Awareness of the Nature and Forms of Written Language

As children hear books read aloud, they begin to sense the connection between speech and written language. Gradually, they understand that print is not infinitely malleable, that a given text is, as Temple and Gillet (1989) term it, "frozen discourse." Awareness that print is fixed in time and place often dawns as a child shares a book with an older reader. The youngster may bend over the book for a close look at an illustration only to be told, "Move back, I can't see the words." Young children demonstrate appreciation of the permanence of print when they insist that every word of a favorite story be read exactly the same each time. When they ask someone to write down their words or read their scribbles, they demonstrate an understanding that oral language and thoughts can be fixed on paper.

At some point, children who have virtually memorized the text of a favorite story can actually match the words on the page with words in their memory. Pointing to each word as they repeat the story, they are developing the concept of a *word* as a series of printed symbols with white space on either side. This eye-voice pointing or **speech-to-print matching** will stand a child in good stead upon school entry, when teachers begin pointing at an array of letters and talking about words.

Reading with children also helps them learn the directional nature of books and print. Initially, very young children make little distinction between the top and bottom or left and right sides of books. One can see them happily "reading" a book upside down and back to front. Eventually however, they become aware that books, and the pages within them, have a top and a bottom, and that the pictures and stories proceed, as a matter of convention, left to right. It is helpful for caregivers to choose books for children that demonstrate these features. As illustrated by the literacy story that opens this chapter, Kathryn had already internalized much of this directional knowledge of print by age three and a half.

Young children also develop literacy through **environmental print**. In chapter 7, I mentioned that one of my young daughters recognized the Shell logo as the word for "gas." Parents and other caregivers have many opportunities to alert children to the print that is all around them. Trips to the supermarket can be occasions for learning as children pick out their favorite breakfast cereals by finding familiar letters and words. During long trips in the car, our preschool children often played the alphabet game, searching for sequential signs containing the letters of the alphabet. Upon passing a Safeway store, one child might shout, "There's an *A*"; a moment later, another might spot a bus stop and call out, "There's a *B!*" and the game would continue to that elusive Z.

Children who are read to a great deal eventually differentiate between the informal language of speech and the formal language of print. Listening as such children pretend-read to their stuffed toys or dolls, one can hear the cadences and phrases of book language emulated to perfection: "Once upon a time, in a land far away there lived a wicked giant...."

Awareness of Speech-Print Relationships

As mentioned above, children who grow up in literate environments and who are often read to soon understand that the print on the page represents oral speech, at least in a general way. The development of more sophisticated print-speech relationships usually depends on the child's interest in writing, coupled with caregivers' response to that interest.[3] Because young children are highly egocentric, they are often more interested in learning how to express themselves through writing than in learning how to read what others have written.

The most basic understanding children construct about print is that there is a difference between words and pictures. They demonstrate this understanding, for example, when they want an adult to print a caption for a picture, or when they attempt to do so themselves.

Actual writing usually begins with scribbles—large, rounded gestures and scratchy straight lines. Perhaps children begin with scribbles because this is what they see when adults handwrite on paper. Soon, however, a few printed letter shapes appear, frequently the familiar letters in the child's name. Children who have alphabet books read to them and who play with magnetic or other three-dimensional letters will often begin incorporating other letters in their writing as well. They also learn that a letter can be written in various ways (tall, short, thin, fat) and still be the same letter.

Soon, children realize that directionality is important not only for the book as a whole, but also for the writing inside. They learn:

- that print begins at the top of a page and continues to the bottom
- that we write from left to right on the page
- that individual words are also constructed left-to-right
- that directionality is important to the identity of letters

As mentioned, English writing has important **conventions.** Not only do English conventions differ from those in such languages as Hebrew, Mandarin, or Arabic, but those conventions are arbitrary and thus difficult to master. Many parents and teachers express concern when young children confuse the letters *b* and *d*, for example. But in most of life, the direction we view an object makes little difference to its identity. A person or a car remains the same whether we see it left-to-right or right-to-left. Thus directionality is not often a useful cue for differentiating objects in the environment. With letters and numbers, suddenly directionality *does* matter. The numbers *9* and *6* are different, as are the letters *b* and *d* and the words *on* and *no*. It takes many children a long while to figure out and remember those distinctions; in fact, directional confusion commonly persists well into grade 2. Thus parents and teachers must guard against concluding too hastily that a child is dyslexic.[4]

Young writers often progress to using **invented spellings** to represent words.[5] At least initially, these "inventions" tend to use consonants to represent entire words. Thus *RBBT* stands for *RABBIT* and *HSPTL* for *HOSPITAL*. This dependence on consonants reflects the fact that consonants have a far more stable and regular sound-symbol correspondence than vowels, and are thus easier for children to represent. More importantly, such invented spelling shows that a child is developing an awareness of the **phoneme-grapheme** (sound-letter) relationships in English. At some point, children must understand that the letters of our alphabet stand for the sounds of our oral language; that is, they must discover the **alphabetic principle** of English writing.

There is growing evidence that reading acquisition is greatly aided by awareness that words can be segmented into phonemes, or sound units. Such understanding is called **phonemic awareness**. In 1990, Marilyn J. Adams published an influential work concluding that phonemic awareness or segmentation is crucial to learning to read. Much research on this issue has been conducted in the decade since, but the results are somewhat difficult to interpret. Some studies indicate that children with a greater degree of phonemic awareness become better readers; others confound this finding by showing that reading instruction is the cause of heightened phonemic awareness.[6]

Prompted by the highly publicized research on phonemic awareness, educational publishers have produced a veritable barrage of disembedded phonemic awareness training programs. While writing this chapter, I received a slim catalog from an educational publisher touting 82 reading resources, primarily for kindergarten through grade 6. Over one-quarter of the resources (22 of the 82) were directly aimed at phonemic awareness or mentioned it as a major benefit. Many were tests to assess particular aspects of phonemic awareness, including:

- rhyming discrimination and production
- segmenting sentences and syllables

- isolating initial, medial, and final sounds
- deleting compound words, syllables, and phonemes
- substituting vowels
- blending syllables and phonemes
- grapheme-phoneme matching
- decoding

Not surprisingly, this same catalog offers resources and programs to address each element of phonemic awareness, should a child be found deficient. Many of the sample pages illustrated in the catalog looked to be pencil and paper workbook exercises and games focusing almost exclusively on reading at the word level and below. From what I could determine, these materials, ranging in price from U.S. $35.95 to $234.95, would give children virtually no experience with listening to or reading interesting connected text. I was not prepared to spend the money required to evaluate the resources in detail, but I suspect my skepticism would not change a great deal were I to purchase them.

Does that mean that teachers should avoid experiences that increase children's phonemic awareness and other metalinguistic knowledge (see chapter 7)? By no means. It's how the learning is accomplished that makes all the difference.

Assessment of Emergent Literacy

This book is not a full-fledged language arts textbook, but rather a framework document that sets out principles and discusses issues pertinent to language arts instruction in Christian schools. Many language arts texts from a variety of publishers offer teacher educators and teachers specific information about assessment and instructional practices. An annotated selection of these resources is listed below. Here I would simply remind teachers that informal methods of assessment in your own classroom have a much greater potential for subsequent instructional payoff than formal, standardized tests. The latter may tell you where a particular child ranks relative to other children but will say little about that child's understanding of the connections between oral and written language, or about his or her specific instructional needs. The ongoing, informal assessments I have in mind include observing children closely in the following learning contexts:

- when being read to
- in shared-book experiences
- during shared writing **(language experience approach)**[7]
- when writing
- during functional interactions with print

Methods of gathering information in these contexts include checklists, interviews, and **portfolios**. A portfolio is simply an organized, representative collection of a child's work over time that signals learning growth and further instructional needs. Chapter 2 provides additional suggestions for using portfolios in assessment and evaluation.

The *Bader Reading and Language Inventory* (1998b, 3rd ed.) contains some useful tools, particularly in the section on "Preliteracy Assessment" (109–120). Included are these assessments:

- Literacy Awareness of Beginning Concepts about Print
- Blending and Segmentation (phonemic awareness)
- Letter Knowledge
- Hearing Letter Names in Words
- Syntax Matching

Bader also includes a useful section on portfolio assessment (159–167).

The *Language Arts Handbook* (Den Boer 1996), published by the Society of Christian Schools in British Columbia, also contains excellent material, including a variety of checklists, for assessing emergent literacy skills.

Instructional Practices for Emergent Literacy

Some general guidelines for planning literacy instruction for young children:

- Create a print-rich classroom literacy environment.
- Include daily reading and writing with and by children.
- Accept approximations ("You don't need to be perfect right away").
- Allow for differences ("Why should we all be expected to be at the same place in our learning when it's perfectly OK to be different heights and weights?").

Crucial instructional practices to include in daily reading and writing:

- Appropriate time for *prereading*, interaction *during* reading, and sharing of reading experiences *after* reading
- Shared-book experiences using predictable *big books*
- Shared writing using the language experience approach, interactive writing, and independent writing

Suggested Resources for Assessment and Instruction[8]

◊ Lloyd Den Boer, ed. 1996. Emergent reading and writing. In *Christian pathways for schooling: Language arts handbook.* 2nd ed. Langley, BC: Society of Christian Schools in British Columbia: 33–108. An excellent two-volume resource using a language-centered framework. Developed by Christian teachers in Canada, it contains a wealth of practical material for all areas of language arts teaching. Available from the Society of Christian Schools in British Columbia at 7600 Glover Road, Langley, B.C.

◊ Charles A. Temple and Jean W. Gillet. 1989. *Language arts: Learning processes and teaching practices.* 2nd ed. Glenview, IL: Scott, Foresman. A "bread and butter" language arts textbook that provides a balanced approach to assessment and instruction. More than a dozen years old, the text is still remarkably current.

◊ Joyce Bainbridge and Grace Malicky. 2000. *Constructing meaning: Balancing elementary language arts.* 2nd ed. Toronto, ON: Harcourt Canada. A Canadian text (also readily available in the United States through Harcourt) with a balanced perspective on instructional issues spanning all aspects of language arts teaching. I use this text in teaching university-level introductory language arts. Chapter 3, "Emergent Literacy," provides excellent information and resources for assessment and instructional strategies.

◊ Susan M. Burns, Peg Griffin, and Catherine E. Snow. 1999. *Starting out right: A guide to promoting children's reading success.* Washington, DC: National Academy Press. Also available online at <http://www.nap.edu/>. The Committee on the Prevention of Reading Difficulties in Young Children supported this book, as did the Commission on Behavioral and Social Sciences Education of the U.S. National Research Council. Directed at children from birth through grade 3, the work is endorsed by an impressive list of literacy scholars representing a broad spectrum of orientations. It includes many diagnostic checklists, over fifty activities to do with children, one hundred recommended children's books, and a guide to computer software and CD-ROMs as well as Internet sites related to literacy and young children.

◊ Irene C. Fountas and Gay Su Pinnell are two teacher educators who provide excellent resources for teachers. I highly recommend the following, published by Heinemann:

Guided reading: Good first teaching for all children. 1996.

Word matters: Teaching phonics and spelling in the reading/writing classroom. 1998.

Guiding readers and writers (grades 3–6): Teaching comprehension, genre, and content literacy. 2000. Recommends 1,000 leveled books.

The primary literacy video collection: Classroom management. 2001. Video 1, *Managing the day* and Video 2, *Planning for effective teaching*.

◊ Dorothy S. Strickland and Lesley Mandel Morrow, eds. 2000. *Beginning reading and writing*. Copublished by the International Reading Association and Teachers College Press of Columbia University. A book full of great ideas that suit a language-centered approach to early literacy instruction, each chapter written by early literacy expert(s). The six chapters of part 1 discuss the foundations for the early literacy curriculum, while part 2's nine chapters deal with instructional strategies for beginning readers and writers.

◊ Patricia M. Cunningham. 2000. *Phonics they use: Words for reading and writing*. 3rd edition. Addison Wesley/Longman. Cunningham's third edition of this book is the best publication on phonics instruction I have seen. The first chapter contains many language-centered teaching ideas for developing basic emergent literacy skills, including some fun lessons to enhance phonemic awareness. I will refer to this book again in chapter 11, where the focus is on reading.

◊ Thomas G. Gunning. 2001. *Assessing and correcting reading and writing difficulties*. Allyn & Bacon. Chapter 7 of Gunning's text "Emergent literacy and early intervention programs" defines the key components of emergent literacy and discusses ways to assess and foster those skills. The book describes several key intervention programs, as well, including Reading Recovery.

◊ Bader, Lois A. 1998b. *Reading and language inventory*. 3rd ed. Merrill/Prentice Hall. Bader focuses on informal reading inventory (explained in chapter 11), but also provides a good sampling of other diagnostic tests (mentioned above), including those that will measure many emergent literacy skills. These may be useful for one-on-one assessment of a small number of children who need special attention.

Conclusion

Children can grow into literacy in much the same way they grew into oracy—*if* preschool caregivers consciously surround them with meaningful reading and writing. This is *not* a plea for parents and other caregivers to engage in highly planned, direct instruction of skills, but rather an encouragement for each of us, teachers included, to share our literate lives with children in joyful ways. Teachers of young children need to be aware that not all children can draw on a background of rich home literacy experience. Fortunately, schools can adopt many instructional strategies to mimic and extend the best home literacy practices and help children emerge into literacy with confidence.

Questions for Discussion

1. What are some of the conceptual differences between **reading readiness** and **emergent literacy**?
2. A grade 1 student named Matt writes the story in the box on the following page and reads it back to you as transcribed on the right. What does this sample of Matt's writing and reading tell you about his literacy knowledge? Specifically, what does Matt understand about literacy, and what concepts and skills does he still need to acquire or develop?

matt wus·a·pona Tim·'Thr·wus·Three-Bas Fodi-B·S momo and·boyB-and Thu·lif hge-Cvr.arr	*Transcription of story as read by student:* Once upon a time there was three bears. Father Bear, Mom and Baby, and they lived happily ever after.

3. What are some of the key ways reading with preschool children can enhance their understanding of fundamental literacy concepts?
4. Why is it important for young children to understand the **alphabetic principle** of English writing?
5. What is **phonemic awareness**? How is it different from **phonics**?

For Further Consideration

1. Find a three-to-four-year-old and share a storybook with the child to determine his or her understanding of print and of books. [A good resource for this is Marie Clay's *The Early Detection of Reading Difficulties: A Diagnostic Survey with Recovery Procedures,* 2nd ed. (1979). This book comes with two other small booklets, *Sand* and *Stones,* which have been designed to help discover children's book knowledge and understanding of print conventions. If Clay's book is difficult to obtain, the resource by Lois Bader (1998b), mentioned in this chapter, is also useful.]
2. Visit a preschool or kindergarten class for a half day. List all the **environmental print** in the classroom, plus all the activities that you judge to be helpful in developing the children's literacy understandings. Be specific about the understandings fostered. Are there elements of the classroom organization and instruction that you deem to be *unhelpful* for literacy development? What is the balance between **embedded** and **disembedded** language use in this classroom?

Endnotes

1 The history of reading education is replete with similar examples. Many claims made about "necessary prerequisite skills to reading" are specious in that frequently children who read do not possess these so-called prerequisite skills. Clearly, then, they are false prerequisites.

2 In some sense, emergent literacy might last a lifetime. For example, at age 56, I don't know how to make sense of the stock market listings in the business section of my local newspaper. Thus, there are still certain literacy forms that I can choose to learn, or would need to learn should I become a stock investor. Illiterate adults are often at an emergent literacy stage and need to develop basic literacy awareness just as young children do. Generally, however, we consider the emergent literacy stage to end when children understand the basic conventions of reading and writing, usually by the end of the primary grades.

3 Marie Clay's booklet *What Did I Write?* (1975) provides a fascinating look at young children's development of writing, illustrated with many samples.

4 Dyslexia is discussed in chapter 11.

5 Chapter 12 deals extensively with learning to spell.

6 See Coles (2000) for a critique of misinterpretation and inappropriate application of the research on phonemic awareness.

7 See Stauffer (1980). In the language experience approach (LEA), the teacher scribes a child's own language verbatim, and it becomes the text that the child subsequently learns to read. The rationale for the LEA is that the child understands what he or she has said, and the child can learn to read easily what he or she understands. Also, the child who sees his or her oral language encoded into print is usually interested in learning to read this personal writing.

8 Unless otherwise specified, these resources include useful ideas for teaching the language arts in the elementary grades generally, including but not limited to emergent literacy.

Part 3

The Four Language Arts: Principles and Teaching Practice

Components in a Language-Centered Instructional Framework

One of the challenges of writing a book that promotes a holistic approach to the teaching of the language arts is that it is sometimes difficult to practice what one preaches. Although I view listening, speaking, reading, and writing as inter-related aspects of the language arts curriculum, it is not possible to deal with them as a single entity. Even within each of these components, it will be necessary to reflect on certain subcomponents. Thus, for purposes of analysis, I will examine the language arts components and subcomponents separately, although the blurring of subdivisions will often be unavoidable. However, this approach is not to be viewed as a recommendation to teach these components separately or sequentially. Although there certainly is a place for instruction in the distinct skills in the language arts curriculum, as much as possible such instruction ought to be embedded in meaningful activities.

Just as the language arts cannot be neatly chopped up into sequential bits and pieces, so too the experiences of children in school cannot be neatly organized by age and segmented into conventional parcels. However, age-grade organization is so pervasive in Western schooling that I have adopted such terminology here for the sake of convenience. Although different areas of North America divide the grade levels in slightly different ways and have varying regulations on the age of school entry, I will use the divisions most familiar to me: primary (ages 5–8, grades K–3) and intermediate (ages 9–11, grades 4–6) constitute *elementary schooling.* Ages 12–15, grades 7–9, make up *middle school.*

Because this is not intended to be a complete language arts textbook, the following sections will *not* provide detailed student activities for each of the components and subcomponents described. However, throughout I will provide general teaching examples and references for more detailed resources.

Skills and Skills Instruction in a Language-Centered Framework

Because this book consistently contrasts a language-centered approach with a skills-centered one, readers may infer that implementing a language-centered approach leads to the neglect of skills teaching. Thus it is germane to consider briefly what is meant by a *skill,* or *skills*. One dictionary definition of *skill* is "an ability to do something well through knowledge, practice, or training." The issue is thus whether language-centered teaching does or does not lead to an ability to listen well, speak well, read well, and write well. But what do we mean by *well*?

A major part of the traditional meaning of *well* in language arts is whether children have a grasp of specific **conventions** of language. Conventions are generally accepted rules, practices, or common usage. They are largely arbitrary and have a great deal to do with social custom and etiquette. For example, what does it mean to read well? Until the middle of the twentieth century, it meant being a fluent *oral* reader. Since reading meant oral reading, reading silently was considered peculiar, and most reading pedagogy concentrated on making children fluent oral readers. This **elocution concept** of reading made sense in a culture in which the minority, or people who became literate, were expected to serve the illiterate majority by reading to them. However, with the increase in literacy rates in the West during the twentieth century, the emphasis in reading pedagogy shifted to rapid *silent* reading (although vestiges of the elocution concept cling to elementary reading instructional practices to this day). The conventional understanding of reading has thus largely changed from an oral to a silent process, and the idea of what counts as reading skill has changed to follow suit.

Another example of changing conventions is illustrated by comparing the King James Version (KJV) of the Bible with a modern translation. Such a comparison will quickly convince the reader that conventions of syntax, spelling, and usage in written English have changed substantially during the almost

400 years since the KJV was first published.

A living language is a dynamic vehicle of expression and communication, and no pontificating by a linguistic elite or even legislating by a government (as in France) will ever fix the conventions of a language forever. However, at any given point in cultural time, there are appropriate and inappropriate ways of using a language in various settings, just as there are appropriate and inappropriate ways of dressing in different circumstances. The duty of the schools is to help students gain control over the conventions of their language so that they can use their language for personal benefit and service to others.

Since language skills have to do with learning conventions, they are partly a matter of language **pragmatics**. Chief among the socially important conventions of written language are **spelling** and **grammar**. Related to these are **phonics** (the principles and practices of relating letters to sounds and vice versa) and other **word recognition skills**, which will be dealt with in chapters 11 and 12 of part 3.

It is important to reiterate the danger of viewing the skills and conventions of language arts as isolated competencies disembedded from meaningful use. Thus, for example, spelling is often taught as a separate subject using lists of words from a speller rather than as an integral part of the writing (rewriting) process. The spelling bee is the quintessential example of treating spelling as a disembedded skill separate from any relevant linguistic purpose. Likewise, skill in grammar has become identified with diagramming sentences and identifying words as parts of speech rather than with word placement (syntax) and its influence on the writing process and product. Again, this is not to suggest that a language teacher should never have a phonics, spelling, or grammar lesson, only that such lessons should always be given in service to some larger communicative purpose. Skills and conventions serve as means to ends, and those ends are listening, speaking, reading, and writing with sensitivity, competency, and understanding. Teaching (and testing) skills in isolation from their actual use in the hope that students will transfer such disembedded, isolated knowledge to their own expression is generally unsuccessful. We can never assume a transfer of learning. The best way to ensure the transfer of skills is to teach them in real contexts.

Chapter 9

Listening

Listening depends on hearing and is the primary language ability. Listening is essential for learning to speak and important for reading and writing as well; yet listening is probably the least developed component in the language arts curriculum. Specific teaching strategies can help students sharpen their listening skills, but good listening is as much a function of the affective climate in the classroom. This chapter explores the classroom factors that enhance children's listening abilities and suggests resources teachers can use to invite and evaluate listening.

The most common form of communication is listening. We listen more than we engage in any other form of communication. Everyone who is free of severe hearing impairment knows how to listen.[1] Through listening, infants first become aware of language; thus, developmentally, listening precedes speaking.

In general, linguistic reception not only precedes production but also exceeds it by a considerable margin. Children's receptive listening vocabularies greatly exceed their productive speaking vocabularies. Similarly, their receptive reading vocabularies exceed their productive writing vocabularies. This principle is important for teachers to bear in mind. Children cannot, for example, be expected to read with comprehension a text they cannot comprehend aurally. Similarly, children should not be expected to spell and correctly use words that are not already in their listening, speaking, and reading vocabularies.

Listening is also important because it applies to daily life. Personal relations with other people depend on good listening; in fact, one of the best indicators of a close relationship is willingness to truly listen to one another. Likewise, many careers depend on good listening. Nearly all jobs require listening to directions and information; in some human service professions, listening is a major part of the workload.

For centuries, the Judeo-Christian tradition was primarily oral-aural. The spoken word lies at the center of God's interaction with humanity. Through hearing (and responding) we come to know who God is and what God demands of us: *"Hear, O Israel: the Lord our God, the Lord is one. Love the Lord your God with all your heart and with all your soul and with all your strength"* (Deuteronomy 6:4–5).

Because listening, like speaking (and in contrast to reading and writing), is thought to be "natural," educators pay little attention to its development in school. Certainly, to acquire the massive amount of linguistic knowledge they bring to school, children must know how to listen. Yet, if we omit listening instruction from the language arts curriculum because children have already mastered it, why is listening often a source of concern and frustration? Why is it necessary to remind students to listen? And why do teachers find themselves repeating directions and instructions so frequently?

A Simple Listening Model

To pinpoint potential sources of listening difficulties in the language arts curriculum, consider the process of listening. As modeled by John Stammer (1977), auditory intake is a three-level process. The first level, **hearing**, involves physically activating the ear apparatus. The second, **listening**, involves paying attention to or concentrating on the message. The third level, **auding**, involves understanding the message and relating it to previous experiences and concepts. Of these three levels, auding or listening comprehension is the object of most classroom concern, yet auding cannot occur unless the two lower levels of auditory action take place. A person must both hear and listen to the message before translating it into something meaningful. The following simple model illustrates:

Sound → Hearing → Listening → Auding

The remaining discussion will refer to Stammer's listening level as **paying attention** and to auding as **comprehending**.

Classroom Atmosphere and Listening

Since paying attention is critical to comprehending, we must consider what kind of teaching invites attention. One of the most important prerequisites to improving attention in a classroom is a positive listening environment. Our earlier discussion of the psychological and physical dimensions of classroom organization (chapter 4) touched on this issue.

This book as a whole stresses the need for teachers to model and demonstrate the life we want students to live, and that includes listening. If a teacher gives individual students the opportunity to speak, and listens with undivided attention when they do, the students will gradually come to do the same. Yet research on classroom talk is unanimous in finding that teacher talk exceeds student talk by a ratio of about ten to one.[2] This finding suggests that teachers are not very good listening models for their students and that the classroom is seldom a place of mutual sharing. If the teacher is the chief speaker, translator, questioner, and filter for the class, students have little need to speak and listen. To provide opportunities for children to speak to a listening audience, the amount of teacher talk in a classroom must shrink. Teachers at all levels, kindergarten through graduate school, should post the words TALK LESS—LISTEN MORE prominently on every page of their plan books and lesson outlines.

Ideally, classroom organization and teaching style invite students to speak with both teacher and peers. Students should feel free to ask questions of the teacher and of each other. Group discussions and other collaborative activities can foster good listening habits, such as respecting the opinions of others, waiting one's turn, and responding appropriately.

In large measure, a classroom environment conducive to listening is a function of personal relationships, both between teacher and students and among class members. Conceiving of the class as a community rather than a random collection of individuals helps to foster oral-aural sharing. Here are some suggestions everyone can follow to make the classroom a learning community (Victoria: Ministry of Education 1988):

- Respect the opinions of others
- Be a considerate listener
- Negotiate rather than arguing stubbornly
- Share discoveries and queries
- Interact in group discussions
- Recall facts
- Repeat instructions
- Respond to what is heard

The classroom's physical arrangement can either invite or hinder listening. In the traditional classroom, with its rows of desks, students look at the backs of classmates' heads. Certainly, that setting is not conducive to the eye contact so essential in oral-aural communication. A U-shaped desk arrangement is more effective in allowing students to look at each other as they speak and listen.

Listening and Making Sense

Listening, like other forms of communication, is a matter of making sense. We pay attention to sounds that make sense to us and ignore the rest. Making sense in this case includes sensing purpose. As Frank Smith (1979) says, "Where language does not make sense, where it has no apparent purpose, not only will children fail to learn from it but they will actively ignore it" (119). Given that connection between purpose and paying attention, what teaching strategies and learning activities will guide learners to listen?

Paying attention is not a skill in the usual sense of the word; it is not easy to segment and analyze it into teaching components. Reminding students to "pay attention" can call everyone's attention to something important, but unless the students regard it as important, the reminder will have an extremely short-term effect. Furthermore, if such reminders are overused, students begin to ignore them. They tune them out or no longer "hear" them.

Force can achieve some immediate results. Threat of negative consequences may elicit immediate behavioral effects, motivating students to pay attention out of fear. In the long run, however, fear is counter-productive to genuine learning and is the antithesis of Christian love that "drives out fear" (1 John 4:18).

Even less effective than reminders and force is sermonizing about paying attention. Although children may give intellectual assent to the virtue of paying attention, their attention does not increase greatly as a result.

The most effective way to help children pay attention is to engage them in learning experiences worth attending to. Children are no different from adults in this respect. If something being said has purpose and personal relevance—if it makes sense—it will receive attention.

Purpose and Listening

In any communicative setting, at least two sets of purposes are at work: the speaker's and the listener's. In the classroom, communication involves the purposes of both teacher and students, and because there are many students, there are also multiple purposes. When we see no apparent purpose for paying attention, we stop listening and drop back to the level of hearing; thus providing a purpose for listening is crucial. Declaring that listening is a duty is not purpose enough; students need an immediate purpose that relates to life.

In creating purpose for listening, teachers need to do two things. First, they must clarify their own purposes. Second, they must examine the match between their purposes and student purposes. Teachers should ask themselves, *Why am I teaching this to these students at this time?*

Two classroom practices that can help align the purposes of teacher and students are **decision making** and **open-ended tasks**. Decision making involves offering students choices, beginning with two similar options and slowly building toward multiple, wide-ranging choices. Thematic teaching, with its multidimensional approach to topics and ideas, is well suited to providing options. Open-ended tasks are questions that have a number of possible answers, or problems that can be solved in more than one way. By creating choices and open-ended tasks, the teacher can continue to set guidelines and choose topic areas while inviting students to actively shape their learning. These practices do much to contribute to a healthy listening environment.

Some teachers fear that offering students choice will reduce classroom control. Obviously, the nature of the choices and the way they are presented must reflect both developmental considerations and students' previous experiences. Middle school students are better able to handle choices and open-endedness than are primary students, especially if these approaches have been part of their experience since kindergarten. Although giving up some decision-making power can be frightening to teachers, the rewards are great. Children who learn to make their own learning decisions, however small, make some commitment to their choices. The result is a more purposeful experience.

Likewise, providing open-ended tasks challenges the more comfortable belief that every question and problem has one right answer. Of course, when there is only one answer, grading students is easier. But far too often the students' purpose becomes finding the easiest way to get that right answer. When many answers or solutions are possible, students are more likely to dig deeper and thus experience discovery, personal involvement, and learning.

Decision making, open-ended tasks, and other meaningful activities directly encourage students to listen. When students have purposeful learning experiences, they have a personal reason for going to school—and a purpose for paying attention to what is said in the classroom.

Listening Activities

Implementing the general listening principles described above will go a long way toward creating a classroom conducive to listening. But there are other factors to consider in fostering listening comprehension in K–9 classrooms. The importance of context, background knowledge, and student confidence should not be underestimated.

Education research contains considerable debate about whether specific listening skills can be taught. A study by Dewitt-Brinks and Rhodes (1992) reviewed and meta-analysed twenty-four empirical studies of listening training originally conducted between 1950 and 1989. The meta-analysis found no clear evidence that listening skills can or cannot be taught. The study did conclude that listening is a multidimensional phenomenon, and that training programs rarely capture the complexity of the physiological and psychological processes involved.

Does this mean that any specific teaching about listening is a waste of time? No, but it does suggest that teachers must be very clear about just what aspect of listening they are attempting to foster through direct instruction. There is a limited place for specific activities to foster careful and critical listening. Used at developmentally appropriate levels, those activities can range from learning how to follow spoken directions to analytical and critical listening. Following are some resources (listed from most recent to older) that provide helpful general information about listening as well as specific teaching suggestions:

◊ Mary M. McCaslin and Thomas L. Good. 1996. *Listening in classrooms.* New York: Harper Collins.

◊ William F. McCart. 1994. *Learning to listen: A program to improve classroom listening skills in a variety of situations.* Toronto: Educators Publishing Service.

◊ Mary R. Jalongo. 1991. *Strategies for developing children's listening skills.* Bloomington, IN: Phi Delta Kappan Educational Foundation.

◊ Penny Ur. 1984. *Teaching listening comprehension.* New York: Cambridge University Press.

◊ Ida M. Hood. 1983. *Is anyone listening? A resource handbook for teachers.* West Vancouver, BC: R. J. Watts and Associates Ltd.

◊ Thomas G. Devine. 1982. *Listening skills schoolwide: Activities and programs.* Urbana, IL: ERIC Clearing House on Reading and Communication Skills, and the National Council of Teachers of English.

◊ Andrew D. Wolvin and Carolyn G. Coakley. 1979. *Listening instruction.* Urbana, IL: ERIC Clearing House on Reading and Communication Skills and Annandale, VA: Speech Communication Association.

◊ David H. Russell and Elizabeth F. Russell. 1979. *Listening aids through the grades.* 2nd ed. Enlarged by Dorothy G. Hennings. New York: Teachers College Press.

◊ Paul G. Friedman. 1978. *Listening processes: Attention, understanding, evaluation.* 2nd ed. Washington, DC: National Education Association.

Evaluating Listening

Teachers need to be alert to the possibility that a student who is not paying attention may have a hearing impairment. A school nurse or family physician can confirm or rule out any suspicion of hearing loss by testing the child with an audiometer. Teachers or teacher aides can also check children's ability to discriminate among phonemes by administering the Wepman *Auditory Discrimination Test* (Wepman 1958) or a similar test such as one found in Bader (1998a). In the Wepman test, children of ages five to nine listen to pairs of words and tell whether they are the same or different. Their responses help the teacher determine whether they are able to discriminate between closely related phonemes, such as the */b/* and */p/* in *bit* and *pit.*

While measures of hearing have been perfected, measures of paying attention have not been invented and probably never will be. Here again, "kid watching" is perhaps the teacher's best available tool. The following behaviors are typical of children who are paying attention:

- looking at the speaker much of the time
- sitting relatively still in a normal position
- responding to humor with smiles or laughter and to other emotional content with appropriate facial expressions

- limiting comments to those appropriate to the content
- refraining from disturbing others

Teachers can construct checklists or rubrics to assess various listening behaviors. Figures 9-1 and 9-2 are examples.

Figure 9-1: Listening rubric to assess traits of a listener whose intention is to encourage a speaker by showing interest

After listening to a story, a student:			
Beginner	*Intermediate*	*Proficient*	*Accomplished*
Can answer non-subjective, factual questions such as the names of the characters, the stated setting of the story, and the subject matter of the story.	Can summarize the story in an organized fashion with a beginning, middle, and end.	Can retell the story in a sequence of events with descriptive details, dialogue, and characterization.	Can retell the story skillfully with a sense of metaphor, making it relevant to listeners.

Once students become alert, competent listeners, it is possible to assess how much they comprehend. The rubric in figure 9-2 can be used to evaluate students' ability to listen to a story.

Figure 9-2: Rubric to evaluate story listening skills

Listener	Never	Sometimes	Usually	Always
Apparently focuses attention on the speaker.				
Responds appropriately to dramatic or comedic moment with silence, laughter, and body language.				

Standardized tests of listening comprehension exist, but they suffer from the weaknesses of most standardized instruments. First, they often lack clarity over what should be measured. If we are gauging students' listening ability by asking questions about what they have heard, should we ask for strictly literal responses or for critical and analytic responses as well? A test using only factual questions cannot measure the total listening process, but if the test uses critical and analytical questions, individual experiences and values will affect results. In addition, the length and interest level of the material students listen to can influence test results.

One must also consider the question of test reliability. Published tests may be useful in measuring groups the size of an entire class, but testing error is usually too great for individual scores to be valid. Therefore, although standardized tests may provide general indicators about the whole class and clues about individuals, their limitations suggest the need for teachers to make careful observations during daily interactions with individual students. Teachers can make checklists and rubrics that include descriptions of listening comprehension such as the following:

- follows spoken directions
- understands spoken information
- uses critical and analytical listening powers

Conclusion

Listening at the level of paying attention and comprehending is an active process that requires effort and commitment. We live in a culture where respect for others is not always shown. Trash talk and rude interruptions are hallmarks of popular culture, particularly on television and in sports. What passes for political debate is often little more than a shouting match. Schools have a difficult task in countering such situations, yet courteous and respectful listening is a prerequisite for a learning community. Teachers must model positive listening behavior before they can expect their students to reciprocate. By working hard to create and maintain an atmosphere of respect and care, teachers can go a long way toward combating the oral-aural malaise that grips our society.

Not all cultures and families have the same understanding of appropriate and desirable listening and speaking behaviors. Teachers will need to encourage their students to:

- contribute freely to conversations or group discussions
- share ideas and feelings
- look at the person being addressed
- ask questions for clarification
- invite others to contribute to the conversation
- take turns
- assume a leadership role when appropriate
- volunteer to begin a discussion
- deal respectfully with any difference of opinion
- remain courteous throughout

Questions for Discussion

1. What conditions must be present before a child can be expected to read a word like *hippopotamus?*
2. Why is it often so difficult for children to pay attention to what is being said in class? What makes it difficult for you as an adult to pay attention?
3. This chapter mentions research indicating that in traditional classrooms, teachers out-talk their students by a ratio of 10 to 1. What do you think might be a more beneficial ratio? Why?
4. What are some steps teachers might take to organize their classrooms so that they talk less and listen more?

5. What may be the range of possible answers to the question *Why am I teaching this to these students at this time?*

6. Is sharing decision making in elementary school an abrogation of a teacher's God-given responsibility to be the instructional leader in the classroom?

7. Might giving students choices in their learning result in neglecting parts of the curriculum? What if they make unwise choices?

For Further Consideration

1. Invite a hearing specialist to come to class to demonstrate the use of an audiometer.

2. Administer the Wepman *Auditory Discrimination Test* (Wepman 1958) or the *Bader Listening Test* (Bader 1998a) to three children between ages five and seven who are deemed at risk in reading. Then administer the same test to three children in a similar age range who are considered to be linguistically advanced. Are there significant differences?

3. As a class project, have pairs of students examine different teaching resources designed to teach listening skills, and provide brief reviews using the headings below. Photocopy the reviews for each class member to provide everyone with a useful booklet of resources.

   - Complete Bibliographic Information
   - Recommended Grade Level
   - Specific Description of Teaching Activity
   - Brief Evaluative Comment

Endnotes

1 Learning to read is more dependent on hearing acuity than on visual acuity. Teachers should be especially alert to possible hearing problems among their students. Speech and articulation problems may be signs of hearing loss. It is difficult for children to develop phonemic awareness if they cannot hear the fine distinctions between closely related phonemes. Any child suspected of a hearing problem should have his or her hearing evaluated by a qualified person.

2 Research findings on language use in classrooms from kindergarten to college present a rather grim picture in which teachers ask thousands of predominantly low-level questions while students predictably respond with short, convergent answers. For examples of such findings, see Daines (1986), Gambrell (1987), and Shake (1988).

Chapter 10

Speaking

Many college-educated adults report that one of their greatest fears is speaking in public. Children who speak fluently and confidently on the playground often mumble barely coherent responses in the classroom. Even preservice education students, who will soon make a living talking to students, fear giving an oral presentation to their peers. Whereas chapter 6 examined oral language acquisition in general, this chapter looks at speaking as a public performance and explores what the school can do to make students more confident and flexible as speakers in a variety of situations.

"Actions speak louder than words."

"Sticks and stones will break my bones, but words will never hurt me."

How often have we heard such statements, or perhaps even made them ourselves? We habitually separate words and deeds, giving far more importance to the latter. Yet, the Scriptures do not make such a radical distinction. As James makes clear in speaking about the tongue (3:1–12), our words not only reflect what lives in our hearts but have great power to affect others. It is simply not true that "words will never hurt me," for words are both the bane and the balm of our lives. An apt answer and a word fitly spoken (Proverbs 15:23) bring real joy, just as a word spoken in anger can lead to judgment (Matthew 5:22). Christians are called upon to live in integrity of word and deed. Jesus is our prime example of that integrity; He not only *speaks* the truth but *is* the truth.

Because teachers conduct much of their work with words, their words will be judged "more strictly" than others (James 3:1). It is especially important that teachers' words and deeds be congruent, since teachers are primary models for their students. Speaking with care, clarity, and confidence is a hallmark of good teaching for us and a goal for our students.

Teaching and Talking

Teachers often exhort students to speak up, or to speak more slowly, more clearly, more respectfully, more grammatically. Many teachers try to involve their students in discussions but find the task more difficult than they imagined. When the teacher poses a question and invites discussion, students may sit silently, seeming to have no ideas, and respond to further prompting only in monosyllables. Teachers find themselves talking too much, perhaps to cover potentially embarrassing silence. At the other extreme, a class may be restless. Instead of listening to each other and contributing to a shared discussion, students carry on a disjointed series of shouted exchanges with the teacher.

A few children come to school with speech problems related to enunciation and articulation. They may need the specific help of a speech therapist, who will address concerns beyond those discussed here. Others may speak ungrammatically, ignoring norms for standard English. How we handle children's non-standard English is a contentious issue. I advocate flexibility.

One important aspect of oral flexibility is the ability to speak competently in standard English—not because standard English is the "correct" or "normative" code but because such competence is useful in many everyday life situations. Thus, teachers must help students gain facility in standard English, without denigrating their home dialects. This is better done by modeling and demonstrating than through explicit grammatical instruction, particularly in the lower elementary grades.

Improving Classroom Communication

Before considering ways to improve the oral communication environment in classrooms, we ask this prior question: Why should students talk in classrooms? This is not a facetious question. Anyone observing a traditional classroom might well assume that student talk is discouraged rather than encouraged. Typically, teachers do all the talking except when they expressly call for student response to a specific question. Yet modern educators emphasize that students internalize their learning by being involved and committed. They relate useful knowledge to the view of the world on which they base action, itself a result of past experience. This interrelating is largely carried out through talking and writing.

Classrooms dominated by teacher talk reflect a simple transmission model of instruction that does not acknowledge the importance of students' own language in their learning. Much of our earlier discussion about the transmission model for listening applies to speaking as well, since listening and speaking are reciprocal processes. For both, the atmosphere or psychological climate in the classroom is crucial, directly shaping communication and learning.

The issue of oral communication in the classroom is thus one of finding ways to encourage and equip students to speak well and appropriately. Mainly, oral communication is a matter of pragmatics, or speaking appropriately given the setting, participants, and purposes.

Fostering Verbal Confidence

In any classroom, some students are outspoken and verbal, some speak out occasionally, and some join class discussions reluctantly. Most classrooms also contain a wide range of verbal aggressiveness, from total lack of verbal aggressiveness to its continual use for attracting attention. Both extremes are common indicators of low verbal confidence.

Many children (and adults) feel that they have nothing important to say, or that they can't express themselves as well as others. With few exceptions, their belief is not caused by physical speech defects or insufficient grammatical control of the language. Instead, lack of verbal confidence reflects factors ranging from overprotective parents to negative experiences in early schooling. Some students may be unaccustomed to using language in the analytical ways valued at school (see chapter 7), and therefore they feel verbally limited. Whatever the cause, they enter school with low self-esteem, which affects verbal confidence.

People typically deal with lack of confidence in one of two ways. Some hide feelings of inadequacy by remaining silent whenever there is any risk. Those who use this mechanism speak out only when they are with an understanding parent, a small group of friends, or others with whom they feel safe. Other people mask their lack of confidence behind attention-getting behaviors, often becoming "class clowns" or otherwise causing disturbances in the classroom.

We develop our self-concept primarily through personal interactions, basing feelings of importance and success on the degree of acceptance we receive from others. Parents have a primary influence in shaping their children's self-concepts, but teachers come a close second. Many classroom teachers contribute to students' lack of verbal confidence by ascribing little value to what students say in the classroom. When the teacher is the chief speaker, translator, questioner, and information provider, anything the students say receives little recognition, and we know that recognition is a major ingredient in building confidence.

Building confidence in a classroom setting is not an easy task. Students' self-concepts are rather deeply ingrained by the time they enter school. What is more, a teacher has less than 30 hours a week to counteract out-of-school influences and must interact with many learners.

Still, teachers can do much to build student confidence. Potential action falls into two categories: (1) setting up a learning environment conducive to talk and (2) using teaching activities specifically designed to build verbal confidence.

The Environment

A classroom's learning environment is at least as important as the content taught. That environment is determined by such matters as physical arrangement, daily schedule, the knowledge transmitted, and the materials used to teach it. The greatest influence on the learning environment, however, is often the interaction between learners and teachers.

Much of what was said in earlier chapters about creating a classroom atmosphere conducive to listening (chapter 9) is also relevant to building verbal confidence. In general, for worthwhile speech to take place, there must be something worthwhile to talk about. Students hiding their lack of confidence behind a barrage of words need to be able to contribute to discussions in constructive ways. Students who do very little talking need opportunities to talk about familiar and comfortable things. In these and other situations, oral activities that deal with students' areas of interest provide motivation. A variety of sharing sessions can be structured into the curriculum using the primary "show and tell" or circle-sharing model. Within the language arts areas, sharing can happen in small-group discussions of stories or books, guided in part by teacher questions. Conferencing about a self-chosen piece of writing is another way to foster verbal confidence by focusing on students' personal interests.

Second, the classroom environment nurtures oral confidence when students are aware that something useful is happening. At home, children acquire most language unconsciously while intent on accomplishing something else. The classroom cannot always reproduce the home environment, but it can help students see that something useful is happening as they communicate. Thus, much of the talking students do in school should contribute to recognized objectives. Discussions in science, social studies, and other academic subjects can be planned so that student talk contributes to an objective for that subject. Brainstorming as a whole class or a small group can stimulate a variety of ideas on a subject, or suggest avenues for solving a problem. Students can experience the usefulness of collaborative talk by planning a real event, such as a class trip, dramatic production, science project, or display.

Third, a powerful tool for creating a positive classroom environment is to recognize that student talk is productive. This requires, first, providing time and opportunity for students to talk to each other as well as to the teacher. It also means allowing students to speak for themselves and resisting the temptation to interrupt them, translate their message to the other students, or repeat the message so that more students hear. These behaviors discourage students from listening to each other. When students are allowed to speak for themselves without interruption or repetition, they are more likely to feel that what they say is important.

Fourth, providing an accepting classroom environment contributes to oral confidence. It is often difficult to decide whether students' improperly worded statements should be accepted as they are or corrected. There is a time for accepting a student's speech and a time for correcting it. Clearly, one of the times for avoiding a critique is when someone who lacks confidence is venturing to speak. Such students need an environment in which it is safe to speak. Parents focus on the semantic content rather than the grammatical form of their young children's speech. While verbal confidence is still developing, teachers are wise to do the same. Positive support is more likely to produce confidence and oral skill than correction.

Functions of Talk

In chapter 6, we discussed the concept of oral language **functions** as suggested by Michael Halliday and Joan Tough. Understanding these language functions can help teachers design oral language-learning activities that will encourage their students to develop a wide variety of language uses. The example below, based on a grade 6 social studies unit on Ancient Greece, provides suggestions for stimulating oral language functions.

Figure 10-1: Oral language activities for a grade 6 social studies unit on Ancient Greece

Instrumental: The Delian League was a group of Greek city-states that banded together to protect each other from aggressive forces. Your class constitutes the members of the city-state of Athens, the largest and strongest member. Chios, also a member of the Delian League, has requested your help in battle against Persian aggressors. In a group debate, decide whether or not you should get involved in the war and help Chios.

Regulatory: You, as citizens of Athens, are concerned

about the civil rights of slaves in Athenian society. In small groups, discuss the present slave regulations and devise a new set of civil rights that will allow slaves the same rights as Athenian citizens. You will present these civil rights to the assembly.

Interactional: You, as a citizen of Troy, have been summoned to an important meeting, and you are awaiting a message from the town crier (played by the teacher). The town crier arrives and says, "There is a giant wooden horse outside the city gate, left there as a peace offering from Greece. We must decide among ourselves whether to accept this horse. We must also decide what to do with it if we decide to accept it." As a class, discuss how you will make this decision. What will you as a group say?

Personal: You are Athenian slaves waiting to be sold. A reporter (played by the teacher) interviews you to determine your emotional reactions to being sold.

Heuristic: Citizens in Ancient Greece believed in a direct democracy where all free adult males were equal and were contributing members of the government. Some of you are members of the Athenian assembly, while the rest are reporters who interview the assembly about why they have chosen a direct democracy rather than electing one leader.

Imaginative: You are in charge of entertainment at an Athenian banquet. You have decided to compose poetic "Who am I?" riddles about mythical Greek gods. In groups of three, compose and audiotape these riddles.

Representational: You are a member of the Athenian Tourism Bureau. Your job is to make a TV commercial to entice people to visit Athenian Greece. In small groups, compose and dramatize a television commercial.

Oral Language Activities

Classroom activities for building verbal confidence should be sensitive not only to the age and interest levels of students but also to their level of oral confidence. For example, it is not always true that a primary grade child will have less verbal confidence than a student in middle school. Verbal confidence is largely dependent on **psychological risk factors**. The greater a student's exposure to personal scrutiny, the higher the risk presented by an oral activity. The overall strategy for building verbal confidence is to introduce low-risk oral activities first, gradually increasing the level of risk as confidence increases. Many of the activities suggested below fall into the category of **drama**, but not drama conceived of as a full-fledged dramatic production. Rather, the dramatic activities described here are informal and carried out in the regular classroom, with the class members as sole participants and audience.[1]

Low-Risk Activities

Informal Discussion Teachers should not underestimate the importance of allowing children to try out ideas in informal discussion. The educational philosopher Alfred North Whitehead spoke of the need for students to engage in a "romance" phase of learning before proceeding to "precision learning." Often it is important that students simply share in small groups what they already know about a topic or theme before assessing their prior knowledge in ways that are more formal.

Choral Speaking This form of oral communication is particularly useful in helping children develop oral skills, both reading and speaking, within the supportive context of a group. Poetry lends itself particularly well to choral presentation because poets write with heightened consciousness of how language sounds. Most poetry needs to be read orally to realize its full emotional and aesthetic effect.[2] Following are some guidelines for choral speaking and reading with children:

- Make the pleasure of the participants, not the audience, the objective.
- Select poems that are appealing (rhythmic, tuneful, imaginative, humorous, clever).
- Try to choose selections children like rather than those you think they should like.
- Involve children in deciding the choral arrangement (who says what and how).
- Have a student leader start, cue, and direct different responders.
- Initially, select poems that are simple and familiar.
- Choose children who are bolder about speaking in front of a group for individual parts, and let shyer children be part of the chorus.
- As much as possible, involve children in discussing voice expression and inflection so that they become conscious of voice as a flexible instrument.

Reader's Theater As in choral speaking, children read from written sources, but here the source is an actual play. Although the number of characters in the play limits the number of children who can be directly involved, other students can learn audience skills and serve as constructive critics. The readers do no physical acting; instead, they make the script come alive through vocal expression and inflection. The readers must work hard at developing effective voice characters, and the audience members must be active listeners, using their imaginations to complete the picture.

Puppetry Because puppeteers are hidden from audience view, puppetry can be especially useful in fostering oral language skills among children who may be uncomfortable speaking in front of groups or who fear classmate ridicule. The personality of the puppet serves as a buffer between the child and the audience, reducing the students' nervousness and insecurity. Puppetry is usually easy to introduce because many children are exposed to it before they begin school. Well-known nursery and fairy tales and fables have a few strong characters and familiar story lines that lend themselves to puppet productions. Children can listen carefully to the tale and discuss the characters and the plot or moral. They may want to write their own script to retell the story, which in turn will raise questions about dialogue and proper voices for the characters. The puppets can be simple or elaborate, depending on how much the students want to do and how often puppets are used.

Puppetry can also be used to break boundaries between grades and nurture a sense of community and cooperation. Older students can help younger ones make puppets, cooperating in an excellent art project. Primary-grade children can gain confidence by sharing their puppet shows with older children. Students in middle school often enjoy making elaborate and sophisticated puppets, and performing puppet plays for children in the primary grades.

Higher-Risk Activities

Impromptu Theater and Role Playing In impromptu theater, a certain idea or stimulus becomes the basis for a short improvised scene in which students play certain roles. As such, it is a high-risk activity that requires considerable self-confidence. One primary class made a play based on a story they had just read about Africa. The story featured many African animals. Children volunteered to be certain animals—a lion, an elephant, a python—and spent time discussing how each animal would move. Then the teacher prepared a simple script about a hunter who went on a safari and met each of these animals. Through careful listening, children playing the hunter and the animals acted out the script as the teacher read it. After the initial reading, the class discussed the effectiveness of the actors' movements and made helpful suggestions. Then the play was repeated with the same actors, and eventually with other children who volunteered for the roles.

In another example, a group of fourteen-year-olds discussed privilege and deprivation, and from these discussions an impromptu drama was developed. In the play, an over-privileged family refuses to give to charity ostensibly because the gift might not help the people it was intended for. Throughout the process, students had to rethink the ideas under discussion and evaluate the relative effectiveness of the impromptu piece in demonstrating the ideas.

A grade 4 class read Lloyd Alexander's story *The King's Fountain* (1971). In this story, wonderfully illustrated by Ezra Jack Keats, a poor man tries to find someone wiser, stronger, and cleverer than himself to dissuade the king from building a fountain that will cut off the city's water supply. Finding no one in the village willing to challenge the king, the poor man decides to go himself. A member of the class volunteered to be the poor man and solicited advice from classmates about what to say to the king. The teacher helped the students see that a king must be addressed in very respectful and, if possible, formal language. The teacher then adopted the role of the king and invited the "poor man" to make his case. After the class provided a positive critique of the supplication, other class members volunteered to take their turn as supplicants, each time incorporating previous suggestions for what to say and how to say it.

Formal Reporting Presenting an oral report exposes the student front-and-center with only a minimum of support, particularly when the student uses only brief notes. Such an activity requires good preparation and a lot of coaching. Adding supports or props can alter the risk of formal reporting. A PowerPoint presentation or other visuals, for example, decrease the risk because those supports draw some audience attention away from the presenter.

Storytelling This is the highest-risk oral activity because all eyes are directly focused on the storyteller, who usually has no diversionary props. The story's plot must be well rehearsed and practiced so that the teller can concentrate on the dramatic elements of the telling. Storytelling is one of the most intimate of oral language activities, revealing as much about the storyteller as the story. Jesus was a master storyteller. Through His parables and picture stories, we imagine God's kingdom and our place in it. Although Jesus' stories are about the deepest issues of life, there is something homey, familiar, and even childlike about them. They are like the words of a loving parent speaking to children. Stories are an effective teaching method. Teachers at all grade levels should make the effort to develop their storytelling skills.

Resources

Below are some helpful resources (listed in order of publication date) that feature specific teaching suggestions for many of the oral language activities mentioned above.

◊ Patricia G. Smith, ed. 2001. *Talking classrooms: Shaping children's learning through oral language instruction.* Newark, DE: International Reading Association.

◊ Helen Raczuk and Marilyn Smith. 1997. *Invitation to readers theater: A guidebook for using reader's theater to celebrate holidays and special events throughout the year.* Edmonton, AB: U-Otter-Read-It Press.

◊ Lloyd Den Boer, ed. 1996. Using language to learn. *The language arts handbook,* vol. 1, 2nd ed. Langley, BC: Society of Christian Schools in British Columbia: 157–169.

◊ Neill Dixon, Anne Davies, and Colleen Politano. 1996. *Learning with readers theater: Building connections.* Winnipeg, MB: Peguis Publishers.

◊ Deborah Butler and Tom Liner. 1995. Chapter 9 of Talking it out: Oral language. In D. Butler and T. Liner. *Room to grow: Natural language arts in the middle school,* Durham, NC: Carolina Academic Press: 253–285.

◊ Bernice E. Cullinan, ed. 1993. *Children's voices: Talk in the classroom.* Newark, DE: International Reading Association.

◊ Carole Tarlington and Patrick Verriour. 1991. *Role drama.* Markham, ON: Pembroke Publishers.

◊ Nellie McCaslin. 1990. *Creative drama in the classroom.* 5th ed. White Plains, NY: Longmans.

◊ Susan Hill. 1990. *Reader's theater: Performing the text.* South Yarra, Australia: Eleanor Curtain Publishing. [Available in North America from Peguis Publishers, Winnipeg, Manitoba, Canada]

◊ Irene N. Watts. 1990. *Just a minute: Ten short plays and activities for your classroom.* Markham, ON: Pembroke Publishers and Portsmouth, NH: Heinemann.

◊ Linda G. Geller. 1985. *Word play and language learning for children.* Urbana, IL: National Council of Teachers of English.

◊ John W. Stewig. 1983. *Informal drama in the elementary language arts program.* New York: Teachers College Press.

◊ Carole Tarlington and Patrick Verriour. 1983. *Offstage: Elementary education through drama.* Toronto, ON: Oxford University Press.

◊ Nancy H. Brizendine and James L. Thomas. 1982. *Learning through dramatics: Ideas for teachers and librarians.* Phoenix, AZ: Oryx Press.

Evaluation of Speaking

Many of the resources above contain helpful checklists and other tools for assessing the featured speaking activity. See for example Den Boer (1996), appendices E–N, for an array of useful forms for evaluating individual students in such skills as public speaking, participation in oral activities, telling or retelling a story, oral reporting, role-playing, and speaking.

For information about evaluating more general oral language development, see the section at the conclusion of chapter 6.

Questions for Discussion

1. How important is it to speak grammatically? Why?
2. What is your level of verbal confidence? What factors determine whether you are willing to risk speaking before a group?
3. Think of a classroom in which you are a student or a teacher. How does the *physical arrangement* of the classroom enhance or deter good oral communication?
4. Compare the physical arrangement of a kindergarten classroom with that of a grade 7 or 8 classroom. Which do you think is more conducive to good oral interaction? Why?
5. Research shows that the amount of talk by the one teacher in the classroom is from three to ten times greater than the combined oral contribution of the twenty-five to thirty students. Suggest meaningful ways to minimize this imbalance.

For Further Consideration

1. Using a good Bible concordance, look up the references for *word* and *words.* What did you learn about the Scripture's view of words in your life?
2. Examine the language arts curriculum standards for your state or province. How much attention is given to the explicit fostering of oral language development compared with reading and writing? How do you account for this imbalance? Might it have something to do with how much more difficult it is to do large-scale formal assessment of speaking?
3. Read *The King's Fountain* (Alexander 1971) and role-play the activity this chapter suggests.

Endnotes

1 Formal dramatics are to the drama/language arts program what competitive sports are to the physical education program. Although there is a place for formal dramatics, it has very few advantages (other than public relations) over simpler forms of classroom dramatics. Often formal dramatics cannot involve every student in the class because the emphasis is on public performance and a high standard of excellence. Besides, the amount of time and energy expended to put on a formal play cannot usually be justified by the educational benefits to the students.

2 See chapter 12 for additional information about the role of poetry in the language arts program.

Chapter 11

Reading

This chapter explores the "remarkable performance" of reading that so awed Edmund Burke Huey almost a hundred years ago. Chapter 5 set the stage for this exploration by sketching the history of the teaching of reading, while chapter 8 chronicled the emergence of reading in young children. Building on that groundwork, this chapter outlines pedagogical issues related to the teaching of reading and describes specific teaching strategies that support the language-centered approach recommended in this book.

> To completely analyze what we do when we read would almost be the acme of a psychologist's achievement, for it would be to describe very many of the most intricate workings of the human mind, as well as to unravel the tangled story of the most remarkable specific performance that civilization has learned in all its history. (Huey 1908, 6)

In the years since Huey's landmark book on reading was published (1908), reading and learning to read have received more research attention than any other field in education.[1] Every year, hundreds of reading research reports are published in professional and scholarly journals representing fields such as psychology, linguistics, anthropology, sociology, and education. The largest reading association in the world (the International Reading Association, or IRA), headquartered in the United States, has a membership of more than 80,000 teachers, professors, and researchers. Each year the IRA publishes four print journals, several electronic journals, a newspaper, and many books devoted exclusively to reading and broader literacy concerns. Its annual convention routinely draws 15,000 educators.

These numbers reflect the enduring desire by the teaching and research community "to completely analyze what we do when we read." Despite this huge effort, a continuous flood of books, pamphlets, and newspaper and magazine articles decries the sad state of literacy in North America and offers often conflicting solutions to this "crisis."[2] The Internet now contributes its voice, with a plethora of sites dedicated to the debate.[3] The educational publishing industry pours millions of dollars a year into marketing reading materials such as basal series, workbooks, reading games, charts, kits, CDs, and tests. Advertisements in education journals herald the year's new reading series with campaigns similar to the automobile industry's launch of "new" and "improved" models. As explained in chapter 5, the battle between "code emphasis" and "meaning emphasis" shows no sign of abating, with each side claiming that "research is on our side." As of this writing, the pendulum is swinging rapidly back to the "code emphasis" side of the debate, backed by questionable rationale.

Concern about how children learn to read is real. Parents and society in general hold the school responsible for teaching all children to read, and the lion's share of this burden falls on teachers in the primary grades. One of the most eagerly and nervously asked questions at the first parent-teacher conference in grade 1 is, *How is my child doing in reading?* So great are children's expectations of learning to read that some are genuinely disappointed when they have not yet learned to read by the end of their first day at school. Both school-based and private remedial reading clinics are often oversubscribed (and just as often understaffed) as they attempt to meet the needs of students deemed "at risk" or already failing to learn to read.

Why Read?

Most discussions of teaching reading arouse almost religious fervor, and there is no denying that the battlefield of reading pedagogy is littered with the corpses of past failures. Before I contribute further to this "methods" debate, it will be helpful to pause and shift the focus to the more fundamental question of purpose. Why are we so concerned about reading acquisition and ability in the first place? Should we be concerned?

Obviously, success at school requires reading ability. However, is this a compelling enough reason for putting so much emphasis on reading? Should school be so dependent on print? Surely, reading skills should not be taught with the sole purpose of assuring future educational success. If reading is not important to the child as child, then perhaps we should not stress it as much as we do.

Another justification for the time and energy devoted to reading instruction is that we live in a print age and therefore must be literate if we are to survive and thrive. While this argument has considerable force, it is probably overstated. Large numbers of successful North American adults read at fifth- or sixth-grade levels, and studies show that many adults who *can* read at more sophisticated levels seldom do so. Many jobs require only minimal functional literacy, and most of us receive our "essential" information from radio and television. [4]

There must be more compelling reasons for spending so much time and energy on reading instruction. I believe there are. Reading is one aspect of our use of language, and language is a special gift from God that allows us to communicate with each other and with Him. Written language is not only a tool for communicating functional, practical information but is also a means of conveying our deepest joys, fears, doubts, and beliefs about the world and ourselves. God uses inspired writing as a primary way of communicating with us. Reading and writing are powerful, persuasive language tools that serve both good and evil purposes. As Christians, we ought to develop these tools for our children and ourselves so that we can be better servants of our Lord.

A major reason for teaching, learning, and exercising reading skills is to understand and appreciate literature. In the words of Leland Ryken, professor of English at Wheaton College, "the subject of literature is human experience, concretely portrayed. Literature does not exist primarily to convey ideas, but rather to take the reader through an imaginative experience" (Ryken 2002, 15).[5] Literature is a repository of a culture's sense of itself and the longings of what it hopes to be. Literature challenges our imaginations and takes us outside the walls of the world to a reality beyond the limits of our five senses. Surely, Christians should appreciate the importance of literature, for the Bible contains a rich gamut of literary styles: historical writing, narrative prose, parable, poetry, chronicle, tragedy, comedy, lament, satire, epistle, oration, drama, and visionary writing. Literary techniques abound as well, including humor, pun, hyperbole, extended metaphor, and a variety of storytelling styles. To mine the literary riches of the Bible as well as of other literature, we must be good readers.

Literacy and Protestant Christianity

Christianity and Judaism, its precursor, are both religions of "the Book" (as is the third major world religion, Islam). God chose to reveal Himself, in large measure, through the writings of what we now know as the Old and New Testaments of the Bible.[6] Thus, literacy has always been important to God's people. Jesus could read, and knew the Old Testament Scriptures well. The early church was the venue for instruction in reading and writing, particularly for the clergy. The Protestant Reformation greatly accelerated the growth of literacy among the laity through its insistence that believers have direct access to the Bible for themselves.

Martin Luther (1483–1546) was a tireless advocate for universal schooling for the young. In his *Letter to the Mayors and Aldermen of All Cities of Germany on Behalf of Christian Schools,* he said:

> What would it avail if we possessed and performed all else, and became perfect saints, if we neglect that for which we chiefly live, namely, to care for the young? In my judgment, there is no other outward offense that in the sight of God so heavily burdens the world, and deserves such heavy reproach, as the neglect to educate children. We cannot deny that, although the Gospel has come and daily comes through the Holy Spirit, it has come by means of the languages, and through them must increase and be preserved. (As quoted in Lucas 1972, 250)

Luther championed free schools for all children as a sure guarantee of public welfare. Convinced that municipalities should not only maintain schools at public expense but should make attendance compulsory, he argued:

> ... if the magistrates may compel their able-bodied subjects to carry pike and musket and do military service, there is much more reason for them compelling their subjects to attend school. For there is a far worse war to be waged with the Devil, who

> employs himself secretly in harming towns and states through the neglect of education. (Lucas 1972, 251)

Many years later, the Puritans in New England used this line of argument to institute compulsory school maintenance in the famous *Old Deluder Satan Act* of 1647. Its preamble eloquently argued that "it being one of the chief projects of that old deluder, Satan, to keep men from knowledge of the Scriptures, as in former times by keeping them in an unknown tongue, so in these latter times by persuading them from the use of tongues ... learning may not be buried in the graves of our fathers in the church and commonwealth, the Lord assisting our endeavors...." Towns of fifty or more families were instructed to appoint someone to teach "all such children as shall resort to him to write and read; the schoolmaster to be paid either by the parents or masters of such children, or by the inhabitants in general" (Lucas 1972, 476–477). Thus Protestant Christianity and compulsory state-supported elementary schooling, primarily for instruction in literacy, have grown up together for centuries.

The Centrality of Story in the Christian Tradition

> "There were two men in a certain town, one rich and the other poor. The rich man had a very large number of sheep and cattle, but the poor man had nothing except one little ewe lamb he had bought. He raised it, and it grew up with him and his children. It shared his food, drank from his cup and even slept in his arms...."
>
> "Now a traveler came to the rich man, but the rich man refrained from taking one of his own sheep or cattle to prepare a meal for the traveler who had come to him. Instead, he took the ewe lamb that belonged to the poor man and prepared it for the one who had come to him." (2 Samuel 12:1b–4 NIV)

Those who know the Old Testament Scriptures will recognize this as the story told by the prophet Nathan to King David after his adultery with Bathsheba and subsequent arrangement for the death of her husband, Uriah. Upon hearing this story, David is incensed and exclaims, "As surely as the Lord lives, the man who did this deserves to die ... because he ... had no pity"

(vv. 5b and 6). Nathan replies, no doubt in a thunderous voice and with pointing finger, "*You* are the man!" (v. 7).

Nathan's story elicits an indignant response from David and dramatically convicts him of his own guilt. It is hard to imagine that a stern lecture accusing David of being a lecher and murderer would have resulted in his freely given confession. Stories clearly have the power to move us in ways that exposition rarely does. As Lee Shulman said (in Sparks 1992), "We've learned in research that narrative quality is often more compelling than an expository presentation of the same ideas" (16).

The use of stories or narrative in teaching has a distinguished history. Christ's use of parables to teach His disciples and the crowds that gathered around Him is well known. In modern times, a number of Christian educators have argued for the need to better utilize narrative in understanding and teaching scriptural principles. Thomas Groome's (1980) model of shared Christian praxis depends on an understanding of Christianity as "a Story which includes the whole faith tradition of our people however that is expressed or embodied" (192). He purposely capitalizes "Story" to emphasize that we are not referring to "just another 'story,' as if someone made it up," but to "our Story which is grounded in historical events and has as its high point, for Christians, God's historical presence in the life, death, and resurrection of Jesus Christ" (192).

John Bolt (1993) emphasizes that the biblical theme of creation-fall-redemption-restoration reflects a view that the overall structure of Scripture is a narrative. For him "the crucial question of education is who tells the story and how it is told" (156). Arguing that "the underlying theme of postmodernity [is] a loss of narrative unity" (156), he attributes the decline of storytelling as a pedagogical practice (a decline traced in chapter 5 of his book) to the influence of rationalism. He argues persuasively for returning narrative to its rightful place in Christian education, quoting Elie Wiesel: "God made man because he loves stories" (158). Bolt uses John Shea to explore this quotation in a manner that bears repeating here:

> If God made man because he loves stories, creation is a success. For humankind is addicted to stories. No matter our mood, in reverie or expectation, panic or peace, we can be found stringing together incidents, and unfolding episodes. We turn our pain into narrative so we can bear it; we turn our ecstasy into narrative so we can prolong it. We all seem to be under the sentence of Scheherazade. We tell our stories to live. But there is a deeper suggestion in Wiesel's phrase. God not only loves to hear our stories, he loves to tell his own. And quite simply, we are the story God tells. We are born into a community of stories and storytellers. In interpreting our traditional stories of God we find out who we are and what we must do. In telling the stories of God we ourselves are told. (158–159)[7]

Thus, to reiterate, a major reason for helping Christian children become literate is to give them the tools with which to access the Story of their faith. Moreover, reading well also helps children access the stories of their neighbors, worldwide, whom we all are called to love and serve.

Theories and Models of Reading

A centipede was happy quite
Until a frog in fun
Said, "Pray which leg comes after which?"
This raised his mind to such a pitch,
He lay distracted in the ditch,
Considering how to run.

—Anonymous

If we are literate, we usually take our ability to read and write for granted; yet it is very difficult to explain exactly what it is we do when we read. Like the centipede, the complexity of our skill distracts us, or we focus only on its simplistic aspects.

Several years ago, a student assistant and I interviewed 500 children in grades one to six about their reading (Bruinsma

1990b). Among the questions we asked were "What is reading?" and "What do you do when you read?" Most students found these questions very difficult to answer. Responses to the first question tended to be object-related: "Reading is when you look at a book [or words or letters]." Responses to the second question typically related to phonological decoding: "When I read, I sound out the words."

Remarkably, when these same questions were posed to about a dozen college students, the responses were not much more elaborate or insightful. Few students at any level focused on the semantic purpose of reading; that is, on the interaction with printed symbols resulting in understanding. But what is this understanding that good reading engenders? Whose understanding is it? The reader's? The author's? These questions prod us to consider just what it is that humans do as they read.

In recent years, a great deal of theory and research has centered on the relationship between language and reading. Three general points of view have emerged, and reading experts tend to lean toward one of these camps. The central issue is how the reader uses language to read. The popular names for the three theories are **bottom-up, top-down,** and **interactive**.

Bottom-up Theories

The several bottom-up theories share a common belief that reading is a process of recognizing words and their individual meanings, then piecing these together to derive sentence and paragraph meaning. Central to word recognition is the ability to recognize letters and letter clusters, and associate them with sounds. Thus, word recognition may include using phonics or "sounding out" techniques as well as recognizing whole words on sight. The reader starts at the "bottom" with letter and word recognition and ends at the "top" with meaning. According to this view, readers simply need to understand the language of the text well enough to piece together the individual word meanings. The process is similar to listening to yourself to find out what you are saying. As readers identify word after word, silently or orally, they listen to themselves to find familiar language and derive sentence meaning.

Bottom-up reading pedagogy stresses the need for carefully sequenced instruction, so that students first decode smaller bits of language such as letters and sounds, then ever larger chunks such as words and sentences, and finally whole texts at increasing levels of complexity. Often, the reading act is conceptualized as a large number of subskills that must be taught in the correct order (a **skills hierarchy**) to allow readers to build up to the fluent reading of whole texts with comprehension. As might be expected, bottom-up theories of reading closely ally themselves with a skills-centered approach to teaching.

Top-down Theories

Top-down theories propose that the process of reading begins with meaning rather than with words or letters. Readers already have a good idea what a group of words says before they begin to decode, particularly if the words appear in a strong context. From their understanding of the author's message in previous words, sentences, and paragraphs, readers can predict approximately what the author will say in the next group of words before focusing on them. Only enough information needs to be gleaned from the words themselves to confirm or alter the prediction. Thus, top-down theories hold that proficient reading starts at the "top" with meaning and goes "down" to word recognition, to the extent that such detail is necessary.

This viewpoint ascribes to readers' unconscious knowledge of language a great deal of the credit for functional reading. Understanding how language works, on a much larger scale than individual words, makes predicting possible. Readers are unaware that they are using context or giving limited attention to individual words, for their attention is focused on the meaning of the passage as a whole.

Two properties of language contribute clues that enable readers to make predictions: semantics and syntax. Semantics contributes clues because the redundancy so common in language allows the reader to follow or contribute to the author's sequence or line of logic. Syntax provides clues because sentence patterns and informal rules of language allow the reader familiar with those standards to predict the form or structure of the next group of words. For example, it is quite easy to predict a meaningful word to fill the blank in the sentence, *The dog _________ loudly at the cat.* The word could be *barked, yelped,* or *growled.* Our prediction is based on what we know about dogs and cats (semantics), as well our realization that a verb is necessary to complete this sentence (syntax). If the sentence is presented as *The dog b__________ loudly at the cat,* the task becomes even easier. The reader will in all likelihood choose the word *barked* using semantic knowledge plus the additional **graphophonemic** knowledge that the letter *b* stands for the phoneme heard at the beginning of the word *barked.*

Notice how long it takes you to answer the question below:

> How quickly can you
> find the error in
> in this sentence?

Most experienced readers scan the sentence several times before noticing the repeated word. Does this simple example recall personal experiences with proofreading? Most of us overlook obvious errors when we proof our own writing. We know what the text is supposed to say and don't notice what is really there. In the example above, we subconsciously edit out the second *in* because of our (largely subconscious) knowledge that English syntax seldom uses the word *in* two times in a row.

Top-down reading theorists insist that reading pedagogy should begin with whole texts rather than letters, sounds, and words. At beginning levels, children should be exposed to texts with repetitive syntactic patterns and other devices that make the text highly predictable. Many traditional fairy tales and nursery stories have such patterns. After talking about the story to build background knowledge, the teacher reads it a number of times: first, the teacher models the reading while pointing to the text;

next, the students echo the teacher; and finally, the students read the story independently. The children are introduced to bits and pieces of the text—letters, sounds, words, punctuation marks—only after experiencing the whole, meaningful text. Throughout the process, the teacher frequently invites students to predict what will come next, thereby encouraging them to take an active part in making meaning of the story.

Interactive Theories

Proponents of interactive theories claim that good readers simultaneously use word recognition and higher level meaning clues. Meaning is the objective, but the process involves both sources of clues. The degree to which each is used depends on how the person interacts with the text. For example, a student who reads about a familiar subject brings a great deal of meaning to the text and uses a predominately top-down reading approach. On the other hand, a reader who is dealing with an unfamiliar subject and is depending on textual clues for meaning uses a more bottom-up approach. According to interactive theories, good readers use bottom-up word recognition, syntactic awareness, and semantics in a compensatory way, depending on their ability to access levels of information from the text and within themselves.

Interactive theories view readers' use of language much as top-down theories do. Readers use the same two properties of language (semantics and syntax) to get meaning *from* and bring meaning *to* the author's message. They are largely unaware of how they process context and individual words. The difference between these two theories lies in the degree of readers' dependence on linguistic and extralinguistic knowledge. In top-down theories, readers depend heavily on meaning and structure clues found in the language of the context, and use individual words only to check predictions. In interactive theories, readers depend somewhat less on specific decoding strategies because word recognition and clues from context interact with each other. Interactive theories are more closely allied with a language-centered approach to teaching language arts. Figure

11-1 illustrates the three theories described above.

Figure 11-1: Three theories about language and reading

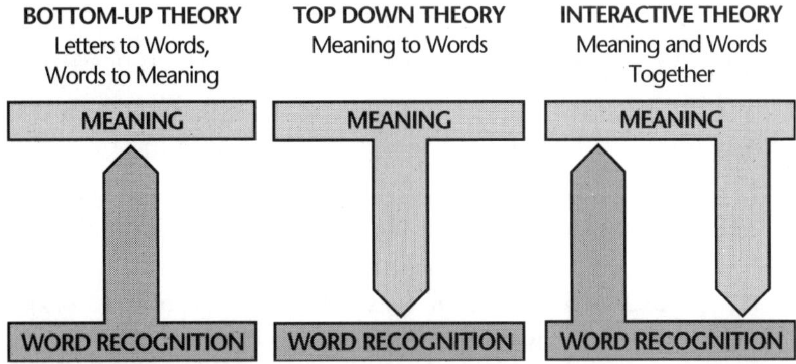

Evaluating the Theories

One problem with the three competing theories is that they do not apply equally well to all forms of reading. Obviously, fluent readers with more life experience and large sight vocabularies can take greater advantage of their knowledge of the syntactic and semantic aspects of printed language, while beginning readers may need to pay more attention to the "lower" levels of text processing. Fluent readers may occasionally come across words that are totally unfamiliar, or meet subject matter to which they cannot bring any background knowledge. In such cases, even fluent readers rely on precise decoding of the text to obtain meaning.

The interactive theory is perhaps best in describing the flexibility good readers employ as they match their approach to the reading task at hand. A fluent reader interacting with print that matches background knowledge and syntactic understanding can use a very top-down reading process. Encountering text with unfamiliar concepts, style, and/or syntax, that same reader will use a more bottom-up approach.

The interactive theory also explains why beginning readers need to pay more attention to the symbol-to-sound relationships embodied in smaller chunks of print. The challenge for teachers is to move children as quickly as possible from heavy reliance on a bottom-up approach to automatic word recognition. Automatic word recognition allows readers to allocate cognitive processing efforts to meaning making rather than decoding.

A helpful way to think about the relative role that bottom-up and top-down strategies play in effective reading is to examine how struggling readers approach text (Campbell 2003). When listening to such readers, one often notices a pattern to their **reading miscues** (the term *miscue* refers to oral reading errors). By analyzing these miscues, teachers can decipher the mix of language **cueing systems** the reader is using, whether **graphophonic, syntactic**, or **semantic.**

Some struggling students read slowly, trying to sound out every word. Their miscues often sound or look like the words on the page but do not make sense. For example, a student who reads: "The *house gulped* down the road" instead of "The *horse galloped* down the road" is clearly using graphophonic more than semantic cues, and has a **print-based miscue pattern**. This student is applying a largely bottom-up approach to reading.

Other struggling readers omit and insert words that are not present in the text, and their miscues make sense but do not look or sound much like the words on the page. Such a student might read *"The pony ran down the path"* for *"The horse galloped down the road."* This reader is not paying enough attention to print, but is using semantic cueing and background information to bring meaning to the text. Such a reader has a **meaning-based miscue pattern** and is applying a largely top-down approach to reading.[8]

In some sense, the latter is a "better" reader than the former, having at least realized that the text must make sense. Still, the latter is an inaccurate reader who may miss important text-based information. Strategic readers know how to use both bottom-up and top-down processes to maximize their interaction with print. That is, strategic readers are interactive readers. The **Print Communication Model** of figure 11-2 summarizes the contribution the three theories make to understanding the reading process.

Figure 11-2: Print Communication Model

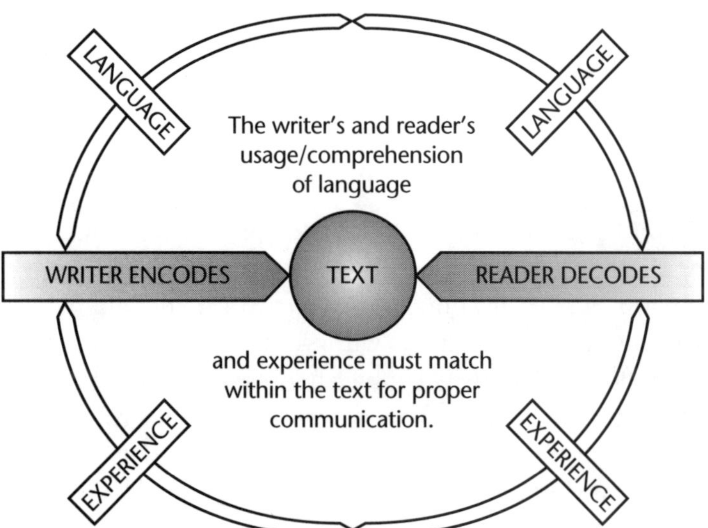

The **Print Communication Model** begins with a WRITER who employs a certain LANGUAGE FACILITY to ENCODE (write) a TEXT about his/her KNOWLEDGE and EXPERIENCE of a topic. The READER must DECODE this TEXT (i.e., figure out what the writer is saying) but must also bring his or her own LANGUAGE FACILITY and BACKGROUND KNOWLEDGE and EXPERIENCE to bear on the reading process. If the reader is to comprehend the text, there must be a reasonable match between the writer's use of language and the reader's language facility and experience. If the writer encodes knowledge and experience in a manner that is far below the reader's ability (incorporating vocabulary, syntax, and information completely familiar to the reader), the reading will be easy, perhaps even boring. If, on the other hand, the language used and the type or level of the knowledge explored are far beyond the reader's ability, he or she will be frustrated and unable to comprehend the text. In the first instance, the reader can use a top-down approach to understand the text. In the second case, even a careful bottom-up approach may not help the reader decode the text well enough to understand it. The challenge is to have students engage reading material in which the language and knowledge are encoded just a bit above their current ability—that is, just within their **zone of proximal development** (Vygotsky 1978).

Reading in the Primary Grades

The **Print Communication Model** attempts to show that reading with comprehension depends on several factors. Readers must contribute their knowledge of the world and language *to* the reading so that it interacts with the author's text structures and functions. Obviously, young children bring fewer understandings than do older children. It is the teacher's role to provide demonstrations and experiences that will help children bridge the gap between what they already know and what they still need to learn.

Chapter 8, on emergent literacy, discussed what we know about how children begin to understand the nature and functions of print in its various forms. Emergent literacy is a developmental process mediated by the child's sociolinguistic environment. Research shows overwhelmingly that children who are read to regularly at home also learn to read most easily at school. Their literacy experiences at home have fostered a basic awareness of important concepts essential to acquiring literacy. To review, these concepts include awareness of the purposes of written language, the nature and forms of written language, and basic speech-print relationships (including phonemic awareness).

What if the foundation of literacy has not been laid at home? Then the school must provide that foundation. Among other things, this implies the need in the primary grades (and especially preschool and kindergarten) for many **shared reading** experiences. In shared reading, the teacher or another more proficient adult reads appropriate print with children, including books, signs, labels, charts, and environmental print. Sharing of books (and especially large format or **big books**) is an especially important activity, inviting children to become aware of the structure of books, speech-print relationships, directional conventions, and story grammar. The scenarios that opened chapter 1 provide glimpses of shared-book teaching/learning experiences.

For children with a strong home literacy background, shared reading provides a natural extension of previous experience with print. For those not so fortunate, shared reading introduces the central literacy experience of story and the central literacy object—books. Shared reading further helps to develop the literacy knowledge that fosters emergent literacy understandings.

Other literacy experiences must be woven into the curriculum as well. Teachers can help children understand the many uses of print by providing pencils and crayons for writing, giving books for presents and prizes, pointing out letters and words on signs, teaching young children to recognize the letters of the alphabet, and helping children print their own names. Such activities have the added benefit of enhancing children's motivation to read.

Just as surrounding children with meaningful talk in a supportive environment invites them to speak, so environments rich in print and books, coupled with enthusiastic teachers who share their joy in reading, spur children to read.

Teaching Principles for Reading in the Primary Grades

Time for reading "Practice makes perfect" is one of those clichés we ignore precisely because it is a cliché. A cliché is often used to exhort us to do things that are supposedly good for us but that we do not much enjoy, such as practicing scales on the piano. Nevertheless, it is true that we get good at reading only when we do a lot of it. We learn to read, and to read better, by reading. Therefore, an essential pedagogic principle in primary (and middle) grades is that the school must provide time for reading if the students are to become proficient readers. School is probably the only significant cultural institution that both values reading *and* has a captive audience. True, our culture pays lip service to the value of reading, but a host of voices subvert that intent by directing youngsters' attention to other activities. Unless teachers consciously program significant blocks of time for sustained reading, children simply will not develop reading proficiency. Thus some of the most valuable time a school can schedule is schoolwide reading time, variously called Sustained Silent Reading (SSR) or Sustained, Quiet, Uninterrupted Reading Time (SQUIRT) or Drop Everything And Read (DEAR).

Variety of reading materials Beyond time for reading, schools need an abundance of interesting material to read. We have already discussed the importance of materials for literacy instruction (see chapter 4), but it bears repeating that a classroom must contain a variety of books and other print materials. Children need exposure to a diversity of excellent writing that suits their varied interests. Materials should represent a range of genres and topics at various levels of difficulty. Because the school's central library may be accessible to children only at specific times, it is essential to have well-stocked classroom libraries. For a primary classroom of twenty to twenty-five students, a collection of one hundred pieces of reading material is an absolute minimum. Furthermore, this material requires frequent change throughout the year. The school library can serve as a central repository from which to select materials for classrooms and should house more expensive, general-purpose references. Local public libraries (and children's librarians) are additional sources for fresh supplies of books and periodicals. Literacy teachers must be knowledgeable about **children's literature** so they can make intelligent and appropriate choices. For students and teachers with limited knowledge of children's literature, I recommend Post (2000) and Russell (1997) as useful starting points.[9]

Activities At the primary level, the following daily activities provide structure:

Recording Writing ideas on the board, chart paper, or pocket charts as an outgrowth of class discussions shows children that speech can be represented by print while providing self-generated material to read (and write). This is the heart of the **Language Experience Approach (LEA)** pioneered by Stauffer (1980) many years ago.

Oral reading Reading orally to the children at least twenty minutes each day gives them a valuable literary experience and helps them develop an ear for the sound of good reading. (Do not assign oral reading by individual children in round-robin fashion. See a critique of round-robin oral reading, below.)

Sustained silent reading Both children and teacher read silently for a period, providing the crucial practice discussed above.

Chanting and singing Besides teaching the sounds of language, chants and songs help develop phonemic awareness and make language easier to memorize. Such memorized material is easier to reread and provides a mental store from which to draw for writing.

Themes The teacher builds lessons around an organizing idea or theme, sometimes working on a single concept for several days or even weeks. See chapter 4 for additional information on integrated themes. Following a developmental sequence of language learning, exploration should move *from:*

- developing ideas orally through discussion in home dialects
- listening to the language of literature in books
- taking dictation from students
- encouraging independent writing by the students
- reading familiar material

to

- reading unfamiliar material

Of course, teachers must work out these activities in specific ways for their own classes.

Teaching Word Recognition

Fluent reading depends on rapid word recognition. Good readers recognize nearly all the words they encounter instantaneously and use most of their cognitive processing energies for comprehension (Stanovich 2000). Poor readers struggle for various reasons, but failure to recognize a large number of words on sight, coupled with limited strategies for decoding unknown words, acts as a major bottleneck to comprehension. Thus, helping students develop extensive sight vocabularies and effective word recognition strategies is an important task for all elementary and middle school teachers.

A Few Cautions

Before continuing, I hasten to add that recognizing words rapidly is only the beginning of reading comprehension. Recognition is not the same as comprehension. Being able to recognize words quickly (or sound them out rapidly) is of little use if the words are not already in the reader's listening vocabulary. Thus, a precursor to recognizing (and understanding) words in print is making sure the child knows the meaning of the words in their aural/oral context. Most words are **polysemous.** That is, they have many meanings depending on their grammatical placement in a sentence, their use (literal or figurative), and even their history. Take the word *dog* in the following sentences:

- My dog loves to chase rabbits.
- Why do you dog my every footstep?
- He returned my book in a dog-eared condition.
- I was upset when he referred to my girlfriend as a dog.

While it is essential to the reading of each sentence that readers recognize the word *dog*, doing so does not automatically guarantee an understanding of *dog* in all contexts. Therefore, it is of the utmost importance that the word recognition strategies described below are set within a meaningful framework.

One other important caution regarding word recognition needs emphasis. It is relatively easy to teach word recognition skills; what is more difficult is ensuring that those strategies are embedded and alive rather than technical and boring. With diligence, most teachers can master a set of word recognition teaching strategies and design classroom lessons around them. The danger is that these strategy lessons become *ends* in themselves rather than *means* of helping students become more fluent, competent readers. Besides tending to be deadly dull, disembedded instruction in word recognition can rob students of the time they need to *apply* their learning to real reading.

Two Key Resources

Many resources are available to help pre-service and in-service teachers develop word recognition ideas and skills. Below are two excellent resources that provide interesting and innovative approaches. They reflect current research on how children learn to read (and write) words, and they situate the teaching of word recognition strategies firmly within a larger semantic context. I have cited both before, but they bear mentioning again.

◊ Irene C. Fountas and Gay Su Pinnell. 1998. *Word matters: Teaching phonics and spelling in the reading/writing classroom.* Portsmouth, NH: Heinemann. Fountas and Pinnell are superb teacher educators who know how to provide information to students and teachers in clear and practical ways, using many examples in a framework that is thoroughly language-centered. The book helps teachers design ways to guide young readers and writers in the various strategic skills that contribute to competent word recognition. Chapter 8 deals explicitly with what the authors call "word solving" strategies.

◊ Patricia M. Cunningham. 2000. *Phonics they use: Words for reading and writing.* 3rd edition. Boston: Addison Wesley/Longman. Pat Cunningham has done the literacy teaching community a great favor by writing a short book that cuts to the heart of what is (and isn't) useful in the much-debated area of phonics instruction. The teaching strategies described here are thoroughly backed by the best research, as illustrated by a short chapter describing underlying rationale. The activities themselves are clearly described and developmentally appropriate, and they always keep meaning and contextual reading front and center. As noted in the introduction, the following five principles guide the book's suggested activities:

1. Because children are "active" learners, they should not just sit and listen or watch but should be actively engaged in doing something.
2. Because children are at various stages in their word knowledge, a good activity has to be multilevel—have something for everyone. All activities in *Phonics They Use* have various things that can be learned from the same activity, depending on what each student is ready to make sense of.
3. Because children have different personalities, learning preferences, and ways in which they learn most easily, activities include as much variety as possible—chanting, singing, rhythm, rhyme, drama, movement, games, and so on.
4. Jargon and rules should be kept to the absolute minimum required to communicate.
5. The sole purpose of learning to decode and spell words is to enable reading and writing. All activities stress transfer to reading and writing. Phonics activities are short and focused so that children spend most of their language arts time engaged in real reading and writing (Cunningham 2000, xi).

Cunningham's concluding appendix, "Phonics No One Can Use (Getting Ready for the Teacher's Phonics Test)," is alone worth the price of the book and points out the uselessness of much of what passes for phonics knowledge.

Because the issue of teaching phonics is so important, I offer two additional helpful resources on this topic:

◊ Dorothy S. Strickland. 1998. *Teaching phonics today: A primer for educators.* Newark, DE: International Reading Association.

◊ Karin L. Dahl, Patricia L. Scharer, Lora L. Lawson, and Patricia R. Grogan. 2001. *Rethinking phonics: Making the best teaching decisions.* Portsmouth, NH: Heinemann.

Word Recognition Teaching Strategies Pinnell and Fountas (1998) provide a useful list of the strategies children must develop to become good word solvers. These strategies are classified under a few basic headings:

Teaching high-frequency words High-frequency words are also known as **sight words**, but that term is confusing as it has at least three meanings. The term *sight words* refers to *the, is, that,* and other words that occur with very high frequency. The phrase also refers to words such as *of* and *one* that can't be learned through phonics but need to be memorized and learned by sight. Finally, *sight words* refers to the fact that good readers recognize almost all words immediately.

High-frequency words are those core words that make up a very high percentage of the words in running text. It often surprises people to know that only about one hundred frequently occurring words account for almost sixty percent of all the words they are likely to meet in print. Five hundred words account for about eighty percent of printed English (Thomas 1979). Certainly, at the outset of learning to read, children should come to recognize a core of these high-frequency words. Pinnell and Fountas (1998) provide appendixes listing the twenty-five, fifty, one hundred, and five hundred most frequently occurring words in English, coupled with ways to teach them.[10]

Teaching phonics Phonics is a way of teaching word recognition (and spelling) that stresses symbol-sound relationships. It is important to distinguish phonics from **phonemics,** an aspect of the science of linguistics that studies the patterns of relations among phonemes in a language. Similarly, phonics is not **phonetic analysis**, a linguistics term for classifying individual speech sounds. Phonics and phonic analysis are *not* scientific disciplines; rather, they are *diverse ways* of coming to terms with the alphabetic principle of the English language.

Recall from chapter 5 that the *alphabetic principle* refers to the fact that the graphemes (letters) of written English represent (in a complex fashion) the phonemes, or distinctive sounds, of oral English. That phonics represents not *a way* but *diverse ways* of relating letters and letter combinations to sounds, and vice versa, is clear when one considers the many types of phonics instruction that exist. Harris and Hodges (1995) list the following types: analytic, cluster, deductive, explicit, extrinsic, intrinsic, implicit, inductive, synthetic, and whole-word (186). The two main types of phonics are **analytic phonics** and **synthetic phonics**. In the former, the teacher presents whole words that are then broken down into their constituent sounds. In the latter, the student learns the sounds represented by letters and letter combinations, and then learns to blend these sounds to pronounce words. Numerous arguments exist to support both approaches. In addition, debate continues about whether phonics should be taught directly (explicitly) or indirectly (implicitly).

Whatever one may say about phonics, it is not simple. Frank Smith (1994) cites research showing that a body of 20,000 common English words requires more than 300 different spelling-to-sound correspondences to account for correct pronunciations. The spelling-to-sound correspondence of 6,000 of the most common English words requires about 166 rules and 45 exceptions, the exceptions accounting for 600 of the most common words in English such as *the, was,* and *of.* At best, correspondence rules have about a seventy-five percent chance of being correct if there is but one sound in the word. The average word contains about four sounds, pushing the error rate considerably higher. Using phonics rules, pronunciation for these 6,000 common words is correct only about 25 percent of the time.

A recent 189-page programmed textbook (Hull and Fox 1998) designed to help teachers learn the phonics rules for reading contains 14 pages of terminology, 60 pages on consonants, 48 pages on vowels, 18 pages on syllabication and accent rules, and 13 pages on onsets and rimes (also known as **spelling patterns** or **phonograms**). While teachers need to know more than their students do, it is not clear how such knowledge will be useful to them as they attempt to help students become better at decoding words.

The book by Cunningham cited above acknowledges the complexity of the rules needed to account for the common spelling patterns in English, particularly vowel pronunciations. Cunningham reduces this complexity by focusing on research by Marilyn Adams (1990) supporting the view that readers decode words by applying spelling patterns from the words they know. Thus, a reader who knows the word *made* will recognize that the vowel sound in the word *blade* is the same as in *fade, shade,* and *grade.* Concentrating on the sounds of most common spelling patterns or word families (referred to as **rimes** by linguists) and the consonants that precede them (known as **onsets**) makes the basics of phonics quite manageable. Figure 11-3 lists 37 high-frequency spelling patterns that allow children to read and spell more than 500 common, high frequency words.

Figure 11-3: Thirty-seven high-frequency spelling patterns with key words (Cunningham 2000, 94)

ack (black)	ail (pail)	ain (train)	ake (cake)	ale (whale)
ame (game)	an (pan)	ank (bank)	ap (cap)	ash (trash)
at (cat)	ate (skate)	aw (claw)	ay (tray)	eat (meat)
ell (shell)	est (nest)	ice (rice)	de (bride)	ick (brick)
ight (night)	ill (hill)	in (pin)	ine (nine)	ing (king)
ink (pink)	ip (ship)	it (hit)	ock (sock)	oke (poke)
op (mop)	ore (store)	ot (hot)	uck (truck)	ug (bug)
ump (jump)	unk (skunk)			

Figure 11-4 provides information about the major beginning consonant letters that children need to learn (single consonants, digraphs, and blends).

Figure 11-4: Key beginning letters and their sounds (Cunningham 2000, 90)

- Single consonants: b c d f g h j (including the /j/ sound in *gym)* k l m n p r s (including the /s/ sound in *city*) t u v w y z
- Digraphs (two letters, one sound): sh ch wh th
- Other two-letter, one-sound combinations: ph wr kn qu
- Blends (beginning letters blended together, sometimes called clusters): bl br cl dr fl gl pl pr sc scr sk sl sm sn sp spr st str sw tr

Note: Do *not* use terms like *digraph* with young children as it confuses them and takes their concentration away from learning and using the sounds of the letters.

Cunningham's book provides a multitude of helpful and meaningful teaching activities for instructing children in these and many other useful decoding skills. The essential point to remember is that phonics is a *means* to an end, not the end itself. By the end of the primary grades, children should have internalized most of the graphophonic knowledge they need in order to recognize most of the words they will meet in their reading. While instruction in vocabulary should continue throughout children's schooling, explicit instruction in phonics should diminish greatly after grade 3.[11]

Evaluating Primary Reading

Assessment should focus on the individual child in the normal classroom context. For this reason, I do not favor the use of standardized tests, which are primarily useful in assessing groups or programs. Several tools are available to help teachers put together as complete a record as possible for each child.

Early in kindergarten or grade 1, it is useful to get a sense of a child's concept of the printed word. Helpful resources are Marie Clay's previously cited "Concepts about Print Text" in *The Early Detection of Reading Difficulties* (Clay 1979a) and Lois Bader's

Reading and Language Inventory (Bader 1998b, 2002). These resources provide ways to assess whether a child knows how books work, can identify words, letters, and punctuation marks, and is already reading.

The best gauge of individual literacy progress is the child's own work. Teachers should keep a **portfolio** for each student, containing dated work samples. On the inside of the portfolio file folder, they can write anecdotal observations of the child's literacy activities. (Teachers can simplify this process by keeping gummed labels handy at all times for recording dated observations, then pasting the labels in each child's file at the end of the day.)

Teachers also need to create an audio record of each child's reading. The student should choose something familiar, while the teacher chooses something just slightly above the child's ability.[12] Tape the reading in a relaxed private or semiprivate setting, capturing a five-to-seven-minute sample. (Parents or older student volunteers can also collect this information.) Analyze the reading in a manner similar to an **informal reading inventory (IRI)**,[13] using a simplified **miscue analysis** to determine whether the child is reading for meaning and to analyze the child's response to graphophonic and syntactic cues.

A related strategy for assessing children's interaction with print, quicker to administer than an IRI, is the **running record.** Developed by Marie Clay (1993) as part of the *Reading Recovery* program, the running record involves periodically listening to a child read material at instructional level. Using a lined paper, make a checkmark for each word read correctly, and note miscued words as follows:

- Write substitutions above the line.
- Mark self-corrections as *SC.*
- Use a dash to mark no response.
- Use a *T* when the child is told the word.
- Use an *A* to indicate that the child asked for assistance.
- Mark a tangled reading as *TTA* (Try that again).
- Mark a repetition with an *R.*

Analyze each miscue as for an IRI. To score the running record, calculate the percentage of errors, and divide the number of errors by the number of words in the selection subtracted from 100 percent. Word recognition at ninety-five to one hundred percent accuracy indicates this selection is at the child's **independent reading level**; ninety to ninety-four percent accuracy signals the **instructional reading level**; and less than ninety percent accuracy indicates the passage is at the child's **frustration reading level**. Pinnell and Fountas (1998), annotated above, detail how to take and analyze running records.

Keeping a log of each book a child reads independently, noting the title and date read, is also helpful for tracking reading development. The log is an essential component of the portfolio.

These methods of assessing primary children's literacy development should provide rich information that is helpful in determining children's strengths and weaknesses, information teachers can share with parents through report cards and parent-teacher conferences.

Reading in the Middle School Grades

Many children in the middle school grades have reached a stage of reading proficiency at or beyond their grade placement. Others are not reading at grade level. In fact, the better the teaching of reading in a school, the greater the spread of reading proficiency as children move up the grade levels. Why is this so? Just as children in a given class vary in shoe size, height, and hair color, so too they vary in learning ability. With good teaching, the "bright" students advance very quickly in reading proficiency; the "slower" children progress less rapidly.

Over time, the spread in proficiency increases; already by grade 5, it is common to have children ranging in reading proficiency from a grade 1 to a grade 8 level. In any heterogeneous class, approximately one-third of the students read within one to two years of their current grade level, about one-third do not read as well as this, and one-third read better. This is not tragic; it is just the way humans are. We must stop trying to treat all students as if they were identical. They are of equal value but not of equal ability. Homogeneous grouping schemes do not alter this fact.

Since God has seen fit to create children with differences, including differences in learning aptitude, we are obliged to honor and work with those differences rather than trying to eliminate or ignore them. An important aspect of the "communion of the saints" is organizing classrooms and classroom instruction so that we can practice such communion. Practicing communion, however, requires recognizing differences in our classrooms, including differences in academic ability.

Before examining ways to accommodate both individual and group needs in the reading of middle schoolers, we will look briefly at the continuing need for skill instruction in reading at this level. Again, we stress that most of this skill teaching should be done in the context of real reading (and writing), although there is certainly a place for well-conceived explicit mini lessons as well.[14]

Skill Instruction in the Middle School Grades

Dealing with "big words" and vocabulary instruction *Big words* is a general term for multisyllabic words that often frighten readers simply because of their length. It is important for children to realize that big words usually contain meaningful smaller components that, if recognized and learned, can reduce the fear of bigness. Good readers quickly decode big words by searching through their store of known words to find other words with the same parts in the same places; that is, they engage in a form of **structural analysis.**

Chapter 4 of Cunningham's book contains useful information and teaching strategies to help middle graders deal with big words and expand their meaning vocabularies in general. Included are helpful lessons on common prefixes, suffixes, and roots that avoid drill and rote memorization. Many commercial spelling programs are, in fact, mostly vocabulary development programs, more useful for that purpose than for teaching correct spelling.

Comprehension Strategies There is a tendency to suppose that once students have well-developed word recognition skills, comprehension automatically follows. Yet many teachers know significant numbers of students who can decode and recognize individual words and can even read fluently but still have only a superficial understanding of the material.[15] American researcher and educator Michael Pressley has demonstrated that there is a significant place for specific comprehension instruction in the language arts curriculum. He and his associates refer to this learning as "cognitive strategy instruction" (Pressley and Woloshyn 1995). Such instruction includes summarizing, mental imagery, generating and answering questions, question-answering strategies, look-backs, question-answer relationships, story grammar, and activating prior knowledge. Many of these strategies not only enhance comprehension in language arts but also deserve use in a wide range of subject/discipline areas in the elementary and middle school curriculum.

Comprehension strategy instruction really teaches thinking skills. Its success depends on teachers' not only knowing the strategies but also implementing them in specific ways across the curriculum. Teaching a strategy once and expecting students to use it consistently is a vain hope. Teachers must demonstrate the strategies frequently and encourage students to use them over an extended period.[16] The following list provides a number of key resources for such instruction:

- ◊ Thomas G. Devine. 1987. *Teaching study skills: A guide for teachers.* 2nd ed. Boston: Allyn & Bacon.
- ◊ Stephanie Harvey and Anne Goudvis. 2000. *Strategies that work: Teaching comprehension to enhance understanding.* York, ME: Stenhouse Publishers.
- ◊ John D. McNeil. 1987. *Reading comprehension: New directions for classroom practice.* 2nd ed. Glenview, IL: Scott Foresman.

◊ Michael Pressley and Vera Woloshyn. 1995. *Cognitive strategy instruction that really improves children's academic performance.* 2nd ed. Cambridge, MA: Brookline Books.

◊ Robert J. Tierney and John E. Readence. 2000. *Reading strategies and practices: A compendium.* 5th ed. Boston: Allyn & Bacon.

◊ Barbara J. Walker. 2000. *Diagnostic teaching of reading: Techniques for instruction and assessment.* 4th ed. Columbus, OH: Merrill/Prentice Hall.

Personalized/Guided Reading

The best way to recognize and cope with individual reading differences within a middle school classroom is to allow for a great deal of **individualized** or **personalized reading.** Personalized reading is a structured approach that focuses on reading and discussing self-selected materials. This approach has the following features:

- Students select their own reading material from a variety of leveled books, with guidance and suggestions from the teacher to extend their interests and tastes.
- They participate in regularly scheduled pupil-teacher conferences that may include a small group of students who are reading the same book or material on the same topic.
- They use trade books, magazines, and other popular materials, including basal reader selections.

During conferences, the students' skill needs are noted, and the teacher provides on-the-spot instruction or incorporates those concepts later in regular small groups or whole-class learning.

Implementing a personalized/guided reading program may be somewhat intimidating to new teachers, or teachers who fear they may not be able to provide enough guidance and instruction without a basal program's pacing and sequencing of skills. As noted above, the best way for students to improve their reading skill is by reading often, widely, and for sustained periods. A personalized reading program sets the stage for just such reading. Despite its many benefits, personalized reading need not take large amounts of teacher planning time. Teachers simply need leveled reading materials for self-selection, plus a simple device to track student reading and conference outcomes.

To implement a personalized reading approach, teachers must first establish a classroom library and, if possible, comfortable areas for reading. They then set aside about thirty to forty-five minutes per day for reading and conferencing. Personalized/guided reading time is thus also sustained silent reading time. During this time, all students read their materials, and the teacher schedules five- to ten-minute conferences. Students come to an area set aside for small-group conferencing, bringing with them whatever they are reading. At the conferences, the teacher and student may choose some of the following activities:

- The student briefly summarizes what he or she has read since the last conference.
- The teacher asks questions to check the student's general reading comprehension.
- The student reads aloud a short portion of familiar material (selected by the teacher or the student), giving the teacher an opportunity to make an informal analysis of reading skills.
- The student brings to the conference any unfamiliar words or phrases in the reading, and the teacher works with the student on ways to discover their meanings.
- During the discussion, the teacher notes problems (word attack, vocabulary, fluency, etc.) to deal with later in small-group instruction and suggests skill strategies or activities for the student to complete before the next conference.
- If the student needs a new book, the teacher describes possible choices, discussing new topics to explore or further reading on the same topic. In this way, the teacher exercises a guiding role, broadening and deepening a student's reading experiences.

To track activities and progress in this personalized reading approach, teachers need to devise simple forms. Serving as a chronological record of students' reading performance and progress, these forms also become the basis for evaluating students and for reporting to parents. Fountas and Pinnell's *Guided Reading: Good First Teaching for All Children* (1996) provides helpful forms and assessment strategies.

Literature Units: Novel Studies

Although our teaching must recognize and allow for individual differences and interests in reading, we cannot forget that the classroom is a community. One of the joys of reading is sharing and discussing common literary selections such as short stories or novels. Teachers in the middle school grades should incorporate a few shared novel studies in each year's language arts curriculum, perhaps related to themes explored in other curricular areas. Below is a basic format and teaching strategies for novel studies, adapted from Den Boer (1996).

Novel reading should be an ongoing activity in every grade, using a mix of independent reading, read-aloud sessions, and focused novel studies. None of these approaches is exclusive, and they often occur simultaneously. Therefore, it is important to remember that the following approaches do not necessarily replace consistent independent reading.

Ideally, a class completes a novel study within four or, at most, five weeks. The approaches presented here can be arranged in a variety of ways and repeated throughout a year, depending on the nature of a class and its curricular requirements. One of the goals of a novel study is to help children develop as readers, internalizing all the strategies that allow for a deeper and more meaningful reading experience. For this reason, the novel study approaches are intentionally presented in a specific order.

The first teaching novel study is planned as a **scaffolding unit** in which the teacher models a response-oriented reading process by monitoring the students' reading and response.

The second and third teaching units gradually enable students to internalize and take ownership of the reading strategies so they can apply them with increasing effectiveness as independent readers. The fourth teaching unit presents structured independent reading, using the journal writing that is emphasized in the other three units.

Novel No. 1: The teacher reads a novel aloud to the class.

Setting the stage/prereading Before reading a novel, the teacher needs to set the stage, particularly for those children whose background differs from that of most in the class. Discussing children's prior knowledge and experiences in relation to the situation of the novel sets the stage most effectively. Children come to a book with a personal reservoir of experiences and knowledge that plays a major role in their reading experience and their responses to the text. Enabling them to tap that reservoir before reading helps them make links between their own lives and the novel. Establishing these links also enhances their reading experience, helping them to reflect on it more meaningfully and consciously. In other words, those links provide a familiar and secure frame of reference that they may otherwise ignore or attempt to reject. This is especially true for children who have had little opportunity to express their personal responses to literature.

As the novel is read Because the teacher reads this novel aloud, it can be one or two grade levels above the average reading level in the class. The novel should be read every day. Each student should have a Reading Response Journal. The following procedure is used.

1. Before beginning, students write their speculations about the novel's title in their journals, answering questions such as these:
    - What does the title suggest to you?
    - What kind of story are you expecting?

Students share their reflections first in small groups, then with the whole class. The teacher may want to record those comments on a class chart for future reference.

2. The teacher reads one chapter (or a section if chapters are too long). Students respond in their journals. Depending on their experience in writing responses to literature, they may need a few prompts, such as these:
   - List any questions you have at this point.
   - Predict what will happen in the next chapter.
   - What are you wondering about so far?

   Students share their written responses in small groups and with the whole class. The teacher records their questions on a class chart that will be ongoing as the novel is read. It is important for the teacher also to keep a journal and share his or her responses. As part of the community of readers, the teacher needs to model the reading-responding process for the students.

3. After a second reading session, the students respond in their journals again. This time, they are encouraged to reflect on their previous questions:
   - Were they answered?
   - How were they answered?
   - What happened to your predictions?

   Students also continue to ask new questions and generate new predictions. The whole class checks the "class" questions, discussing which questions were answered. Predictions will arise out of the questions. Answered and unanswered questions are discussed in small groups and by the whole class.

4. Throughout the reading of the novel, the students and teacher continue to generate questions and predictions individually, discussing them in small-group and whole-class settings. The class reviews the chart questions each day, making the chart the guiding tool for discussion.

As students become more comfortable with generating written responses, the teacher encourages them to extend their responses beyond questions and predictions. A list of "journal starters," posted in full view, helps students focus on specific responses. It is essential that responses are always shared with partners, small groups, and the whole class. The teacher should continue to include her own responses and questions. Besides modeling the reading-response process, teacher participation introduces questions that reflect the goals of the novel study or extend the responses and questions of the students. Even before a given reading session, the teacher may want to set the stage by asking a question for the students to reflect on.

Post-reading A number of post-reading activities help shape student responses:

1. Students list unanswered questions in their logs, share them with others, and add any additional questions suggested by other students.

2. Students add any unanswered questions to the list on the class chart. These are used for additional group and whole-class discussions.

3. Follow-up discussions and activities arise as much as possible out of the unanswered questions generated by the students and the teacher. The teacher strives to use the questions as bridges between student responses and her own goals for the unit. Where this is not possible, the teacher ensures that her own questions are added to the class list. Important here is the teacher's role in guiding and encouraging students to reflect and discuss issues that deal with Christian perspective and the development of Christian discernment. In addition, these deliberate plans can initiate further in-depth study or an activity relating to a particular concept or literary element. It is advisable to focus on a limited number of concepts or literary structures (those that are strongest in that novel) rather than attempting to deal with all the concepts and lit-

erary structures in every novel. Students will learn more effectively if they can concentrate on one area in depth rather than many areas superficially. Of even greater concern, a comprchensive novel study would become long and tedious, taking away the sheer enjoyment of the literature. It is important, however, to ensure that all literary elements are taught over an entire year.

Novel No. 2: Students in each small group read the same novel.

Note: In this novel study, the suggestions presented earlier for "setting the stage" are replaced with several "prereading" strategies since the small groups are reading different novels.

1. Students select a novel from a list of five or six, sharing why they prefer certain titles to others and what they predict the novels will be about.
2. Students choose again, indicating their first and second choices and basing them on a brief synopsis of each novel.
3. Alternative Strategy: The teacher reads a small introductory section of each novel. After each reading, the students write a response, which can be general (like/dislike, predict, wonder ...) or in reply to a specific question (e.g., What kind of a character do you think X is? How do you think the setting of this novel will play an important part in the story?). After these brief readings and their initial responses, the students share which books they prefer, and why. Their first and second choices determine the novel groups, which should be no larger than five students each.

During reading Students read and respond in their journals every day until they have completed the novel. Every day, they meet with their group to complete these tasks:

1. Each member reads his or her last journal response.
2. Any member may respond to those ideas.
3. Groups review their previously asked questions, determin-

ing which questions have been answered (checked off) and how. Questions might include, What do we know now that we didn't know before? Have some of our previous answers/predictions changed?

4. The group records new questions on a communal sheet and discusses possible answers. Students should be encouraged to share their thoughts and opinions openly and freely.

5. Each group decides how far each member should read for the next day. These plans should be flexible among groups but within predetermined parameters so that groups do not read many chapters in one sitting.

Post-reading Groups are likely to complete their novels at different times. A group that finishes can begin follow-up activities, which will differ according to which novel they read.

1. When a group completes a novel, the teacher collects the student journals and responds by commenting or "talking" to them in the margins and at the end. The teacher limits remarks to genuine dialogue, such as items of interest, questions, shared reflections, and surprises. At all times, the students are affirmed and/or nudged to extend and deepen their insights. The teacher includes no value judgments, corrections, or "received interpretations." These response journals provide a window through which a teacher can view how students are engaging with the text, glimpsing their insights, their frustrations, and their wonderings.

2. Follow-up activities should not begin until after students get their journals back, so that their responses and questions can be bridges for further in-depth study. Alternatively, the group can begin reading another novel by the same author or another book (fiction, nonfiction, poetry) that relates in some way to the novel just read.

3. The teacher returns the journals to the students. Students reread their entries and the teacher's comments.

4. In each group, discussions could continue based on:
   - unanswered questions
   - a question that the teacher selects from the students' journals as a bridge to a follow-up activity
   - issues generated from categorized unanswered questions, planned over a number of days
   - plans to present their book to another group
   - a combination of the above

5. Students can be regrouped so that each member has read a different book and presents a "you should/shouldn't read this book" to the others in the group. There are creative ways of doing this kind of book sharing by brainstorming within groups (see Atwell 1998).

6. In group discussions, each group or each student chooses to represent new understandings and knowledge in one of a number of forms. Again, the students should focus on just one or two concepts or elements. To set the scene, teachers should explain choices carefully and relate them meaningfully to each novel being read.

Novel No. 3: Each student reads a class novel independently.

Reading Refer to the Reading section under Novel No.1 for suggestions to prepare for reading:

1. Each student reads the novel at his or her own speed. Goals are set for each day, but students may read ahead.

2. Students write in their response journals after each chapter. If chapters are very long, a page number limit should be set (perhaps no more than 10 to 12 pages per entry). Every response entry should be dated. Students may use the "journal starters" again, if they wish.

3. The teacher reads the novel and responds in his or her journal at the same time.

4. At the beginning of each class, the teacher checks and notes where the students are reading to make sure they are keep-

ing up and responding regularly. Consistent reading and responding will not only contribute to the learning but will assist in evaluation.

Post-Reading

1. As students complete their reading, they hand in their journals. The teacher "talks" to the students in the margins. Again, teacher comments should be nonevaluative and affirming while nudging students to deeper and broader thinking.
2. The teacher returns the response journals. Students reread their responses and the teacher's comments. As they reread, they place checks by the answered questions and circle the unanswered ones.
3. Students form groups of three. They select several of their unanswered questions to use as the basis for this first discussion of the novel. They should be encouraged to use their journal entries and the text. At the end of their discussion, each group lists and submits the unanswered questions they feel are important. These could be recorded on a class chart.
4. As before, use unanswered questions and student responses as much as possible to initiate follow-up discussions and activities. Questions can lead first to individual, then small-group and finally whole-class discussions. Each small group can take a different question, discuss it, and share the results with the whole class for further discussion. Continued journal writing should be encouraged.
5. See Novel No. 1, Post-Reading, for follow-up strategies and activities.

Novel No. 4: Each student chooses a novel for independent (personalized) reading.

After students complete several response-based novel studies, they can use their response journals in conjunction with the independent reading protocol discussed above. This should happen for four to five weeks. During this phase of independent reading, the students and the teacher keep up a written dialogue through the students' journals. In this format, the teacher responds to individual students' journal entries regularly rather than only at the end as was the case in the novel studies presented above. The format proceeds as follows:

1. Students choose a novel from a large classroom supply of novels or short stories and/or from the school library. While reading the novel, students should not read other materials, such as magazines, but focus on literature.
2. Students are required to write to the teacher in their journals twice a week. They can select their own days to write, and they may write more often.
3. The teacher writes back to each student after each journal entry. In other words, the teacher and student have an ongoing dialogue about the literature during the four-to-five-week session. Dialogue between the teacher and student should be genuine, in that the teacher is not evaluating but is sharing knowledge, responses, and personal reactions just as the students do. To help the students develop as readers, the teacher nudges and encourages them to ponder different angles, to ask new questions, to look "deeper and wider." (See Nancie Atwell's *In the Middle* [Atwell 1987, 1998] for more detailed information on dialogue journals in an independent reading program.)

Reading Workshop

The novel study strategies advocated above fit very well with a **reading workshop** approach to reading instruction. A workshop is both a place and an activity.[17] As a place, a workshop is a space filled with tools specific to a craft. It is a place for purposeful activity, culminating in useful and aesthetically pleasing artifacts. For example, most of us can conjure up an image of a furniture maker's workshop filled with lathes, drill presses, planes, saws, chisels, and other hand tools. Smells of various woods and varnishes fill the room. Standing about are items of furniture in various stages of production, from raw lumber to sanded and polished pieces. Although there is clutter, it is purposeful clutter. We sense that the craftsperson knows just where everything is and why. In addition to the master craftsperson, one or more apprentices learn by doing under the watchful eye and skilled guidance of the master.

A workshop is also an activity. Teachers are familiar with such activity from participating in various education workshops. A good workshop uses discussion and demonstration to provide intensive study and application of a particular educational concept or teaching technique.

In both senses of the word, *workshop* implies productive busyness—people and materials coming together to achieve some worthwhile purpose. Classrooms ought to be workshops in both senses, particularly in middle school and above as students develop proficiencies beyond the introductory level.

What is the reality in many middle school classrooms? About fifteen years ago, Nancie Atwell (1987), who pioneered the reading and writing workshop approach, lamented that the American middle and secondary school status quo presents:

> ... a bleak picture revealing little evidence of the collaboration, involvement, and excitement in acquiring knowledge that our students crave—that all humans crave. When I listen to my junior high students, their message is, "We're willing to learn. We like to find out about things we didn't know before. But make it make sense. Let us learn together. And be involved and excited so we can be involved and excited." When I listen to educators talk about junior high, I hear a different message. I'm told that my role is to keep the lid on, to consolidate "basic skills" covered in the elementary grades, to prepare my students for high school, regardless of the logic or appropriateness of the high school program in question." (Atwell 1987)

Since Atwell made these comments, the junior high school structure to which she refers has, in many school jurisdictions, evolved to middle school (Stronks 1990). Yet visits to many Christian middle school classrooms in both Canada and the United States convince me that not that much has changed in the fifteen years since Atwell wrote these words. While kindergarten and primary students are often busily engaged in a variety of self- and teacher-selected activities, middle schoolers have far less independence in their learning. While primary students often have opportunity for movement and personal involvement in classrooms alive with color, excitement, and productive learning, middle schoolers are largely confined to individual desks, completing teacher-directed activities from textbooks and worksheets. An air of passivity pervades many middle school classrooms. Language arts or English is a content course. It mostly involves listening to teachers talk *about* English, writing an occasional essay assigned by the teacher, reading assigned literature texts, memorizing definitions, correcting errors of usage and punctuation in English handbooks, and drilling assorted "facts" about static, inaccurate versions of English grammar. There is little of the purposeful and engaged busy-ness of the workshop described above.

Fortunately, I have also visited Christian middle school classrooms that provide a refreshing alternative to the largely passive teacher/textbook–dominated scenario sketched above. Many have adopted some form of a reading/writing workshop. Briefly, reader's workshop (or reading workshop) requires students to "engage in reading and responding to trade books (in contrast to textbooks). It includes small-group discussions with the teacher to learn or review key concepts about reading and literature" (Harris and Hodges 1995, 206). Reading workshop gives students time for reading, ownership of reading, and response to reading. The entire reading program can adopt a reading workshop approach, or such an approach can be a significant component. In the latter case, three 40-minute periods each week may be devoted to reading workshops. Students are expected to bring a book to class, preferably one that tells a story (e.g., novels, biographies, histories), and read (and write) for the entire period. Students keep a **dialogue journal** in which they write notes to their teacher and to classmates in a **reader response** mode (explained below). The teacher and other students respond to each other's letters and notes. As a bare minimum, a student is usually required to write one response letter per week and a letter to the teacher at least once every two weeks. Whole-class sharing sessions occur regularly as well, giving students time to share with or read to others in class.

Throughout the term, as part of an individualized reading program, the teacher conducts short (five- to fifteen-minute) mini lessons based on these discussions, as well as on conferencing, to help students develop and apply skills and knowledge about reading and writing. Mini lesson topics can foster reading skills such as skimming, scanning, oral reading, and increasing reading speed. They can also deal with content knowledge about story, grammar, and elements such as setting, characterization, plot, conflict, narrative voice, theme, or any other method that writers use to effect a particular response.

Reader's workshop is essentially an extension of personalized and individualized reading as described above. What this approach implies is student freedom to choose what reading to explore, within a specified structure. As Atwell says: "Freedom to choose and time to read in school are not luxuries. They are the wellsprings of student literacy and literary appreciation" (1987, 21).

It is also crucial for students to read for pleasure, because wide reading stimulates good writing. As students experience diverse genres and author styles, they become literary borrowers. The resonating echoes of their reading return, often unknowingly, in their own writing. Atwell (1987) puts it this way:

> Students who seldom read for pleasure, seldom choose their own books, or seldom encounter texts that capture their imaginations or satisfy their needs will not become literary borrowers. Elementary school children who read only the voiceless committee prose of basals don't borrow, nor do middle and secondary school students who read only the prescribed canon of anthologized "classics." It is what captivates students as readers that inspires them as writers. (241)

We need to organize our middle school teaching in ways that help our students take more responsibility for their own learning. Reader's workshop will go quite some way toward liberating the middle school reading curriculum from the oppressive strictures of passive reception. It's an approach that demands teachers who model the importance and usefulness of the subjects they teach in their own lives, demonstrating how they learn and what they know of their fields of study. Teachers must invite students inside academia by showing that *inside* is a worthwhile and interesting place to be. In sum, we need what Christian philosopher Nicholas Wolterstorff (1980) has called a "Christian responsibility view of learning."

Concluding Issues

Reader-Response Theory

What happens when a reader reads a text? The *Print Communication Model* (Figure 11-2) suggests that reading with comprehension is not simply a passive intake of author intent on the part of the reader. Rather, good reading is an active process requiring the reader to incorporate background knowledge, use appropriate comprehension strategies, and monitor understanding.

One important aspect of background knowledge is understanding how to approach texts so as to obtain meaning from and bring meaning to them. This is a matter of the reader's **stance** toward a text. Louise Rosenblatt, an American educator and literary theorist, developed reader-response theory to suggest that a reader's stance toward a text will largely determine the transaction that occurs between the reader and the text (1978, 1985, 1991). Rosenblatt argues that readers adopt different stances or approaches toward text depending on the nature of the text and their purpose for reading it. She posits that a reader's response can fall on a continuum from **efferent reading** on one end to **aesthetic reading** on the other. A reader with an efferent stance will focus attention on the specific information that can be taken from the text. The reader with an aesthetic stance will focus on the "lived-through experience" of the text, the thoughts, images, and emotions it evokes. This latter response is concerned with the personal nature of the reading experience rather than with retaining specific information. Rosenblatt suggests that different texts require different transactions. A writer crafts a poem or novel primarily to evoke an aesthetic response, while a stock market report clearly has an efferent function. Unfortunately, school instruction in the language arts tends to turn every reading transaction into an efferent one. Seldom are students invited to determine their own stance toward a poem or a novel by surrendering to the text, "living through" the reading and allowing it to evoke personal meaning and responses. Instead, the transaction is directed to a predetermined end by text-based activities and right-answer questions, whether framed by the teacher or included at the end of the reading.

So often, our primary desire to make sure our students "get it right" violates the stance that a piece of literature calls for. Yet it is important to realize that the choice between an efferent and an aesthetic stance is not either-or but a position along a continuum. Both responses may be desirable, depending on the circumstance. For instance, a reader may "live through" the saga of Joseph and his brothers as related in the Old Testament (Genesis 37–45), at the same time noting its rich depiction of Egyptian life.

Rosenblatt asserts, however, that in education we too often neglect the aesthetic stance, allowing it to be overshadowed by efferent purpose-setting, efferent instruction, and efferent assessment. I tend to agree. My advice to students in my children's literature classes is to "read first of all with your heart, and then reread with your head." That is, I strongly urge my students first to take the stance of a lover as they read the literature and then, after that first wholehearted reading, return to the text with a more analytic, efferent stance. That subsequent efferent analysis, including the sharing of other readers' views, can also deepen their aesthetic response.

Christian teachers seem particularly reluctant to allow aesthetic responses from their students because of their strong sense of responsibility for guiding them to truth or "the Truth." Far better to take our cue from Jesus who, we are told, "did not say anything to them without using a parable" (Mark 4:34a). When asked why this was the case (see Mark 4:10–13), Jesus makes it clear that He wants His hearers to struggle with the meanings of His parables for themselves. In essence, He tells parables not to make truths easier to understand but more difficult. He wants His listeners to attempt a heartfelt understanding before attempting an interpretation.

Clearly, no one comes to a text with a blank mind. We are social beings with particular cultural experiences. Each brings both unique and common schemata to the task of reading. This brief discussion of reader-response theory alerts the teacher to the need for a gradual relinquishing of control over students' meaning-making, to allow the Holy Spirit to do His work in their hearts and lives as well. We may be the primary guide to an enriched understanding of the landscape painted by the poem or story, but we should allow our students to make at least the initial discovery of this new country.

Round-Robin Reading: One Bird That Should Become Extinct

Earlier in this chapter, I commented that teachers should avoid the oral reading practice known as "round-robin reading." In round-robin reading, also called around-the-group oral reading, individual students take turns reading aloud while classmates follow the reader silently. Condemned as poor teaching practice for more than sixty years (Gilbert 1940), this practice continues relentlessly, not only in reading and language arts lessons but in all subjects. The round-robin reading strategy is assumed to be educationally sound in that each pupil in the group supposedly both sees the words and hears the correct (or corrected) response, thus having the silent response to the stimulus words reinforced.

What is wrong with round-robin reading? First, there's the obvious problem: Not all students are reading along with the oral reader. Some read ahead, while some daydream or look out the window. What's more, round-robin reading provides a poor model for those supposedly following along. As early as 1940, Gilbert clearly demonstrated significant concerns about the eye movements of students silently following oral reading. When silent readers try to keep pace with oral reading, particularly by students less able than themselves, they tend to employ more **fixations**, more **regressions**, and longer pauses than when they proceed at their own rates.[18] The slow reader is frustrated in trying to keep up with the good reader, and the fluent reader is annoyed at having to adapt to the slow reader's pattern.

Furthermore, there is considerable evidence that the characteristics of oral reading are considerably different from those of silent reading. One of these characteristics is **eye-voice span.** A skilled oral reader's eyes must run four or five words ahead of his or her voice. When reading aloud, pronunciation as well as the intonation depends as much on what lies ahead as on what has gone before. Thus, fluent oral reading is much more demanding than silent reading, which requires no such voice-eye lag. In essence, good oral reading really depends on silent reading occurring shortly before the oral performance.

Perhaps it is no wonder, then, that competent silent reading usually proceeds at a much faster rate than oral reading. Thus, a conscientious silent following of oral reading can occur only if the silent readers depress their rate of reading. Such slowing of rate can only interfere with the anticipatory mechanism that readers use to orient themselves to print and to predict subsequent meaning in running text (Wildman and Kling, 1978–1979). Thus round-robin reading runs counter to the goal of learning to read silently with fluency.

A final important reason for eschewing the routine use of round-robin reading is the fear factor. Oral reading is a "high risk" activity, one that can be traumatic for the student required to do it. The shy or fearful pupil, the poor reader, the boy or girl with a speech defect or a foreign accent—all share the feeling of being alone among enemies. Even worse is the practice of allowing these "enemies" to pounce on errors so that they can have "their turn." This "vulture technique" (Singer 1970) can hardly be expected to foster a love of reading. In fact, adult illiterates often report that their avoidance of reading stems from the early embarrassment they experienced when reading aloud in front of classmates in their elementary years.

Oral reading (but not round-robin reading) does have a place in the reading curriculum. It can be useful in the diagnosis of reading difficulties, but for this purpose it is always done one-on-one in a private setting. Oral reading as a dramatic performance skill is appropriate when done by a willing student, after rehearsal. Chapter 10 provides a number of oral reading activities that place oral reading in an appropriate pedagogic context and avoid the high-risk fear factor so often associated with round-robin reading.

Let us make sure that round-robin reading is one bird that soon becomes extinct!

Dyslexia: A Label in Search of a Disease

From time to time, one of my college students will ask to write an exam on a computer with a spell checker "because I am dyslexic." When I ask these students what they mean by labeling themselves as dyslexic, they will usually say something like this: "I have always had trouble with spelling (or reading)." When I ask why they don't just say that, they reply, "Well, that's what *dyslexic* means, doesn't it?" Quite frankly, I am not sure what the term means, but I do know that in most cases it is not helpful to label people without conclusive evidence that the label actually describes a real phenomenon with agreed-upon characteristics.

The meaning of the term *dyslexia* is fraught with imprecision, uncertainty, and contradictory research findings. In the words of Doris Johnston, "We have yet to arrive at a conclusive explanation for the problem" (1995). The *Literacy Dictionary* of the International Reading Association (Harris and Hodges 1995) defines dyslexia as "a developmental reading disability, *presumably* congenital and *perhaps* hereditary, that may vary in degree from mild to severe" (63) [italics mine]. "In many ways," states Campbell (2003), "dyslexia has become a catch-all term to describe reading difficulties in general; the word often means 'reading backwards' or transposing letters." Campbell has provided a brief but helpful discussion of the definition and history of dyslexia, quoted here with permission:

> At the turn of the century, ophthalmologists and physicians drew attention to individuals who could not read and coined their term "congenital word-blindness" (Morgan 1896; Hinshelwood 1917). In the 1920s, Orton, a neuropsychiatrist and pathologist, dropped the term "word-blindness" in favor of "strephosymbolia" (twisted symbols); this label was later amended to "developmental dyslexia," a term that is still widely used. Orton concluded that dyslexia was a functional brain disorder—the failure of one hemisphere to become dominant in the control of language. Orton believed that this disorder lent itself to remedial training.
>
> The notion that dyslexia is a deviation in language development is reflected in the International Dyslexia Association's (1998) definition of *dyslexia*:
>
> Dyslexia is one of several distinct learning disabilities. It is a specific language-based disorder of constitutional origin characterized by difficulties in single word decoding usually reflecting insufficient phonological processing abilities. These difficulties in single word decoding are often unexpected in relation to age and other cognitive and academic abilities; they are not the result of generalized developmental disability or sensory impairment. Dyslexia is manifested by a variable difficulty with different forms of language, including, in addition to a problem with reading, a conspicuous problem with acquiring proficiency in writing and spelling. (4)

> This definition is grounded in the bottom-up theory of reading, which purports that individuals learn to read by progressing through a linear, sequential series of skills.
>
> Instructional programs based on this theory tend to emphasize word identification skills at the beginning stages of reading development rather than comprehension, and tend not to make effective use of students' knowledge as they read. The Orton-Gillingham program, developed by Orton and his colleague Anna Gillingham, is a case in point; this remedial program is based on the belief that learning to read is easier if one starts with small, isolated pieces of information. This method is painstakingly slow.
>
> With the Orton-Gillingham method, the instructor uses the alphabetic approach to establish the concept that words are built out of units of sound. The teacher begins by introducing the letters of the alphabet systematically, using visual, auditory, and kinesthetic techniques. The student learns the sound that is associated with one letter, and how to write it, before proceeding to the next letter. After the student has mastered the sound-symbol associations for a prescribed group of letters, he or she begins to blend them together into words such as *bat, map,* and *him*. Students learn the elements of language (e.g., consonants, vowels, digraphs, blends, and diphthongs) in an orderly fashion. Then they proceed to advanced structural elements such as syllable types, roots, and affixes. As students learn new material, they continue to review old material to the level of automaticity. The teacher addresses vocabulary, sentence structure, composition, and reading comprehension in a similar structured, sequential, and cumulative manner (Gillingham & Stillman 1979). The popularity of the Orton-Gillingham method is disconcerting because it paints all students with one brush stroke and every student receives a similar remedial program.

While some students may suffer from some neurologically based reading disability, their numbers are small and diagnosis is extremely difficult. It would be better for teachers to describe as clearly as possible what reading problem(s) students exhibit without attempting to attach a specific (and often unhelpful) label. Such labels often begin to limit students in their own (and others') eyes while providing little useful information for addressing reading concerns.

Remedial Teaching of Reading

What should one do about the students who exhibit reading problems? This book is not directly concerned with remedial reading education, although many of its principles are relevant. Good remedial teaching is simply good teaching done more intensively with one or just a few students. The danger in remedial teaching is over-reliance on predominately bottom-up instructional approaches, which are most frequently used in special education, influenced as it is by behaviorist psychology.

Recall from the discussion earlier in this chapter that good reading is best seen as an interactive process that makes flexible use of both top-down and bottom-up strategies. The remedial teacher attempts to discover what strategies the disabled reader is (and is not) using and then designs learning activities that complement strengths and ameliorate weaknesses. Often there are patterns to a reader's interaction with print (e.g., print-based or meaning-based miscues), and the task of the remedial teacher is to help the student diminish over-reliance on one of these patterns and learn strategies for the other. The goal of remedial teaching is helping struggling readers understand that reading is a meaning-making activity, closely related to what they are already able to do through oral language.

Most struggling readers are demoralized learners. Especially if they have been struggling for a number of years, their sense of themselves as competent learners is very low. Because it is natural for human beings to avoid unpleasant and unsuccessful experiences, poor readers avoid the very activity that will make them better readers—that is, reading.[19]

The greatest challenge of any teaching, but especially of remedial teaching, is to banish in the student the fear of failure and ridicule. For where there is fear, there can be no real learning. Good teaching, then, is first about love, for "perfect love drives out fear" (1 John 4:18). Successful remedial teaching of reading requires a combination of compassionate motivation and skillful understanding of the process required to address the student's specific reading problem.

There are many good resources for learning about the teaching of remedial reading. Three excellent ones are listed below:

◊ Pat Campbell and Flo Brokop. 1998. *STAPLE: Supplemental training for practitioners in literacy education. Vol. 1. Unlocking the mystique of teaching reading and writing.* Edmonton, AB: Literacy Coordinators of Alberta. This excellent interactive CD ROM and training manual is available from:
  Grass Roots Press
  PO Box 52192
  Edmonton, Alberta T6G 2T5
  Canada

◊ Thomas G. Gunning. 2001. *Assessing and correcting reading and writing difficulties.* 2nd ed. Boston: Allyn & Bacon.

◊ Barbara J. Walker. 2000. *Diagnostic teaching of reading: Techniques for instruction and assessment.* 4th ed. Columbus, OH: Merrill/Prentice Hall.

Conclusion

Successfully and completely describing exactly what it is that fluent readers do has been a formidable task during most of the twentieth century. Although we understand much about the reading process, there is still much to learn. In spite of our partial understanding, most children do learn to read, and we know a great deal about the conditions and teaching approaches that foster reading proficiency. This chapter has sought to present these findings and suggest teaching methods that fit within the Christian framework laid out in chapters 1 and 2. While considerable controversy swirls around the teaching of reading, the goal of this chapter has been to suggest approaches that honor children as responsive image bearers of their Creator.

Questions for Discussion

1. Endnote 2 cites evidence that children in kindergarten through grade 8 read as well as or better than at any other time in the history of the United States. Does this conclusion surprise you? What factors do you think have contributed to the widespread belief that there is a "reading crisis" in the United States and other English-speaking countries?

2. C. S. Lewis once asked a student why he read so voraciously, and the student replied, "to discover that I'm not alone." What do you think this student meant?

3. Why do you read?

4. Pretend that a classmate does not know what reading is. How would you explain reading to him or her? Write down your explanation and share it with a classmate. What theory of reading does your explanation seem to draw on most heavily?

5. Explain figure 11-2 in your own words. What is the relevance of this "Print Communication Model" for the teaching of reading?

6. "When two vowels go walking the first does the talking and says its own name." This phonics generalization can be applied to a word like *meat*. What common word in this phonics "rule" violates the rule itself? How would the word *great* be pronounced, given this rule? What about *belief*?

7. Pronounce the following letters and letter groups, in sequence, to the best of your ability:

   h ho hon hone honest

   What does this exercise suggest about the utility of "sounding out" words from left to right?

8. Reflect on your own elementary and middle school language arts education. Recall, if you can, when you were instructed how to answer questions, how to distinguish among types of questions, and other techniques to help you understand a text better.

9. How would you mesh personal reading, group literature study, and reader's workshop approaches into a workable teaching stratagem?

10. Atwell claims that an "air of passivity" characterizes much middle school language arts instruction. Does this claim reflect your own experience as a middle school student, or not?

11. In your experience as a language arts student, who determined what a piece of poetry or prose should mean? How should variant interpretations of a text be adjudicated? Would you answer this last question differently for the Bible than for other pieces of literature? Why or why not?

12. Was round-robin reading a common practice in your school experience? What was your reaction to it then? What is your reaction to it now, after reading the critique in this chapter?

13. Are you a reader? Do you love to read? Why are these questions two of the most important ones to ask a current or prospective language arts teacher?

For Further Consideration

1. Basing your answer on the argument presented in this chapter along with the discussion of fantasy literature in chapter 4, how do you respond to the idea that we are all characters in God's redemptive narrative? Is your part chosen for you, or by you?

2. Lucas (1972) credits the Protestant Reformation with playing a large role in increasing literacy amongst the laity in vernacular languages. Is there a "down side" to our being able to read the Bible for ourselves without the benefit of a unified interpretive community such as that once provided by the Roman Catholic Church?

3. Tape-record five to seven minutes of reading by a struggling reader. Perform a running record analysis of the person's reading, and attempt to analyze it. What **reading pattern** does the person seem to have?

4. Locate a **big book** version of *Rosie's Walk* (Hutchins 1968) or *Brown Bear, Brown Bear* (Martin 1982). Analyze whether and how it can help emergent readers develop awareness of:
   - the purposes of written language
   - the nature of the forms and conventions of written language
   - basic speech-print relationships

5. If you are a teacher, or if you have the opportunity as a student to visit a primary or middle school classroom, do a quick, informal assessment of
   - how many minutes per day students in this classroom actually read in a sustained manner
   - how many different books are available for children to read in this classroom
   - how much choice students have in the material they read

6. This chapter contains about 14,400 words. Choose a section of about 3,000 words (about one-fifth of the chapter) and, with a partner, do a word frequency count of that chunk of text. How many different words does this 3,000-word segment contain? What are the fifty most frequently used words, and what percentage of the total words do these fifty words represent? What are the implications of your findings for teaching word recognition?

7. Do a further study of **dyslexia** and report what you found concerning the validity and usefulness of the term in educational settings.

Endnotes

1 Huey's 1908 book is available in a 1968 reprint. It is worth reading not only for historical interest but because it anticipates so many of the issues and controversies that still occupy the field today.

2 The available evidence does *not* support the contention that there has been a decline in the reading ability of North American students. See Klenk and Kibby (2000) for a summary of research demonstrating the "indisputable fact that children in grades K–8 today read as well as, or better than, children at any other time in the history of the United States" (667).

3 I hesitate to provide a listing of these websites because they are so notoriously short-lived. A couple of American sites that will probably be around for a while are the National Right to Read Foundation <www.nrrf.org/synthesis_research.htm>, and the American Federation of Teachers <www.aft.org/edissues/downloads/rocketsci.pdf>. Both sites reflect the current swing back to a "code emphasis" that I mention in the text. The fact that I list these sites and the reports they present should not be construed as agreement with their stance.

4 **Aliteracy** means having the ability to read but failing to do so. Recent surveys of North American adults with a high school and/or college education indicate that most have not read an entire book for pleasure since graduation. An additional problem is **hyperliteracy**, which refers to people whose literacy abilities far exceed what is required in their daily work. Many highly literate people have jobs that require only minimal literacy skill. Some sociologists of work have argued that such hyperliterate workers are problematic for employers because they are typically bored and thus perform poorly.

5 See Ryken (2002) for an excellent article on "The Bible as Literature."

6 God's other means of revelation are His creation (cf. Romans 1) and His Son, Jesus. Both of these means are testified to in the Bible.

7 The section in chapter 4 (Fantasy in the Christian Classroom) explored this same idea of the Christian life as story.

8 Other miscue patterns are possible as well. For a very helpful way of categorizing miscue patterns and using such information for remediation, see Campbell (2003).

9 Ideally, all pre-service teacher education programs should require students to complete a course in children's literature.

10 Canadian researcher Ves Thomas (1979) also provides lists of the 1000, 1500, 2000, 2500, and 3000 words that account for about eighty-seven percent, ninety percent, ninety-three percent, and ninety-five percent, respectively, of the most frequently used words in English writing. There has been a remarkable stability in these frequency counts in a variety of studies over the past seventy-five years. The lists also have tremendous relevance to the teaching of spelling (see chapter 12).

11 An extremely useful omnibus handbook on many word-related matters is Edward B. Fry, Jacqueline E. Kress, and Dona L. Fountoukidis. 2000. *The Reading Teacher's Book of Lists.* 4th ed. Paramus, NJ: Prentice Hall.

12 Here again, it is important to have many books available, leveled for difficulty, as found in Fountas and Pinnell (1996, 2000).

13 An informal reading inventory (IRI) is "the use of a graded series of passages of increasing difficulty to determine students' strengths, weaknesses, and strategies in word identification and comprehension" (Harris and Hodges 1995, 116). A large number of commercial IRIs are available. I use Bader (2002), which I like because it also contains many other useful diagnostic literacy tools.

14 A good source for many ideas for specific literacy mini lessons is Linda Hoyt. 2000. (174) *Snapshots: Literacy minilessons up close.* Portsmouth, NH: Heinemann.

15 Philip's interaction with the Ethiopian eunuch, as recorded in Acts 8:26–35, provides an interesting biblical example of someone who could decode a text but did not have enough background knowledge to comprehend it.

16 An important component of comprehension strategy instruction includes teaching *study skills*. These include such skills as note-taking from text (and lectures), ways of studying from text such as SQ3R (**S**urvey, **Q**uestion, **R**ead, **R**ecite, **R**eview), as well as other means to learn from content area texts. Helpful references for this kind of teaching are Tierney and Readence (2000) and Vacca and Vacca (2002).

17 This section draws heavily on the work of Nancie Atwell (1987, 1998), coupled with visits to a number of Christian middle school classrooms that incorporate a reader/writer workshop approach.

18 When persons read, their eyes do not move smoothly from left to right along a line of print. Rather, the eyes move in jerky jumps (known as saccades), stop momentarily (fixations), and frequently move backwards as well (regressions). The eye is able to take in information only during a fixation. The length of the saccade represents the eye span. The larger the eye span and the fewer the regressions a reader makes, the more fluent the reading. Thus, eye movement behaviors can be a window on the efficiency of a reader's text processing ability.

19 See Stanovich (1986) for a famous paper on this phenomenon of the "rich getting richer and the poor getting poorer" with respect to reading.

Chapter 12

Writing

Of the four major components of the language arts—listening, speaking, reading, and writing—the latter seems to be the most difficult to master. Yet early childhood educators report that young children are often more interested in learning to write than to read. This chapter explores why learning to write poses special challenges and suggests approaches teachers can use to help students become more confident and competent writers.

> "And now, Tarkheena, tell us your story. And don't hurry it—I'm feeling comfortable now." Aravis immediately began, sitting quite still and using a rather different tone and style from her usual one. For in Calormen, story-telling (whether the stories are true or made up) is a thing you are taught, just as English boys and girls are taught essay writing. The difference is that people want to hear the stories whereas I never heard of anyone who wanted to read the essays.
>
> C. S. Lewis, *The Horse and His Boy*

Isn't that the truth? We all, young and old, love to hear or read a good story, but English-speaking schoolchildren are not known for their eagerness to write them. Instead, we hear endless jeremiads about the inability of high school and college graduates to write even a few coherent sentences of articulate prose. Weary teachers, elementary through graduate school, continue to assign essays and lament the task of grading them. Like C. S. Lewis, "I never heard of anyone who wanted to read the essays." What makes writing so difficult to teach and learn?

Vygotsky on Writing

As early as the 1930s, Russian psycholinguist Lev Vygotsky (1962) suggested that writing comes so hard to the young because it requires a high level of abstraction. Writing, he said, is speech in thought and image only, lacking the musical, expressive, intonational qualities of oral speech. In learning to write, children must disengage themselves from those sensory aspects and replace words (which are already symbols) by images of words (a second degree of symbolization). Speech that is merely imagined and that substitutes written signs for sounds must be as much harder than oral speech as algebra is more difficult than arithmetic.

What's more, writing is often disembedded from an immediate, functional purpose. It is speech without an interlocutor, addressed to an absent or imaginary person or to no one in particular, a situation new and strange to the child. Whereas the motivation for speaking is clear, the motives for writing are more abstract, more intellectualized, further removed from immediate needs.

Writing also requires deliberate analytical action. In speaking, children are hardly conscious of the sounds they pronounce and are unconscious of the mental operations they perform. In writing, they must be aware of the sound structure of each word, dissect it, and reproduce it in alphabetical symbols, which they must have studied and memorized before.

If Vygotsky is correct, is it any wonder that teaching and learning writing are so difficult and time consuming? Perhaps teachers ought not be discouraged or disappointed about their students' slow progress. Perhaps writing is like juggling, playing the violin, or other difficult and arcane arts, and we should expect only a few persons to become competent writers even after twelve or more years of instruction and practice. But is Vygotsky correct? Is written language inherently more abstract than spoken language?

Beginning Writers and Beginning Writing

Studies of young children's writing acquisition have produced much evidence that writing can, in fact, be learned in a developmentally "natural" manner similar to speaking and reading (Baghban 1984; Bissex 1980; Chomsky 1971; Clay 1975). Children who grow up in environments supportive of literacy learning often want to mimic writing. Their earliest writing is frequently a form of "scribble writing," a series of connected scribbles on paper that the child interprets as a story. Such scribbling obviously imitates the cursive writing of adults. Then, as children are read to, they become aware of printed letters and words on the pages of books. Sometimes they learn how to print letters of the alphabet from watching TV programs such as *Sesame Street*, and from playing with wooden or magnetic alphabet letters.

Children may begin to use their emerging letter-sound knowledge to write stories (as in the literacy story in chapter 8). Young children, in fact, are often more interested in learning to write than to read. Reading requires them to attend to what others have to say; writing satisfies their egocentric urge to impose themselves on the world (Chomsky 1971).

As children gain more control of the symbol-sound system of the language, they often use **invented spellings**. When my daughter Ann was four, we would role-play hospital games in which I played the doctor and she the nurse to her many stuffed animals (apologies for that sex-role stereotyping). One day, I found this scribbled note on my desk: HLP DCTR PTR RBBT AS SK NRSS ANN. (Transcription: Help doctor. Peter Rabbit is sick. Nurse Ann.) Although my wife and I read to Ann a great deal, and she had learned to print the letters of the alphabet using a set of magnetic letters as models, I can't recall ever explicitly modeling spelling or writing for her. Somehow, she figured out the sound-symbol relationships on her own. From then on, we often left notes for each other all over the house, and over time Ann developed into a fluent writer.

As Ann's writing illustrates, young children using invented spellings tend to concentrate on consonants and have the most difficulty with vowels. This is understandable, since each English consonant has one or only a few sound values, while each English vowel has multiple values. This consonant-focused spelling is just one example of the gradual, developmental nature of learning to spell and write. Instead of hunting for "errors" in those early writing efforts, teachers need to understand and focus on positive signs of learning. For example, we could say that my daughter Ann misspelled every word (except her own name) in her note to me. It is far more meaningful and accurate, however, to say that twenty-three of her thirty-five graphophonic representations, or about sixty-six percent, are correct. At age four, Ann already showed a remarkable ability at phoneme-grapheme matching.

The Writing Process

During the last few decades, an explosion of research on the writing process has culminated in some very fine resources for teachers. The work and writing of Donald Graves is deservedly the best known of these efforts. His classic 1983 book, *Writing: Teachers and Children at Work,* is wonderfully readable and still very relevant. Graves emphasizes that confidence is the key to good writing and that confidence builds when children move from the known to the unknown in a supportive environment. They will produce good writing only if they are first free to explore many topics orally. When children write, their environment must encourage risk-taking. With beginning writers, teachers should avoid emphasizing correctness or mechanics, since fear of making mistakes paralyzes the flow of ideas. It is also important to allow beginning writers to use highly personal, expressive modes that flow out of shared experiences and talk. The distinctions among modes of writing developed by James Britton (1970, 1992) are helpful here.

Britton's Model of Writing

Britton suggests that all writing falls into one of three modes based on the **voice** of the writer. *Voice* refers to the combined effects of the writer's purpose, style, tone, and other intangibles, such as commitment, energy, conviction, and personality. Britton identified three voices of writing: expressive, poetic, and transactional.

Expressive writing tends to use a subjective voice to express the author's thoughts. Expressive writing includes personal journals, a letter to a friend, or a diary entry. Writing in this mode tends to be informal, articulating ideas that are close to us and perhaps not fully shaped.

Poetic writing uses the imaginative voice of poetry and fiction to create a work of art. It is more literary and is usually intended for an audience other than the author. Poetic writing often contains aesthetic elements not usually present in either expressive or transactional writing.

Transactional writing takes the objective voice to convey information for a specific purpose. Transactional writing is the most difficult because it is the most disembedded form of writing, and its mastery comes later than that of expressive and some forms of poetic writing. Most expository writing is transactional, including essays, reports, and business letters. Good transactional writing can balance information with personal perspective, but traditional transactional writing emphasizes the need for objectivity and personal distance. For example, my academic and professional training never allowed the use of the first person in such writing.

Britton noticed that young writers frequently move from one voice to another. When writing a report on a pet, for example, they may add a personal anecdote about their own pet, thus combining the expressive and transactional voices. Similarly, they may shift from the expressive voice to the poetic and back to the expressive when writing a story, adding themselves as a character and writing in the first person. Britton terms this the **transitional voice**. As writers mature, they usually learn to select an appropriate voice for their writing and remain consistently within that voice, although good writers continue to make effective use of the transitional voice when it suits their purpose.

In advice that would likely please C. S. Lewis, Britton encourages teachers to begin fostering writing development with expressive modes, moving later into the poetic, and finally introducing transactional modes.

Teaching Writing as a Process

Work in the '80s by Donald Graves (1983), along with that of Lucy Calkins (1986, 1992) and Nancie Atwell (1987, 1998), prompted a major shift in the teaching of writing in schools. These teacher-researchers demonstrated that writing is not a single act springing from the writer's head to the page, producing a finished product in a straightforward, linear fashion. Rather, writing is a *process* that has a multiplicity of steps, many of which are recursive. Writing is as much a process of learning as an end product. Unlike its oral counterpart, writing waits on the page, where the writer can return to ponder, adapt, or share. Writing is by nature a preservative, holding meanings fast. Being slower than talk, it can freeze the thinking process in time, yet its staying power is coupled with an independence not present in speech. Even taped talk is not the same; it is usually not meant for later reflection, and its content is static.

Writing teaches partly because it defines ideas more clearly but also because it generates new ones. We write ourselves into a subject. The reading self prompts the writing self with second thoughts and new ideas. Notice how a writer gropes after the next phrase by reading back over the preceding sentences. It is a way of cueing into the next idea. We also reread to identify false notes, inaccuracies, errors of logic, and inconsistencies. We act as a second person, interrogating what is written, arguing back or nodding approval. A productive inner dialogue occurs between ourselves as writers and ourselves as readers. Thus, writing at its best is a reflexive medium that is self-generating; it works on us as we work on it, in what James Moffett (1979) terms "the revision of inner speech." In Moffat's view, this is the only true form of writing, for it involves expressing and shaping one's own thoughts. He also claims that it is rare to find such writing in classrooms. Most teaching of writing tends to stop at the craft level, helping students produce conventionally correct forms but failing to foster their unique, personal voice.

To enable writing to function as a reflexive medium, it is useful to lead students through the writing process in four distinct steps: **prewriting/rehearsal, writing/composing, revising/rewriting,** and **publishing/sharing**.

Prewriting/Rehearsal A writer needs something to write about. Before students write, they need time to develop topics that interest them. Stimulating an interest at this prewriting stage might involve reading, viewing a film, participating in a discussion, going on a field trip, or another direct or vicarious experience. Most of all, it should involve talking with others in both large and small groups to build a bank of ideas and to rehearse possible approaches. If the writing task is in the transactional mode, the prewriting phase includes narrowing a topic, developing a thesis statement, library research, choosing the pattern of writing (e.g., defining. classifying, explaining, tracing causes and effects, comparing and/or contrasting), and preparing a rough outline. Other important considerations in prewriting include defining the audience and selecting tone and voice. The prewriting phase is a time of idea incubation, exploration, and preparation.

Writing/Composing In the second stage of the writing process, students should generate a fast draft. The emphasis here should be on *fast*. This is not the time to worry about crossing t's and dotting i's, but a time to get ideas on paper. The writer's thoughts, feelings, and ideas about the topic should flow unimpeded. Attention to mechanical detail at this point results in stilted, mechanical writing.

Rewriting/Revising It is a truism that good writing is largely a matter of good rewriting. Still, many students seem not to have learned this in school. Instead, they view rewriting as punishment for not having done a good job in the first place, or as a necessary chore to make the writing look neater. In fact, rewriting is the heart of the writing process. One way to convince students of this fact is to bring a professional writer to class to talk about writing and, if possible, to show multiple drafts of a piece of writing.

The word processor has made the rewriting phase much less arduous than in the pre-computer days of longhand revision or cut-and-paste typewriter drafts. Elementary school children need to learn effective computer keyboarding as soon as possible to facilitate the rewriting process, although working on paper with cross-outs and write-overs may remain an important mode for many students.

Teachers also need to model the rewriting stage in their own work so that students can literally see and hear how to do it. Rewriting begins with a personal rereading of a piece. Students must be encouraged to ask themselves questions such as the following:

- Does my writing make sense?
- Do I like it?
- Does it say what I want it to say?
- Is it smooth, clear, and precise?
- Is it interesting?

Next, students should share their writing with peers. This step requires students to understand how to receive others' writing with kindness and courtesy. Peer reaction is not first of all a matter of faultfinding but of helpful critique. I find that triads work well in providing useful peer response. The three students sit in a circle. One student reads his or her piece, and the other two each write one feeling word as a reaction (for example, *frightened, confused, happy*). Then the writer reads the piece again. This time the other two students each write two sentences in response, one beginning with "I like ..." and the other with " I didn't understand...." The students share their comments with the writer, and the writer thanks them for their contributions. The process continues until all three have shared their writing with the group.

After these initial personal and peer responses, the writer reworks the piece in light of what was said. The piece may go through a triad reaction session again, or it may be ready for close **peer editing.** In close peer editing, three students again sit in a circle, with each student carefully copyediting one piece of writing and then passing it to the next person. The assumption is that six eyes are better than two in catching all the mechanical glitches. Finally, the writer sits down for a session of revising and polishing to get the piece "just right."

Note that in many cases, especially in writing shorter pieces, the prewriting and rewriting phases take considerably more time than the actual writing or composing phase. Tools such as the dictionary and thesaurus are particularly useful in the rewriting phase. Note also that the entire process takes a lot of time. If students are going to become good writers, that time is essential. We signal the importance we ascribe to activities by the amount of time we devote to them. Good writing requires and deserves extended periods of time.

Publishing/Sharing With the exception of personal journals and diaries, we write so others can read what we have to say. Authentic writing demands an authentic audience. A teacher cannot serve as the only audience for student writing; students soon realize that no one person can sustain a genuine interest in all the writing that emanates from a class of twenty-five or more writers. To see themselves as writers, students need opportunities to make their work public. That's what publishing is all about. Publishing can be as simple as reading one's writing to a small audience of peers, or as complex as sending a piece out to a newspaper or magazine. It may include making a book for younger children, writing an article for the school newspaper, creating a poem for a class anthology, or producing a play from a student-written script. In short, a multitude of options exist for authenticating the task of writing.

Of course, not everything a student writes needs to be published. Some writing represents false starts, partly finished pieces, or simply less than the best a student can do. Nevertheless, students need regular opportunities to select their best pieces for more or less formal evaluation, public exposure, and celebration.[1]

Forms of Writing

Text may take many forms or structures. One major distinction that can be helpful is that between *expository* form and *narrative* form.

Expository writing intends to explain (or "expose") something. This writing is not designed primarily to convey feelings or personal observations but to pass on information. It requires the writer to be well organized, clear, and coherent. Examples include reports, textbooks, memos, notices, and—especially in college and university—the ubiquitous term paper (or research paper).

Narrative form derives from storytelling, linking thoughts and events in a way that makes sense to us. When writers develop a story, they craft the narrative to fit a certain structure. In Western culture, story structure usually contains an introduction (including a setting and introduction of characters), a middle section with a problem or conflict (or series of conflicts), and an ending that achieves some resolution of the problem. This basic structure is termed **story grammar**. Beginning writers are often able to chain events together, but they struggle to develop a theme that will bind the events into a story. They need explicit help in noticing the elements of story grammar in their reading, and in writing these elements into their work.

Even more difficult for the young writer is learning to manage the various **text structures** found in expository writing. Text structure refers to the way text is organized. For example, science writing often requires a problem-solution text structure. Newspaper editorials or advertisements need a persuasive text structure. Although the classification of text structures is somewhat arbitrary, at least six basic structures deserve attention: **description, persuasion, comparison-contrast, sequence, cause-effect,** and **problem-solution.**

Awareness of text structures benefits both reading comprehension and writing. It is helpful to find simple examples of these structures and point out their characteristic features. Mapping the structure on a chart or **semantic map** can follow. Campbell and Brokop (1998) provide an excellent interactive CD-ROM program that includes practice in both recognizing and writing various text structures.

Helpful Resources for Teaching Writing

◊ Frank Smith. 1982. *Writing and the writer.* Hillsdale, NJ: Lawrence Erlbaum. Smith's book explores the relationship between the writer and what the writer happens to be writing. It is not directly concerned with the teaching of writing but provides fascinating insights for anyone interested in the complex psychology of writing.

◊ Donald H. Graves. 1983. *Writing: Teachers and children at work.* Portsmouth, NH: Heinemann. This is the classic book developing a process model of writing and teaching writing. Graves argues that "the literate life of the teacher has the greatest effect on the literacy behavior in the classroom." A wise, insightful book full of useful information.

◊ Lucy M. Calkins. 1992. *Living between the lines.* Portsmouth, NH: Heinemann. Calkins' book has been very influential in developing a workshop approach to writing. In addition to providing a great deal of pedagogical advice, it resonates with the author's personal voice and is a joy to read.

◊ Nancie Atwell. 1998. *In the middle: New understandings about writing, reading, and learning.* 2nd ed. Portsmouth, NH: Boynton/Cook Publishers. This is a major revision of Atwell's 1987 book about the reading and writing workshop, which became a classic for middle school instruction. In this edition, Atwell recommends a more activist role for the teacher in teaching writing.

The following books are practical resources for teaching all aspects of writing within a broad process perspective. They include many helpful suggestions for evaluating writing.

◊ Charles Temple et al. 1993. *The beginnings of writing.* 3rd ed. Boston: Allyn & Bacon.

◊ Dorothy S. Strickland and Lesley M. Morrow, eds. 2000. *Beginning reading and writing.* Newark, DE: International Reading Association.

◊ Susan D. Lenski and Jerry L. Johns. 2000. *Improving writing: Resources, strategies, and assessments.* Dubuque, IA: Kendall/Hunt Publishing.

◊ Ralph Fletcher and Joann Portalupi. 1998. *Craft lessons: Teaching writing K–8.* Portland, ME: Stenhouse Publishers.

◊ Joann Portalupi and Ralph Fletcher. 2001. *Nonfiction craft lessons: Teaching information writing K–8.* Portland, ME: Stenhouse Publishers.

Teaching Poetry[2]
by Joel and Amanda Kleine

Language users have an innate poetic sense. We express emotions through intonation, gather thoughts into flowing and rhythmic sentences, and create rhymes and songs to help remember simple things. Parents expose young children to poetic language through nursery rhymes, prayers, riddles, and songs. Children's faces light up when they recognize the rhythmic playfulness of words. As they begin to interpret speech and speak for themselves, the basis for much of their language learning is poetic. Drawn to poetry by its playfulness, beauty, and rhythm (Cullinan, Scala, and Schroder 1995), children glimpse two of God's greatest gifts to humanity: creativity and language.

Poetry, more than many other literary genres, uses these gifts to create such joy, excitement, and praise that children naturally react without hesitation. Poet and educator Georgia Heard (1989) writes, "When I read poetry to kindergartners and first graders, they sway and nod their heads and snap their fingers. I don't have to say, 'Poetry is rhythmic, boys and girls; why don't you dance a little?' They know the music of the poem because they feel it in their bodies" (5). It is vital that teachers seize upon children's excitement for poetry and encourage it to grow.

Of course, it is relatively easy to educate the enthusiastic student. It is, however, naive to think that all students will be excited about reading and writing. Even in the primary grades, teachers come across students who have little desire to read, perhaps because of earlier frustration and failure. Many educators find poetry a valuable vehicle for reaching those unmotivated students. A poem's conciseness is a breath of fresh air for the struggling reader. Its density of content and rhythmic overtones invite the reader to take on a piece and discover that poetry is not only manageable but meaningful (Perfect 1999). The resulting increased confidence will, with encouragement, build a stronger reader who is willing to explore different forms of writing.

As students explore various forms, they begin to seek literature that not only appeals to them as entertainment but also relates to their current situation. Poetry is "a bridge between ourselves and the poet, ourselves and others ... because it speaks so often of our common human condition and experiences" (Perfect 1999, 729). Difficult issues such as death, divorce, and loss can be dealt with as ably as the humorous or mundane. Poems give students a quick yet deep glance into the mind of someone else who may be thinking and feeling exactly as they are. Thus, children gain an affirmation of self and are motivated to express themselves in the same way.

Teachers are charged with the important task of encouraging a sense of community within and outside the classroom. That community builds when students play together outdoors, when they learn together in group assignments—and when they study poetry. As students discuss poems, they learn much about each other's perspective, background, and feelings. Poetry helps students realize new things about themselves, about their relationships with others, and about their Creator.

General Practices

The most exciting aspect of language is its interactivity. We read, listen, view, reflect, and respond to the words of others. These five interactions are equally vital to a healthy poetry learning experience. Too often children have little opportunity to view, reflect, and respond to poetry, as teachers focus on reading and listening. The following is a sample of general teaching practices that will help create an effective poetry learning experience for both teachers and students.

1. Allow students to experience poetry at different levels. Much like a well-written novel, a poem can and should be enjoyed at a variety of levels, for every layer contributes to the overall experience. Given opportunity, each child will find those aspects of a poem that are personally intriguing. As Spiegel (1991) writes,

> Children should be free to explore both the form and the meaning of a poem and to be creative in their own unique responses. One child may be intrigued by the rhythm, but another may be entranced by the sounds of the words. One child may focus on the author's use of imagery whereas another reacts to the message as a whole. (429)

This is the beauty of poetry: The level on which it is enjoyed depends on the reader and shifts as the reader/writer matures. A young child may note that a poem's words sound funny together, and be intrigued by the sheer silliness of the piece. As children mature, the level of meaning deepens, and the issues and emotions embedded in the poem become relevant.

In many classrooms, poetry is read aloud just once before being deconstructed to reveal the author's mechanics, techniques, and intent. Perhaps the emphasis on mechanics is understandable, since defining those details is easier than interpreting the content because each reader's interpretation is unique. But as Spiegel (1991) suggests, that approach places undue emphasis on form at the expense of content:

> Children [are] urged to count syllables and words rather than explore the power of a form to convey a message. Thus, what [is] reinforced in this mechanized approach [is] a superficial aspect of poetry, the form, at the expense of the message. (428)

Imposing this controlled approach is not suitable to the freedom of poetry, for it directs students to consider just one of a poem's many layers.

This is not to say that one should avoid teaching the mechanics of poetry but that students should be encouraged to enjoy the poem as a whole before looking at its pieces. Further, when focusing on mechanics or poetic techniques, teachers should pay particular attention to the many concepts that are transferable to other styles of writing. Exploring descriptive words, hyperbole, simile, metaphor, imagery, and other writing techniques not limited to poetry hones students' "abilities to use language in interesting ways in their own writing" (Strickland 1997, 201). Those insights also help students recognize and understand the creative language found in their reading.

2. Read a poem more than once, without interruption. A poem must be experienced as a whole piece before its parts can be appreciated. As a poem is read the first time, students will listen to it. To enhance the experience, teachers should resist the temptation to explain words on the first reading, a practice that disrupts the flow of the words and sounds. On the second reading, students will recognize phrases and be able to construct meaning from the poem (Heard 1989). As McClure notes, "The emphasis [should be] on enjoying the poem as a whole, developing an appreciation for how the parts—rhyme, rhythm, imagery, and figurative language—[contribute] to that whole" (1990, 47). Next, let students view the poem. Poetry is a visual as well as an auditory art, and its shape often aids students in piecing the work together.

3. Integrate poetry with other subjects. A plethora of poetry anthologies are available focusing on the works of particular authors, or subjects, or genres. Children who have difficulty with the academic challenges of certain subjects may remember more through learning or writing a poem focused on that topic than through any dogmatic lesson. A teacher might choose a poem of the week or poet of the month, or introduce poetry centered on a theme such as humor, change, death, seasons—or whatever is relevant in the classroom at the time.

4. Encourage writing. Even at a young age, students should be involved in writing poetry. Too often, the focus becomes reading others' poetry rather than encouraging students to plunge their hands into the rich soil of imagination and word play. Many teachers shy away from poetry writing because it defies many grammar rules they strive so hard to instill. Yet as Spiegel notes, a poetry unit will "be strengthened if there is a writing component that encourages children to try their hands at writing poetry themselves" (1991, 428). Teachers ought not to be afraid to let students explore the beauty of language. The results are often surprising and captivating.

Children experience an openness and willingness when writing poetry. For many, it is a moment when they can finally express the happiness or sadness they feel about a particular aspect of their life. Students are "aching to talk about the mysteries of both life and death" (Dakos 2001, 34). As they learn that written expression is valuable, they begin "to seek the written word as a means to explore and understand the complexities of their personal lives" (Myers 1998, 270). Thus writing poetry can cause a child's relationship with literature to flourish in a very personal way, potentially creating a lifelong appreciation of language.

Besides writing their own poems, students studying poetry can respond through journaling or drama. After reading a poem through, students may need to organize their thoughts before discussing them; writing allows that to happen. Teachers should encourage them to concentrate on evaluative responses in their journals rather than imposing mechanical recall questions on them. The range of dramatic responses students can construct includes mini-plays, monologues, and reader's theater.

5. Don't impose your ideas. Much of the wonder of poetry is its mystery. Poetry invites individual readers to interpret something appropriate for their life. When teachers explain a poem, they offer an adult perspective, which many elementary students do not understand. Imposing that adult interpretation without allowing students to construct their own reflection narrows their understanding of how to interact personally with poetry, stunting their intellectual and emotional growth. As Amy McClure (1990) writes, "We have been too concerned about teaching children that there's a 'right' way to interpret poetry and that interpretation is the only thing one does with poetry. In effect, we've taken poetry out of the hands of children and put it into the hands of adults" (48).

Instead, educators need to celebrate and nurture the mind of the child. Doing so demands a constructivist approach that invites students not only to see the poem as a reflection of the author's opinions, feelings, and emotions but to make it their own by tying it into personal experience. For as Spiegel notes, "if meaning is imposed by the teacher or if the teacher dictates what should be of interest in a particular poem, children are denied important opportunities to create meaning for themselves" (1991, 429). Teachers need to offer guidance by facilitating open discussion rather than forcing a desired outcome (McClure 1990).

6. Set high expectations. When developing a poetry unit for elementary students, teachers often rely on works that appeal to young children. Shel Silverstein, Dennis Lee, Jack Prelutsky, and others form the foundation of typical elementary poetry studies. Students enjoy the zaniness of the content, and teachers enjoy the variety of anthologies these authors have produced.

While humorous poetry is valid and entertaining, it is important to move beyond lighthearted themes and simple poems. According to Heard (1989), teachers should "stay away from poems that have strong rhymes. This is the kind of poetry students already know; in fact, often it's the beginning and the end of what they think poetry is. [The job of the teacher] is to expand those boundaries" (5). Teachers need to challenge their students to experience poems that require deeper personal reflection.

Conclusion

The teacher's role is to facilitate creation experiences that are valuable for each student. As teachers face a growing diversity of needs, it is important that they attempt to provide learning tools and experiences that will develop each student's gifts. Poetry is a valuable tool that can be integrated with other teaching methods and subjects, providing a unique opportunity for children to experience language as an integral part of all learning.

Poetry is a rich linguistic gift, full of wisdom, enjoyment, and creativity. It offers insight into mysteries within ourselves, others, and the world around us. We become creators as we write and read poetry, thereby fulfilling our calling to reflect God's creativity within us.

Recommended Poetry Resources

Anthologies

◊ E. H. Sword and V. F. McCarthy, eds. 1997. *A child's anthology of poetry.* New York: Scholastic.

◊ Jack Prelutsky, ed. 1983. *The Random House book of poetry for children.* New York: Random House.

◊ Seamus Heaney and Ted Hughes, eds. 1982. *The rattle bag.* London: Faber and Faber Ltd.

Teaching Resources

Practical

◊ R. Routman. 2000. *Kids' Poems* Series. New York: Scholastic. (Four books covering kindergarten through grade 4.)

◊ Michaela Morgan. 2001. *How to teach poetry writing at key stage 2.* London: David Fulton Publishers.

Pedagogical

◊ Fred Sedgwick. 2000. *Writing to learn: Poetry and literacy across the primary curriculum.* London: Routledge Falmer.

◊ Fred Sedgwick. 1997. *Read my mind: Young children, poetry, and learning.* London: Routledge.

◊ G. Heard. 1989. *For the good of the earth and the sun: Teaching poetry.* Portsmouth, NH: Heinemann.

Online Resources

◊ The teacher's corner
http://www.theteacherscorner.net/writing/poetry/index.htm

◊ Online poetry classroom
http://www.onlinepoetryclassroom.org/how

◊ Creative writing for teens
http://teenwriting.about.com/cs/poetrylessons

◊ Scholastic: Writing with writers: Poetry
http://teacher.scholastic.com/writewit/poetry/index.htm

Teaching Mechanics and Conventions

Learning to produce conventionally acceptable written language presents the greatest combination of difficulties of any language task. In learning to write, purely mechanical and arbitrary skills must be mastered to represent the essentially "natural" psycholinguistic activity of oral communication. Mastery of the mechanics of writing includes a number of skills. First, it requires refined muscular control of the hand and arm **(handwriting).** Then the writer must learn an irregular system for representing words in print **(spelling)**, a way of indicating the stress, pitch, and juncture of speech **(punctuation)**, and the syntactic conventions of the language **(grammar and usage)**. Finally, a writer must deal with the slowness and deliberation required by process of writing and rewriting.

These distinct and demanding features tempt us to teach writing as a set of isolated skills—handwriting, spelling, punctuation, grammar, and usage. Yet assuming that skills or rules learned as isolated activities will transfer into lively written language is unwarranted. Skills isolated from the communicative and expressive uses of language become abstract (disembedded) encoding exercises, unrelated to meaning. This reality suggests two principles. First, it is best to develop any skill in the context of meaningful activity, and second, mechanics are important only to the extent that they facilitate meaningful communication between writer and reader. In teaching and evaluating writing, we must focus first of all on meaning. Of course, form greatly affects function, so we cannot ignore mechanics.

To help students understand the importance of mechanics in writing, I often use the analogy of a game or sport. In Western Canada, where I live and work, ice hockey is a major winter preoccupation for many children, as both participants and fans. As most children know, when beginning players take to the ice, they simply try to shoot the puck into the opposing team's net as best they can. Eventually, someone demands penalties for infractions such as offsides, and soon rules are needed because "that's how the professionals play." Gradually the players gain enough skill to enter a formal game, where referees settle disputes using the sport's official rulebook.

As I point out to students, the mechanics of the writing game, like the rules of hockey, are encoded in rulebooks (dictionaries, style guides) and are adhered to by professional writers. As one becomes more skilled in a game, one will get better and better at playing by the rules. When players don't play by the rules, or when the referees do not enforce them, fans are agitated because they expect the players to follow the agreed-upon conventions.

I then point out that, like hockey players, writers have an **audience**. Like fans, readers expect certain rules to be followed—in this case, the conventions of spelling, punctuation, and grammar. Violating those rules interferes with readers' ability to understand the writing. Thus, writing well and correctly is a way of serving our reading neighbors. It is not facetious to argue that paying attention to the rules is one way we love our reading neighbors linguistically, honoring God's command to "love our neighbors as ourselves."

It is important to realize, however, that learning to produce conventionally acceptable written language is a developmental process and thus has an emergent character. Developmental learning always moves from vague to precise, from gross to fine, from highly concrete and contextualized to more abstract, from familiar contexts to unfamiliar ones. In learning written conventions, risk-taking is essential; developing writers must think about what they want to say, explore genres, invent spellings, and experiment with punctuation. Students and teachers need to appreciate that stretched boundaries, imperfections, and even mistakes are part of learning.

Learning and Teaching Spelling

A friend of mine is the personnel manager of a small electronics firm. He tells me that, when reviewing an application for employment, he checks first for spelling errors. If he finds even one error, he eliminates the applicant from further consideration because he doesn't want people working for him who don't take the time and trouble to make sure their spelling is correct. My friend's attitude toward spelling is typical. Correct spelling is the shibboleth of our culture's literate elite; it is a test we employ to judge whether a person is in or out of the club of the educated. Thus spelling ability has important social consequences.

Spelling is an applied skill, valuable only in written expression. Teaching spelling in isolation and for its own sake is hardly defensible. But before we can *apply* a skill, we must first *acquire* it. The rest of this section provides insights about spelling acquisition and instruction by posing and answering a number of important questions.

Is there a pattern to how children learn to spell? Yes, spelling is a developmental skill, although as in all developmental learning, not all children move through the stages at the same rate. **Invented spelling** is one step children take as they move toward a mastery of orthodox spelling. Children invent spelling as they listen attentively to the spoken language around them and attempt to encode words in print. Young children are particularly sensitive to the sounds of words, and they try to put the sounds they hear into symbol form (Read 1975).

En route to orthodox spelling, children generally move through the following five stages of invented spelling. This process can last from age three or four to age eleven or twelve (grade 5 or 6) and even (for some) into adulthood.

1. *Prereading or precommunicative spelling* In this stage, children place whatever letters they can recall and produce in random order, with no apparent understanding of letter-sound correspondence. Thus a child might write *PRLN* and tell you it spells *dog*. At this point, the child has become aware that what is written on a page signifies a particular meaning.

2. *Prephonetic or semiphonetic spelling* In this stage, children have a primitive concept of the alphabetic principle and of letter names. They often use letter names as clues to spelling, resulting in such combinations as *NHR* for *nature* and *U R A RBBT* for *You are a rabbit*. Consonants tend to predominate in their writing.

3. *Phonetic spelling* This stage is most commonly seen in children from kindergarten through grade 3. Guided by a more complete understanding of letter-sound correspondence, children represent sound features of words as they hear them. The spelling reflects the fact that children's articulation of sounds is not always accurate at this stage. Often, they omit preconsonantal nasal sounds such as the letters *M* and *N*. Thus numbers becomes *NUBRS*.

4. *Transitional spelling* In the second through fourth grades, children usually include a vowel in every syllable and overuse familiar spelling patterns. Thus, *make* may be spelled as *MAEK*. They often overgeneralize so that, for example, *MOUSES* is written as the plural for *mice* because adding an *s* is the most common way to indicate the plural form.

5. *Standard spelling* From about grade 5 on, children's spelling demonstrates a more sophisticated understanding of the constraints of syntax and morphology. They spell most common words correctly and are beginning to master irregular spellings. Many spelling errors are still related to errors in pronunciation. Thus, *dentist* is spelled *DENIST* because the child drops the middle *t* when pronouncing the word. Other errors result from mistakes in usage. The most common examples are the misuse of *to, too,* and *two* as well as *there, their,* and *they're.* Children at this age are capable of developing a spelling conscience. That is, they understand that spelling well is a courtesy to the reader as well as a tool for expressing meaning clearly.

When should a child be expected to learn how to spell a given word? A child should be held responsible for spelling a given word correctly only when the word is

1. part of the child's experiential background
2. in the child's listening vocabulary
3. in the child's speaking vocabulary
4. in the child's reading vocabulary

When these four conditions are met, we can be sure that learning to spell a given word is not simply a meaningless exercise in memorization. Unfortunately, when students learn to spell lists of words from a commercial spelling series, lesson by lesson, one or more of these four criteria is often unmet. Spelling lessons become a series of isolated exercises in transcribing and memorizing words that have no powerful or useful conceptual associations for the child or are only a meaningless arrays of letters.

Does extensive reading ensure that a child will be a good speller? Because learning to spell is largely a visual memory skill, reading does help children become better spellers. It is primarily through reading that children come into visual contact with printed words. However, reading is of limited help in learning to spell, for two reasons. First, fluent readers pay little attention to the graphemic (written) structure of words. Their primary concern is with semantics (meaning), not graphemics. Second, reading primarily involves decoding while writing involves encoding. We cannot assume a skill transfer from one to the other. For example, *comeing, coming, cuming, kumming,* and *koming* can all be read as /kuming/, but only one is spelled correctly.

Reading with a writer's eye, however, can improve spelling. Students committed to using reading as a "window" on writing can make themselves consciously aware of a writer's approaches and techniques. To open that window, the student must reread a piece with particular attention to the form of the writing. Being too conscious of form during an initial reading can disengage the reader from the content, but a careful rereading can reveal how a writer uses certain words and grammatical constructions to create the effect felt during the first reading. Skill as a reader does not ensure that a person will be a good speller, but reading can help one learn to identify spelling errors.

Does a child have to know phonics well to be a good speller? The phonemic characteristics of words are a significant help in narrowing down the possible ways of spelling a word. But as we have seen, many words do not have a regular phoneme-grapheme (sound-symbol) correspondence, so learning to spell well requires other strategies besides phonics. It should be mentioned here that phonics is probably more useful for spelling than for reading. "Sounding out" words disturbs the speed and fluency required for reading well; writing, on the other hand, is a slower, more deliberate process of getting thoughts down word by word. Using sound-to-symbol encoding relationships in English spelling is a useful strategy in the revising phase, but it can provide only limited approximations. Children whose only spelling strategy is "sounding out" tend to get mired in the *phonetic spelling stage* described above.

What words should children be taught to spell, and when should they be taught to spell them? Children should be helped to spell those words they need and want to use in their writing.

We can determine the **core vocabulary** needs of children at various ages by surveying masses of writing done by and for children and by doing frequency counts of the words they write. Fortunately, that work has been done, and teachers have ready access to the information. The late Ves Thomas of the University of Calgary in Alberta did some of the best research on a core spelling vocabulary. His book *Teaching Spelling: Canadian Word Lists and Instructional Techniques* (1979) is a standard text in the field. The information to follow in this section draws heavily from Thomas's work.

Thomas collected six thousand samples of student writing (grades 1 to 6) from the ten Canadian provinces. These samples produced a total of 521,195 words, representing 13,904 discrete words. He also analyzed 540 letters to *The Canadian Magazine.* These 540 compositions produced a total of 55,260 words, representing 7,277 discrete words. About fifty percent of the latter overlapped with words found in the student writing. Thomas compared his findings with those of earlier studies of word and word frequency counts done in the United States (by Horn in 1927 and Rinsland in 1945) and found an amazingly high congruence among the studies.

Thomas found that a total of only one hundred discrete words accounted for fully fifty-nine percent of all the words written by both children and adults in his study. The data show that if children learn to spell fifty of the most frequently used words, they will be able to spell about half of all the words they are ever likely to use in their writing. Learning to spell 3,000 words will allow them to spell about ninety-five percent of all the words they are ever likely to use. These numbers are surprisingly low and make learning to spell a core vocabulary list a manageable task. Through careful analysis of his data, Thomas distributed the 3,000-word core vocabulary list over seven grades (2 through 8) with a low of 300 words to be learned in grade 2 and a high of 600 in grade 8. This means that, in a Canadian school year of about 180 days, children in grades 2 through 8 should learn to spell about 8 to 17 words each week. Thomas's little book provides lists of the most frequently written words (from most to least frequent, and frequency by grade level). It also includes lists of the 25 most frequently misspelled words by grade level *(too* and *their* rank first and second, respectively, in grades 1 through 6) and the 200 most frequently misspelled words overall. In addition, Thomas provides 15 pages of sensible teaching strategies, as well as diagnostic tests of spelling errors, corrective techniques, record-keeping forms, and 24 pages of instructional games and special activities. In short, Thomas's book contains almost everything a teacher needs to develop a complete spelling program.

As figure 12-1 shows, the number of words needed to account for different percentages of running text in widely separated American and Canadian studies remains remarkably stable. Many recent computer-assisted counts corroborate the stability of word frequency over time. A good source of words in addition to those provided in Thomas (1979) is *The American Heritage Word Frequency Book* (Carroll, Davies, and Richman 1971).

Figure 12-1: Frequency of word usage from a 1945 USA and a 1975 Canadian study (data from Thomas 1979)

Number of Different words	Percentage of USA, 1945	Total Word Count Canada, 1975
50	N/A	49%
100	60%	59%
500	82%	80%
1000	89%	87%
1500	93%	90%
2000	95%	92%
2500	N/A	94%
3000	N/A	95%

Does a core list encompass all the words a child needs to be able to spell? No. In addition to a core vocabulary, children need to learn to spell words of personal interest, as well as technical, subject-specific words. For example, a grade 2 child writing a story about rockets and space travel may well want to use the word *astronaut*, a word not found on a grade 2 high-frequency word list. Similarly, many specialized terms in subjects such as math, social studies, and science do not appear on high-frequency word lists. Yet it is important for a student to be able to spell those words *when they are needed.*

What is the best strategy for teaching spelling? The most important principle is this: teachers should not take time teaching what a child already knows.[3] It is counterproductive for all children in the class to work on the same list of spelling words. Instead, teachers should employ a three-step spelling strategy involving **pretest**, **study**, and **post-test**. In all cases, students must self-correct their spelling because it is important for them to *see* where they have made errors.

A week's spelling program in a grade 4 class might work something like this: On Monday, the teacher dictates a list of 12 core words for the entire class to spell. This is the pretest. Students self-correct their pretest and identify misspelled words. From Tuesday through Thursday, they study the *misspelled* words, plus a number from their personal spelling list and other subject-specific words. On Friday, they are again tested on the entire list. In the study portion of the strategy, students follow these six steps:

1. Write the word correctly on a card and look at it carefully.
2. Pronounce the word accurately.
3. Think about the word with particular reference to the misspelling.
4. Cover the word and write it from memory.
5. Check the spelling.
6. Repeat steps 1–5 as necessary.

The key to learning to spell is developing visual images of each word and storing those images in long-term memory. In so doing, we create a mental template against which to compare the same word when we later write it.

How much time per day should students spend on learning to spell? Research has conclusively shown that ten to fifteen minutes of concentrated study daily is the most effective. The effectiveness decreases if the time period is lengthened or the frequency decreased. We are speaking here of time spent in relatively isolated spelling study of high-frequency core vocabulary and personal and/or technical words. Of course, spelling correctly is an important part of the writing process. In fact, when a next-to-final draft of writing is completed, any misspelled words should be entered into a student's personal spelling notebook, joining other words studied during the ten-to-fifteen-minute formal spelling class.

How can a teacher ensure that words learned during formal spelling study transfer to students' writing? Quite simply, it is not possible to ensure transfer. In fact, we should expect students to make more errors in their connected writing than on tests derived from spelling lists. After all, connected writing focuses on meaning, while the spelling tests focus on spelling. As editing and proofreading become a normal part of the writing process, however, students involved in a systematic program of spelling as outlined above will learn to identify spelling errors more efficiently.

Are there specific spelling practices to avoid? Unfortunately, yes. Here is a brief list of largely unhelpful (and in some cases downright harmful) practices used in teaching spelling:

- writing words in the air
- rebuking children for asking how to spell words
- telling children to spell words the way they sound
- using the writing of spelling words as a form of punishment[4]

- having children exchange papers when checking pretests and mastery tests
- unscrambling words

Instead, teachers are wise to choose these *helpful* spelling practices:

- providing real audiences for student writing
- teaching proofreading skills and insisting on their use
- being a good model by writing with and in front of students
- teaching spelling both formally and informally
- helping students to develop a spelling conscience

Perfect spelling is a goal to aim for, although it is seldom reached. I probably spell about ninety-eight percent of my words correctly. In almost any other endeavor, ninety-eight percent accuracy is an enviable record; in spelling it is mediocre. Were I to apply to my personnel manager friend, he might well reject my application outright, except that I would ask someone else to check the spelling before submitting it. Even professional writers have editors or at least spell-checking programs on their word processors. Students vary in the acuity of their visual memory and thus in their spelling ability. With sensible instruction, appropriate modeling, wide reading, writing accompanied by personal and peer editing, and a good dictionary, most manage to break through the spell of spelling successfully.

Recommended Resources for Teaching Spelling

◊ Jo Phenix and Doreen Scott-Dunne. 1991. *Spelling instruction that makes sense.* Markham, ON: Pembroke Publishers.

◊ Mary Tarasoff. 1990. *Spelling strategies you can teach.* Victoria, BC: Pixelart Graphics–Active Learning Institute.

◊ Ves Thomas. 1979. *Teaching spelling: Canadian word lists and instructional techniques.* 2nd ed. Toronto, ON: Gage.

Research Studies on Spelling

◊ Charles Read. 1986. *Children's creative spelling.* London: Routledge & Kegan Paul.

◊ Rebecca Treiman. 1993. *Beginning to spell.* New York: Oxford University Press.

Punctuation and Capitalization

Punctuation and capitalization serve written language in the same way that stress, pitch, and juncture serve oral language. Writing conferences and mini lessons are the best ways to teach these skills. Worksheets of drill-and-skill exercises are not effective. During instruction, it is useful to refer children to the literature they are currently reading. A class novel can provide a quick reference for teaching paragraphing, the capitalization of names and places, and the writing conventions associated with direct address.

Sammy is writing a story and wants to use dialogue for two characters. He writes, "Who's going to run home for help and who's going to stay here he asked." He is not sure about the placement of his quotation marks and asks his teacher for help. Realizing that several children are struggling with this same skill, she decides to address the issue with a mini lesson. Using a comic strip copied to an overhead transparency, she demonstrates how the actual words spoken by a character are shown inside a balloon. "In a story," she says, "quotation marks are used instead of a balloon; only the actual words spoken belong inside the quotation marks." Using another overhead transparency, the teacher demonstrates her point with a section of a familiar story that includes dialogue. Using Sammy's original piece, the class now works with the teacher, putting the quotation marks where they belong. This collaborative approach is better than working with students in isolation. To reinforce the learning, students will need reminders of such lessons from time to time, or repetition with other examples.

Grammar and Usage

The etymology of the word *grammar* is the Latin *gramma*, meaning either a small grain or a written character or letter. Thus, the study of grammar involves the "bits and pieces" that make up a language. More technically, grammar is the study of how a language is used, including the form and syntax of its words.

Before 1700, there were no books on the structure of English. Grammar meant Latin and Greek grammar, and grammar schools were schools in which the teaching of Latin and Greek predominated. The educated elite of Europe believed Latin and Greek to be superior languages and considered the vernacular languages, including English, inferior. The eighteenth century witnessed the rise of a mercantile middle class that wanted the advantages of an education but had no particular fondness for the traditional classical languages. In that century, more than 250 books on English grammar were published. Unfortunately, in an effort to enhance the status of English through association with classical thought, these grammar books attempted to describe the structure of English in terms of the structure of Latin. But Latin is an inflected language that relies predominantly on word endings and sound (and spelling) changes within words to signal grammatical relationships. In an English sentence, by contrast, it is primarily the *position* of words that determines their grammatical function. Most early grammars of English, as well as current traditional English grammars, artificially impose Latinate grammatical categories on a language that operates by quite different principles.

Various twentieth century English grammars have been developed. Much of our grammatical terminology stems from **traditional** or **prescriptive grammar**, which has its roots in the Latinate grammars mentioned above. Some basic labels for word functions (such as *noun, verb, adjective, adverb, preposition*) are useful in streamlining communication about grammar, but little else about traditional grammar is useful.

Structural grammar developed from structural linguistics, an attempt to describe the structure of each language without preconceptions. To capture that structure with scientific accuracy, structuralists believed, grammar must not appeal to meaning because *meaning* is an imprecise term. The great American linguist Noam Chomsky took issue with the structuralists' flight from meaning, pointing out that grammatical function is often impossible to describe (or even determine) without referring to meaning. For example, "Snoopy is eager to see" and "Snoopy is easy to see" are structurally identical; only by appealing to meaning can we differentiate these two sentences grammatically. Chomsky developed the theory of **transformational grammar** to describe the processes by which deep grammatical structure (unconscious grammatical knowledge) is transformed into the surface structure grammar that we speak and write.[5]

The foregoing serves as a preamble to pondering whether grammar instruction (of any kind) should be a formal part of the English language arts curriculum. Constance Weaver (1979) comments on this question in her book *Grammar for Teachers:*

> One valid reason for teaching grammar may simply be that language is such a marvelous human achievement it deserves to be studied. Another reason may be that, properly approached, the study of grammar can help students discover how to collect data, formulate and test hypotheses, draw generalizations—in short, it can help students learn to approach something as a scientist does. However, the most common reason for teaching grammar has been the assumption that it will have a positive effect upon students' ability to use the language. Unfortunately, this assumption seems unwarranted. (88)

Of all the pedagogical issues in English education, the relationship between students' grammatical knowledge and their speaking and writing ability has been the most thoroughly researched for the past ninety years. The findings are unequivocal. The impressive fact is that:

> [I]n all these studies, carried out in places and at times far removed from each other, often by highly experienced and disinterested investigators, the results have been consistently negative so far as the value of grammar in the improvement of language expression is concerned. Surely there is no justification in the available evidence for the great expenditure of time and effort still being devoted to formal grammar in American schools. (DeBoer as quoted in Weaver 1979, 89)

In the more current *Handbook of Research on Teaching the English Language Arts*, Hillocks reviews studies of written composition done from 1963 to 1982 and concludes:

> School boards, administrators, and teachers who impose the systematic study of traditional school grammar on their students over lengthy periods of time in the name of teaching them writing do them a gross disservice which should not be tolerated by anyone concerned with the effective teaching of good writing. (Hillocks and Smith 1991, 596)

There are two main reason why the formal study of grammar has such a dismal record in improving language expression. First, typical grammar pedagogy teaches students to break language apart, while speaking and writing require the synthesis of the parts into meaningful wholes. Diagramming sentences is typical of that atomizing approach. While instruction in grammar typically concentrates on *analysis* of language, instruction in writing should concentrate on *synthesis.* Secondly, teachers too often assume that knowing parts of language automatically transfers to knowing how to apply this fragmented understanding to constructing whole language. To avoid these two problems, teachers must match instructional and performance tasks, and must consciously equip students to transfer their skills.

Students do not enhance their speaking and writing abilities by memorizing language rules or analyzing sentences but by practicing the use of the language. A wide variety of activities can help students at all levels discover and explore the nature of English syntax (the effect that word order and sentence structure have on meaning). These activities fit naturally in the writing process, particularly the prewriting and editing phases. They involve students in active construction and manipulation of their own sentences rather than in deconstructing and analyzing someone else's sentences in a workbook or manual.

The study of English grammar is, of course, worthwhile in its own right. But studying grammar is best postponed until students are in high school and have the cognitive maturity, research ability, and historical perspective to deal with this fascinating but complex subject. Yet all language arts teachers ought to understand the main types of English grammars and the historical and pedagogical issues surrounding this controversial area of English language teaching.

Resources for Grammar Teaching

◊ Charles A. Temple and Jean W. Gillet. 1989. *Language arts: Learning processes and teaching practices,* 2nd ed. Glenview, IL: Scott Foresman. [1997. 2nd ed., paperbound. Addison-Wesley.]

◊ Gail E. Tompkins and Kenneth Hoskisson. 1995. *Language arts: Content and teaching strategies.* 3rd ed. New York: Merrill.

◊ Constance Weaver. 1979. *Grammar for teachers: Perspectives and definitions.* Urbana, IL: National Council of Teachers of English.

◊ Constance Weaver. 1996. *Teaching grammar in context.* Portsmouth, NH: Boynton/Cook.

◊ Constance Weaver, ed. 1998. *Lessons to share on teaching grammar in context.* Portsmouth, NH: Boynton/Cook.

Teaching Handwriting

When my father was a schoolboy in the Netherlands, he got a perfect mark in *Schoon Schrijven* (literally translated, clean or beautiful writing) on his grade 5 report card. My grade 5 report card lists a D for penmanship, suggesting a low heritability for this skill. Unfortunately, the quality of handwriting is often judged to be of greater consequence than the content of the writing, a judgment that modern teachers must try to reverse. Still, fluid and legible handwriting is important.[6]

The goal of all handwriting instruction should be legibility for the sake of effective communication. Legibility is related to speed, but a balance between speed and clarity needs to be found. Too much attention given either to the clarity of handwriting or to its aesthetic dimension may slow the writer down so much that form intrudes upon expression.

Compared to such hot topics as reading, composition, or spelling, the teaching of handwriting seems mundane. Yet it arouses considerable controversy, attracting debate about areas such as learning theory, readiness for instruction, guidelines for teaching, manuscript versus cursive writing, and even the tools and surfaces used in handwriting instruction. We will look briefly at each.

Learning Theory and Handwriting Instruction

Until recently, handwriting pedagogy has emphasized breaking down complex behaviors into discrete skills that are actively taught. This has usually meant having children train their small muscles by forming letters first in the air, next on a chalkboard or easel, and then on lined paper. As children develop control over letter formation, they use paper with increasingly narrow line spacing. Usually, children must adhere to a model, constructing letters with strokes and curves in particular sequences. They spend much time practicing printing and then writing individual letters. Newer theories of learning, in contrast, stress the need for children to make sense of whole concepts before exploring details. By extension, children should explore writing as a whole before learning individual letters. Cognitivists also stress the active meaning-making nature of authentic learning and the need for teachers to act as guides for children engaging in their own explorations.

Marie Clay's (1975) book *What Did I Write?* is an excellent example of the cognitivist approach to children's developing concept of writing. Rather than analyzing the task of handwriting into its components from a scientific, adult perspective, Clay has studied young children's perceptions about print both before they can read or write and as they emerge as readers and writers. As a result of her studies, Clay proposes that children move through five stages of understanding and competence that are based on these five principles:

1. *Recurring principle:* making the same marks repeatedly, as in "scribble writing"
2. *Generative principle:* using a small number of different marks repeatedly but in various orders, so that the "writing" begins to look like printing
3. *Linear principle:* arranging figures in horizontal lines across the page, moving right to left just as often as the conventional left to right
4. *Flexibility principle:* realizing that adding marks to some letters merely embellishes them, but adding other marks, or adding marks to other letters, changes their identity
5. *Sign principle:* recognizing writing as a social activity and asking others to read back what they have written

Clay's work shows us that children perceive global features of writing before they can turn out recognizable writing themselves. This fact suggests that children need to explore and experiment with writing before they begin formal handwriting instruction. Given this reality, I recommend that teachers use a fairly systematic approach to formal handwriting instruction within a broadly cognitivist perspective.

Readiness for Formal Handwriting Instruction

Readiness can be thought of as the adequacy of existing capacity in relation to the demands of a given task (Ausubel 1959). This definition implies that readiness is not simply a matter of a child's cognitive and psychomotor development but is also dependent on the parameters of the task. For example, a six-year-old needs more sophisticated motor control to print letters within half-inch lines than to print them on unlined paper. Therefore, a six-year-old may be "ready" to print on unlined paper but not on lined paper. By watching as children "write" in their unstructured journals, teachers can determine at which of Clay's five stages they are operating.

Generally speaking, kindergarten and grade 1 children benefit from opportunities to use crayons, scissors, and brushes in a variety of activities to develop motor control. Children should demonstrate an ability to copy simple shapes before they begin to construct formal letters, although copying can be extremely dull and frustrating for the child who cannot do it well. Trying to form particular letters is frustrating for a child who cannot make a pencil do what he or she wants. A variety of unforced activities using various media and tools is the best cure for manual clumsiness.

The best test of a child's readiness for formal handwriting instruction is whether the child engages freely in play writing. If the child's play writing shows evidence of Clay's generative and linear principles, instruction in letter writing can begin.

Guidelines for Teaching Handwriting

Direct, formal instructional periods should be kept short since small muscles tire easily. Ten to fifteen minutes a day is plenty. It is best to de-emphasize isolated drills and place handwriting practice in the context of real tasks such as writing captions, recipes, game rules, and ads. The teacher's handwriting on the board and for assignments should serve as a model for student writing. In the primary grades, it is also helpful to prominently display models of upper and lower case letters for easy reference.

Manuscript versus cursive Most handwriting instruction begins by teaching children to print manuscript style letters.

Eventually, usually at about grade 3, children are taught how to write in cursive style. Some researchers suggest that the switch to cursive places an unnecessary burden on children and urge schools to teach cursive handwriting from the beginning. Others say there is no need to introduce cursive writing at all, since many adults write quickly and clearly using manuscript letter forms. Because most of the writing children read is in print, or manuscript form, and because this form is easier for young hands to control, it seems wise to continue the custom of beginning handwriting instruction with a manuscript form. However, the evidence on whether instruction should shift its emphasis toward cursive writing is unclear. The D'Nealian system developed in 1987 by Donald Thurber (1984) offers a middle road, forming manuscript letters in a more rounded style that makes the transition to cursive writing less difficult. In the D'Nealian method, most letters can be converted from manuscript to cursive by adding a single stroke.

Tools and surfaces for writing Handwriting is best learned in the context of real tasks, usually with pencils or pens on paper. Five- to seven-year-olds may lack the finger strength and coordination to hold thin pencils and pens, so they should have opportunities to write with chalk on a board or with thick felt pens at an easel. Because young children want to write like adults as soon as possible, it is wise to introduce fat primary pencils (with medium to broad points) or thick ballpoint pens to use on strong paper early in the process of learning to write. Teachers should demonstrate a comfortable finger position, but students invariably develop their own personal grip. Just as children want to write with adult implements, they also want to write on standard-size lined paper. Larger sheets of paper are good for beginners, but standard 8½ x 11" paper should be available for anyone who wants to use it.

The left-handed child We live in a right-handed world, as any left-handed person trying to use a can opener will testify. Yet about ten to fifteen percent of children are left handed. Teachers need to identify those children and help them overcome special handwriting hurdles. Most children come to kindergarten or grade 1 with marked hand dominance. Watching children as they pick up and use familiar implements such as spoons will usually enable a teacher to determine hand preference. If a given child seems to have no preference, it is probably advisable to encourage the child to use the right hand for writing, but a left-hander should never be forced to write with the right hand.

An older left-handed student or the teacher can model the formation of letters, since it is difficult for left-handed writers to follow a right-handed model. Left-handed writers should turn the bottom edge of the paper away from the left side of the body at about a forty-five degree angle and, if possible, lower the writing surface slightly. Students should concentrate on finding a comfortable and legible style no matter how it differs from the standard right-handed model that most students follow.

Evaluating Handwriting

In assessing children's handwriting progress, it is important to use several yardsticks. These might include samples of appropriate handwriting by children at different age or grade levels, a general assessment instrument, a pupil self-analysis sheet, and an assessment of rate. For examples of these guides, see Flood and Salus (1983, 164–171).

Writing in the Middle School

Middle school students, who are in a world between childhood and adulthood, experience the tension of conflicting emotions and other challenges. Ideally, adolescents in a Christian school feel safe enough to explore and express their thoughts and feelings within the context of the community. Although Nancie Atwell (1987) does not write from a professed Christian stance, she speaks to Christian schools when she says, "We're there to help [middle school] kids open a window on adulthood, on what really matters in life; we help by opening our curricula to [middle school] preoccupations, perspectives, and growing pains" (1987, 50).

Writing can be an excellent vehicle for dealing with tension because it offers scope for private reflection and expression as well as public sharing. By establishing an environment of trust in the context of a writing workshop, middle school teachers can break the usual cycle of teacher-assigned topics, followed by perfunctory student writing, followed by teacher grading.

At the heart of this enterprise is the belief that meaning—what is communicated to an audience—is the most important part of writing and reading. This meaning, in turn, depends on the lived experiences of the reader or writer. It is in this context that rules and skills such as spelling, grammar, and usage become important for students. The following writer's workshop principles are gleaned from Nancie Atwell's (1987) work:

- Writers and readers (students) need regular chunks of time to write.
- Writers need to have "ownership" of what they are writing. In other words, they must have a choice in what they write about.
- Writers need response while they are writing. Writers need to read just as readers need to write.

Working these principles out in the classroom requires attention to the language arts strands of *listening* and *speaking* (see previous chapters) because writer's workshop is predicated on the need for students to listen and speak with both teacher and students.

Writer's workshop is an obvious companion to reader's workshop as discussed earlier. Christian teacher Brian Doornenbal (1997–1998) describes it as follows:

> In a writer's workshop, the context in which a student's writing takes place is not determined by a teacher's lesson plan but rather by the student's experience. The students will be writing virtually

> every day that we have writer's workshop (four forty-minute periods per week). They will be writing on topics of their choosing, although they will certainly have the opportunity to get help from their peers or the teacher in discovering a topic. Throughout the writing process, the students will have the opportunity to get responses in conferences with the teacher and with peers. These conferences will have a definite structure that will be made clear to the students at the beginning of the year. The students will keep a writing folder during the year in which everything that they write will be kept. Their folder will also contain forms on which students can keep a record of all finished work, a list of skills they have learned in editing conferences, and a list of topics that they think they might like to write about at some other time. The students' writing is their text for this part of the course, so they must have it at school each day of writing workshop. Finally, two other important aspects of writer's workshop are the group sharing sessions (five to ten minutes at least twice each week) and the publishing of student work.

Clearly, writer's workshop lends itself to the structure and function of the writing process. And, as in reader's workshop, specific teacher-directed skills teaching occurs through periodic five- to ten-minute mini lessons at the beginning of the period.

Evaluating Writing

A grading system for writing has to take into account all the abilities that come into play when a writer writes. Experimenting, planning, choosing, questioning, anticipating, organizing, reading, listening, reviewing, and editing are all part of the process. Of course, one piece of writing can't provide an accurate picture of a student's abilities, so students need to keep cumulative copies of their writing in a folder (portfolio), preferably stored in a classroom filing cabinet to prevent loss. This writing portfolio, in conjunction with the teacher's dated conference notes, can provide a realistic picture of a student's growth as a writer. Interestingly, students often don't care much about grades on individual pieces of writing if they are truly involved in their writing. A student who writes about the death of a beloved dog, expertise as a hockey player, anger about war, or love for a grandparent isn't writing for a grade. What students do want is specific feedback from peers—and from the teacher, whom they see as a more accomplished writer. Thus the heart of writing evaluation is ongoing, periodic response to writing. This response must address issues as diverse as writing itself, from the use of commas to the trick of capturing accents in dialogue.

When teachers ask about evaluation, they are really asking, How do I rate and rank student writing so I can come up with a mark for my grade book and for a report card? Teachers must deal with these political realities. When setting grades for writing, it is helpful to develop a point system that gives varying weights to the qualities stressed that quarter or semester. Atwell provides the following example of such a scheme:

- 20 points CONTENT (supplies appropriate and significant information)
- 20 points CLARITY (organizes and presents content to meet a reader's needs)
- 20 points MECHANICS (spelling, punctuation, margins, paragraphing, legibility)
- 15 points FOCUS (narrows topics)
- 15 points COMMITMENT (uses time productively, confers with others, and proofreads)
- 10 points RISK-TAKING (willing to try new modes, topics, forms, techniques)

Each of these aspects of a piece of writing can be developed into a detailed rubric that gives a student more precise comments on the writing (see chapter 3 for specifics). By constructing a writing evaluation rubric carefully, the teacher can reduce the amount of written response required for each piece.

Whatever scheme a teacher uses, it must be valid. In other words, evaluation has to reflect both the expectations communicated to students in each day's writing class and the personal writing goals each student has set over an agreed period. Working with the *process* of writing only, or evaluating individual writing solely as a *product* by imposing "objective" standards for "good" writing, disheartens students and erodes classroom rapport. Evaluation must be an occasion for student and teacher to analyze the writing together so that both can grow in understanding what it means to write well and to teach writing well.

Questions for Discussion

1. Do you enjoy writing? What is the most difficult aspect of writing for you?
2. Return to the chapter 8 Questions for Discussion, item 2, and re-examine Matt's story in the light of what you have learned in chapters 9–12.
3. What is your response to those who claim that accepting children's invented spellings encourages error-filled writing?
4. Think back to the last writing task you undertook. To what extent did you engage in a process similar to the one described in this chapter?
5. What audience(s) have you had for your writing? How important is it for you to have an audience? What are some realistic and manageable ways for teachers to increase the diversity of audiences for their students?
6. What are the typical elements of a story grammar? Try drawing a "map" for this structure.
7. In learning the writing conventions, what is meant by the statement that "developmental processes always have an emergent character"?
8. In response to children's requests for help in spelling a particular word, teachers often tell them to "sound it out." If "sounding out" is a child's main spelling strategy, what

stage(s) will the child's spelling represent?

9. What considerations must be met for a child to spell the word *hippopotamus* correctly?
10. A grade 1 child writing a story about space travel spells the word *astronaut* as *astronot*. The teacher tells the child to use the term *space man* instead because *astronaut* is not part of the grade 1 core vocabulary list while *space* and *man* are. What do you think of this teacher's response?
11. Why do students' grades on spelling tests *overestimate* their spelling performance in written work?
12. Why are word scramble puzzles and games like Boggle® not particularly helpful in improving students' spelling abilities?
13. "Punctuation and capitalization serve written language in the same way that stress, pitch, and juncture serve oral language." What are stress, pitch, and juncture?

For Further Consideration

1. Analyze the spelling in the writing of some children in kindergarten through grade 3. What spelling stages can you identify?
2. Analyze the writing of students in the early middle grades (e.g., grades 4 and 5) for the **voice** employed, using Britton's distinctions of expressive, poetic, and transactional voices. Which voices are most prevalent in these students' writing?
3. When I visited classrooms to gather information for this book, many teachers told me that one of their greatest challenges is "teaching creative writing." By creative writing, they mean imaginative, expressive, and poetic writing as found in stories and poems. Why do you think creative writing presents such a teaching challenge?
4. Think back over your entire educational career. How many

times do you recall having a teacher share his or her personal writing with your class? Is your response to this question helpful in addressing question 3?

5. A **semantic map** is a drawing or diagram that provides a visual schematic for a process. Find or create a semantic map that illustrates such text structures as description, comparison-contrast, sequence, cause-effect, and problem-solution.

6. Interview some teachers who teach traditional grammar. Politely ask what they believe to be the value of such teaching. What do you think of their reasons? What research findings can you cite that either support or refute their reasons?

7. Research the D'Nealian handwriting system and compare it with the traditional "stick and ball" instructional method.

8. Ask a number of left-handers to describe their experiences with learning to do handwriting. What suggestions do they have for making the process easier for "lefties"?

9. Research the development of the "qwerty" typewriter/computer keyboard. Why are the letters arranged on the keyboard as they are? Is there an ergonomically more efficient way to arrange the keys? If so, why hasn't it been done?

10. Develop a rubric to use in evaluating each of the following types of writing:
    - personal narrative
    - science fiction story
    - limerick
    - persuasive essay

Endnotes

1 There is a tendency for writing workshop advocates to romanticize process writing for its ability to create classrooms that are more democratic in that students are given a personal voice. Seldom addressed is what happens to the classroom and to individuals when some student voices are mean-spirited and selfish. For an honest and critical examination of the difficulties involved in establishing the writing workshop, see Timothy Lensmire (1994).

2 Joel Kleine, a grade 3 teacher at Northeast Edmonton Christian School in Edmonton, Alberta, Canada, and his wife Amanda, a librarian, contributed this section on teaching and writing poetry.

3 This is one of many reasons commercial spelling programs tend to be ineffective. Students spend too much time working with words they can already spell. In addition, spelling textbooks seldom present the teaching of spelling in ways that are consistent with research findings. The activities in such texts do not encourage risk-taking; rather, they encourage reliance only on rote memorization. The books often contain "busy" pages with mixtures of cartoon graphics, bold colors, and many fonts. There are frequently so many activities on a page that it is hard to tell what is really being taught.

4 In fact, using any school subject as a form of punishment is counterproductive. If we use writing to punish children, we imply that writing is not a pleasurable activity. The same is true for the dubious practice of withholding certain subject-related activities from students as a form of punishment. As a child, I soon realized that arithmetic was an important school subject while physical education, music, and art were frills. Whereas a class was frequently punished through the withholding of PE, music, or art, I can never recall a teacher suggesting that if we didn't behave we'd have to miss math.

5 A thorough exploration of grammar and its teaching can be found in Gail Tompkins and Kenneth Hoskisson's *Language Arts: Content and Teaching Strategies* (1995).

6 For a fascinating cultural history of handwriting in America, see Tamara Thornton (1996).

Conclusion

The Introduction stated that "the central purpose of this book is to help Christian teachers and future teachers explore what it means for them to love God and neighbor linguistically." It is up to my readers to judge whether this intended purpose has been realized. At the conclusion of a writing project on a subject as broad as the English language arts, one is aware that so much more could be said about the topic. This sort of book is always a compromise between comprehensiveness and the limitations of the author's time and talent.

Thank you for reading this book. I truly hope that it is both principled and practical for your work as a student, teacher, principal, or parent. If you have any specific comments or questions about the book, or suggestions for how to improve possible future editions, you can reach me as indicated below.

My advice to students who often struggle with how to end a piece of writing is to simply stop when they have written what they intended to say. Here I will follow my own advice.

Dr. Robert Bruinsma
The King's University College
9125 – 50th Street
Edmonton, Alberta T5W 1W8
Canada
robert.bruinsma@kingsu.ca

Appendix 1

Request for Reconsideration of a Book[1]

Complainant represents self ______________________________
or organization ______________________________________

Please write responses on separate paper.

What do you object to about the book? (Please be specific.)

1. What do you feel might be the result of reading this book?
2. For what age group if any would you recommend this book?
3. Is there anything good about this book?
4. Did you read the entire book? If not, what parts?
5. Are you aware of how literary critics have judged this book?
6. What do you believe is the theme or basic message of the book?
7. What would you like the school to do with this book?
   ☐ Do not assign it to my child.
   ☐ Withdraw it from all students as well as from my child.
   ☐ Send it back to the library committee for re-evaluation.
8. What book do you recommend that the library acquire in place of this one?

Signed ______________________________Date______________

[1] Taken with permission from Evelyn Sterenberg and Sharon DeMoor, eds. 1991. *Libraries in the '90s: A Handbook for Christian Schools* (Appendix D). Edmonton, AB: Christian Schools International. District 11.

Appendix 2

Readability: Evaluating Text Difficulty

Textbooks continue to be a major source of information for students. It follows that the teacher should ensure that students are able to read the texts provided for them. In order to assess the appropriateness of a given text for a given student, one needs to know (1) the reading level of the student and (2) the readability level of the text.

Determining the Expected Range of Reading Ability at a Given Grade Level

Students in every class vary in a host of ways. Those in a given class vary by weight, height, shoe size, skin color, interests, scholastic aptitude, and reading ability. An accepted estimate for the **range** of reading ability found in a given classroom can be calculated by using a simple formula:

Range in Reading Ability = 2/3 Chronological Age

R = 2/3 CA

Estimate Chronological Age (CA) by adding the number 5 to the grade level under consideration.

For example: The CA of children in grade 6 is estimated to be 11 [6 + 5 = 11].

Some Examples of Expected Reading Range

Example 1: What is the expected reading range in an "average" grade 3 class?

R = 2/3 CA   CA = 5 + 3 = 8   R = 2/3 X 8 = 16/3 = 5.3

Thus, if the range of reading ability in a grade 3 class is 5.3 grades, the spread around the mean of 3 is 1/2 of 5.3 = 2.7

K-•——1——2——3——4——5——•-6——7

Thus in a typical grade 3 classroom, it is common to find children with reading abilities ranging from emergent kindergarten to grade 5.7 (dots on the scale).

Example 2: What is the expected reading range in the "average" grade 9 class?

R = 2/3 CA   CA = 5 + 9 = 14   R = 2/3 X 14 = 9.3

3——4—•—-5——6——7——8——9——10——11——12——13—•—14——15

Thus, in a typical grade 9 class, the range of reading ability is likely to vary between about grades 4.3 and 13.7 (well into the first year of college, as indicated by the dots on the scale).

Implications

The better the teaching in a school, the *greater* will be the range in reading ability as one moves up the grades. As discussed in chapter 11, the range in reading ability widens because good teaching maximizes the opportunities of all students. The more capable students will advance faster than the less capable, causing the spread in reading ability to increase over time.

There are two implications of the wide range of reading ability in a typical classroom:

1. Teachers need to know the reading demands of the texts they are using.
2. Teachers need to adapt their instruction to meet the needs of readers with a wide range of reading abilities.

Teachers can determine the approximate reading difficulty of a text in a number of ways. A recent method that is gaining acceptance is that of **leveling texts,** especially for primary grade reading materials. At these lower levels, fine gradations of text difficulty are important to ensure that the texts given to beginning readers are "just right" for them. Lori Rog and Wilfrid Burton (2002) suggest the following as criteria to use in developing a leveling system: vocabulary, size and layout of print, predictability, illustration support, and complexity of concepts. It takes considerable effort and commitment to learn how to use a given leveling system. Chapter 4 lists a number of resources that provide published lists of leveled books as well as training for those who wish to learn how to level books themselves.

A simpler procedure for determining the readability of a text is the use of a **readability formula**, and teachers can determine the ability of individual students to interact with a given text using the **cloze procedure.**

Readability Formulas

Various readability formulas and graphs measure the **surface difficulty** of a given text. Surface difficulty involves such factors as word length and sentence length. The operative idea is that word length is a measure of vocabulary difficulty and that sentence length tends to be a measure of syntactic complexity. Thus, readability measures are predicated on the assumption that long words and sentences are more difficult to read than short words and sentences. Elements of readability such as concept load and idea density are not so easily measured however, and for that reason texts with a relatively low readability score may still be conceptually very difficult. Teacher judgment and experience are still important in assessing the suitability of a particular text for a student or class (see comments above about leveling text).

One of the most widely used readability formulas has been developed by Edward Fry of Rutgers University (Fry 1977). Fry transformed his formula into a handy, noncopyrighted graph (see page 355). Using the graph provides the teacher with a rough estimate of the **reading grade level (RGL)** of a text. Many novels for young readers will have a reading grade level indicated inside or on the back cover. The Fountas and Pinnell (1996, 2000) leveling system also provides such information. For example, a designation of RL 2.7 means that the book is appropriate for a child who reads at least as well as the typical student in the seventh month of the second grade. However, teachers must remember that this is an approximate level, *and that there is always a range of reading ability within a given class.*

Cloze Screening

A more relevant thing to know than the approximate readability of a text is how well a *given student* can read a *given text*. In other words, it is important for teachers to discover how well particular students interact with a text. Readability defined in this interactive way is a measure not just of text difficulty but of reader ability as well. How well a given reader can access a given text depends largely on factors *internal to the reader,* including the reader's familiarity with the subject matter (the reader's *prior knowledge*) and the reader's ability to decode text, use context clues, and so forth. A useful measure of a student's ability to interact with text is a technique called **cloze screening**.

Cloze Screening Procedure

Construction of the reading material

1. Select a reading passage of approximately 275 words from material you will be assigning your students. This should be material that they have not yet read.

2. Leave the first sentence intact. Starting with the second sentence, omit the fifth word and type a 12-space line in its place. Delete every fifth word thereafter, until you have 50 underlined blanks. Finish that sentence. Type one more sentence intact.

Administration

Before you pass out the tests, inform the students that they will be taking a test that will try to measure the difficulty of their class reading materials. Show them how the cloze works on the board with sample sentences such as, "It's dark in here, please turn on the ____________." Or, "The man ____________ down the stairs." Emphasize to students that they can get many clues from the context of the reading passage that will help them determine words that fit. Also, tell them that the length of the blank has nothing to do with the length of the missing word.

Scoring

1. Prepare a list of the missing words. Have students mark their own passage. Count as correct every ***exact word*** that students supply. ***Do not*** count synonyms judged satisfactory. Students will spend far too much time trying to judge the appropriateness of "almost" answers. (How to treat synonyms is explained below.)
2. Multiply the total number of exact word replacements by two in order to determine each student's cloze percentage score.

Interpretation

0%–39%	FRUSTRATION LEVEL [TROUBLE]
40%–59%	INSTRUCTIONAL LEVEL [FUNCTIONING]
60%–100%	INDEPENDENT LEVEL [EASY]

At **frustration level** students will not be able to comprehend the text even when all the words are intact. The vocabulary and syntax are too challenging for their reading ability. The challenge for the teacher is to find another way of presenting the material, either by using another text on the same topic at the students' instructional/independent level, or by presenting the information in some way other than written text.

Students who score at the **instructional level** can read the text with teacher assistance. Such assistance may include the preteaching of vocabulary, the provision of reading guides, or other pre-reading help.

Students who score at the **independent level** can read the text without teacher assistance and may, in fact, be able to read more challenging material on the topic.

Obviously, the percentage ranges for the three levels are wide enough that teachers need to exercise judgment when matching texts with readers. Teachers may wish to examine the cloze tests of students who score at the boundary of a particular level. For example, suppose a student scores 58% on a cloze screening. Upon examining the student's responses, the teacher finds that many of them are acceptable synonyms for the missing words. In this instance, it may be warranted to consider this material at the student's independent rather than instructional level.

Fry Readability Graph

by Edward Fry, Rutgers University Reading Center, New Brunswick, NJ

1. Randomly select three 100-word passages from a book or article, beginning at the beginning of a sentence. Count proper nouns, numerals, or abbreviations.
2. Count the number of sentences in each 100-word passage, estimating the fraction of the last sentence to the nearest tenth.
3. Count the number of syllables in the passage. A syllable is defined phonetically so that generally there are as many syllables as vowel sounds in a word. (For example, *stopped* has one syllable, and *wanted* has two syllables.) One way to count syllables is to put a mark above every syllable in each word (two marks over *wanted*, for example). When you get to the end of the passage, count the marks.
4. Plot the average number of syllables and the average number of sentences per hundred words on the graph to determine the approximate grade level. If you observe great variability in sentence count or syllable count in the three passages, you can conclude that its readability is uneven, and you may want to average additional passages. Few books will fall into either of the gray areas, but when they do, grade level scores are invalid.

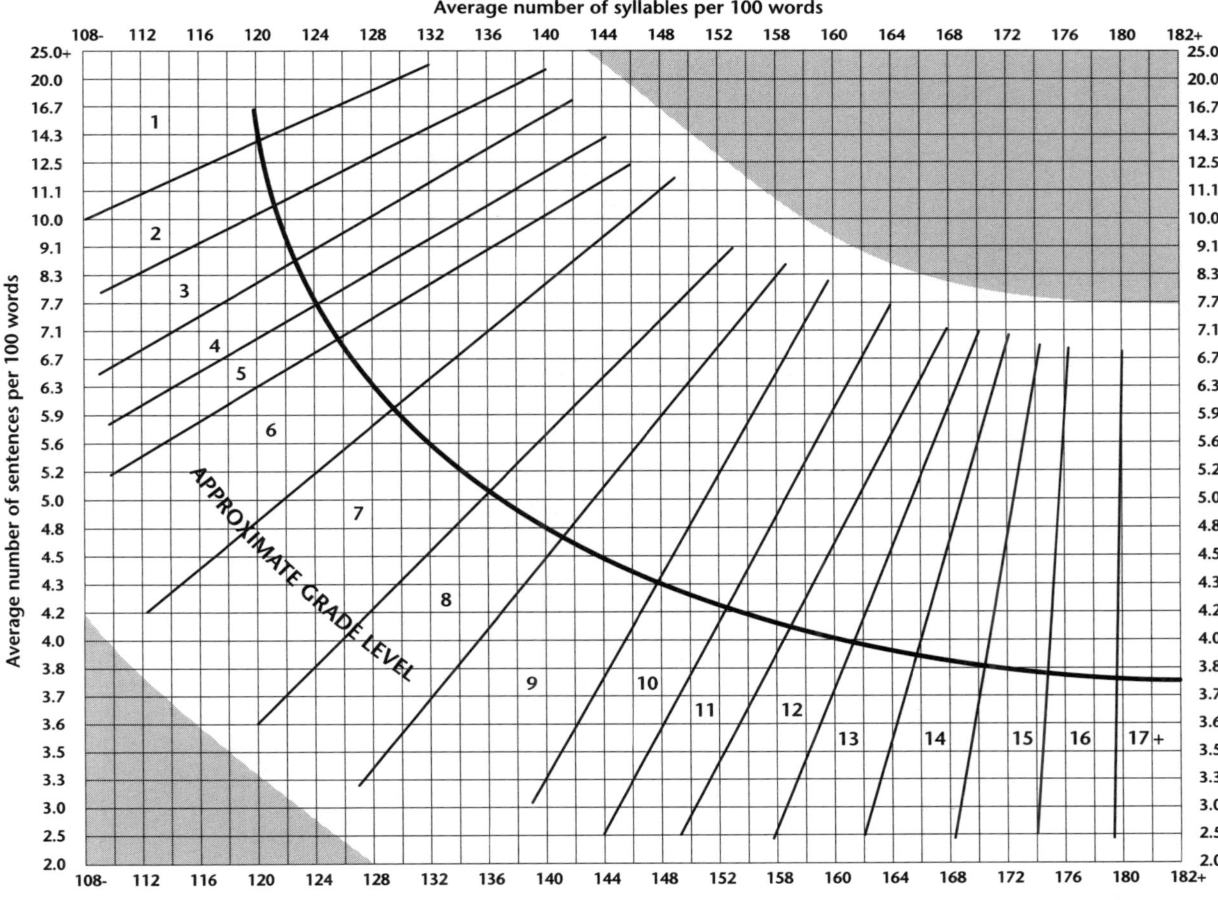
Average number of syllables per 100 words
108- 112 116 120 124 128 132 136 140 144 148 152 158 160 164 168 172 176 180 182+
Average number of sentences per 100 words
25.0+ 20.0 16.7 14.3 12.5 11.1 10.0 9.1 8.3 7.7 7.1 6.7 6.3 5.9 5.6 5.2 5.0 4.8 4.5 4.3 4.2 4.0 3.8 3.7 3.6 3.5 3.3 3.0 2.5 2.0
APPROXIMATE GRADE LEVEL
1 2 3 4 5 6 7 8 9 10 11 12 13 14 15 16 17+

References

Adams, Marilyn J. 1990. *Beginning to read: Thinking and learning about print.* Cambridge, MA: MIT Press.

Adams, Pamela E. 1997. Reading instruction in Christian schools: Does one's view of Scripture influence pedagogy? *Journal of Research on Christian Education* 6, no. 2:233–260.

Alexander, Lloyd. 1971. *The king's fountain.* New York: Dutton.

Atwell, Nancie. 1987. *In the middle: Writing, reading, and learning with adolescents.* Portsmouth, NH: Heinemann.

——. 1998. *In the middle: New understandings about writing, reading, and learning.* 2nd ed. Portsmouth, NH: Heinemann.

Ausubel, David. 1959. Viewpoints from related disciplines: Human growth and development. *Teachers College Record* 60:245–254.

Bader, Lois A. 1998a. *Bader listening test.* Upper Saddle River, NJ: Merrill/Prentice Hall.

——. 1998b. Oral language. In *Reading and language inventory.* 3rd ed. Columbus, OH: Merrill/Prentice Hall.

——. 2002. *Reading and language inventory.* 4th ed. Upper Saddle River, NJ: Merrill/Prentice Hall.

Baghban, Marcia. 1984. *Our daughter learns to read and write: A case study from birth to three.* Newark, DE: International Reading Association.

Bainbridge, Joyce, and Grace Malicky. 2000. *Constructing meaning: Balancing elementary language arts.* 2nd ed. Toronto, ON: Harcourt Canada.

Barton, James, and Angelo Collins, eds. 1997. *Portfolio assessment: A handbook for educators.* Menlo Park, CA: Innovative Learning Publications.

Best, Raphaela. 1983. *We've all got scars: What boys and girls learn in elementary school.* Bloomington, IN: Indiana University Press.

Bissex, Glenda L. 1980. *Gnys at wrk: A child learns to write and read.* Cambridge, MA: Harvard University Press.

Blomberg, Doug. 1980. Toward a Christian theory of knowledge. *No icing on the cake: Christian foundations for education in Australia.* edited by Jack Mechielsen. Melbourne, Australia: Brookes-Hall Publishing Foundation.

——. 1995. Teachers as articulate artisans. *Nurturing reflective Christians to teach: A valiant role for the nation's Christian colleges and universities.* Edited by Dan Elliott. New York: University of America Press.

Bloomfield, Leonard, and Clarence L. Barnhart. 1961. *Let's read: A linguistic approach.* Detroit, MI: Wayne State University Press.

Bolt, John. 1993. *The Christian story and the Christian school.* Grand Rapids, MI: Christian Schools International.

Boman, Thorleif. 1960. *Hebrew thought compared with Greek.* New York: W.W. Norton & Company.

Britton, James N. 1970. *Language and learning.* London: Penguin Books.

——. 1975. *The development of writing abilities, 8–11.* London: Macmillan.

——. 1992. *Language and learning.* 2nd ed. London: Penguin Books.

Brizendine, Nancy H., and James L. Thomas. 1982. *Learning through dramatics: Ideas for teachers and librarians.* Phoenix, AZ: Oryx Press.

Bruinsma, Robert W. 1981. A critique of round robin oral reading in the elementary classroom. *Reading – Canada – Lecture* 1, no. 4: 78–81.

——. 1984. Upside-down "i's" and other conventions of print: A literacy story. *Early Childhood Education* 17, no. 1:22–25.

——. 1987. Metalinguistic awareness and beginning reading: Some instructional implications. *Reading – Canada – Lecture* 5, no. 4:213–219.

——. 1990a. *Language arts in Christian schools.* Grand Rapids, MI: Christian Schools International.

——. 1990b. Learning to read and learning to ride a bicycle: Children's conceptions of reading. *Australian Journal of Reading* 13, no. 2:114–127.

——. 1993. Of dogs and witches: Dangerous books in the Christian school classroom. *Christian Educators Journal* 33, no. 1:15–17.

——. 1994. Phonics and the teaching of reading in Christian schools: A further response to Thogmartin. *Journal of Research on Christian Education* 3, no. 2:285–295.

——. 1995. A rose by any other name: Response to James Rooks. *Journal of Research on Christian Education* 4, no. 2:271–275.

Burns, Susan M., Peg Griffin, and Catherine E. Snow. 1999. *Starting out right: A guide to promoting children's reading success.* Washington, DC: National Academy Press.

Butler, Deborah, and Tom Liner. 1995. Chapter 9: Talking it out: Oral language. *Room to grow: Natural language arts in the middle school.* Durham, NC: Carolina Academic Press.

Butler, Dorothy. 1995. *Babies need books.* 3rd ed. London: Penguin Books.

Butler, Dorothy, and Marie Clay. 1987. *Reading begins at home: Preparing children for reading before they go to school.* Portsmouth, NH: Heinemann.

Calkins, Lucy. 1986. *The art of teaching writing.* Portsmouth, NH: Heinemann.

——. 1992. *Living between the lines.* Toronto, ON: Irwin.

Campbell, Patricia. 2003. *Teaching reading to adults: A balanced approach.* Edmonton, AB: Grass Roots Press.

Campbell, Patricia, and Flo Brokop. 1998. *Supplemental training for practitioners in literacy education (STAPLE Vol. 1): Unlocking the mystique of teaching reading and writing.* Edmonton, AB: Literacy Coordinators of Alberta.

Carroll, John B., Peter Davies, and Barry Richman. 1971. *The American Heritage word frequency book.* Boston: Houghton Mifflin.

Cazden, Courtney B. 1972. *Education and language.* Toronto, ON: Holt, Rinehart & Winston.

Chall, Jeanne S. 1967. *Learning to read: The great debate.* New York: McGraw-Hill. [1996. 3rd ed. Fort Worth, TX: Harcourt Brace College Publ.]

Chomsky, Carol S. 1971. Write first, read later. *Childhood Education* 47:296–299.

Chomsky, Noam. 1957. *Syntactic structures.* The Hague: Mouton.

——. 1959. Review of *Verbal behavior,* by B. F. Skinner. *Language* 38, no. 1:26–58.

Clark, Margaret M. 1976. *Fluent readers: What can they teach us?* London: Heinemann.

Clay, Marie M. 1975. *What did I write?* Portsmouth, NH: Heinemann.

——. 1979a. *The early detection of reading difficulties: A diagnostic survey with recovery procedures.* 2nd ed. Portsmouth, NH: Heinemann.

——. 1979b. *Reading: The patterning of complex behavior.* 2nd ed. Auckland, NZ: Heinemann.

——. 1993. *An observation survey of early literacy achievement.* Portsmouth, NH: Heinemann.

Clay, Marie M., Malcolm Gill, Ted Glynn, Tony McNauton, and Keith Salmon. 1983. *Record of oral language & Biks and Gutches.* Portsmouth, NH: Heinemann.

Cohen, Miriam. 1980. *First grade takes a test.* New York: Dell.

Coles, Gerald. 2000. *Misreading education: The bad science that hurts children.* Portsmouth, NH: Heinemann.

Crawford, P. A. 1995. Early literacy: Emerging perspectives. *Journal of Research on Childhood Education* 10, no. 1:71–86.

Cullinan, Bernice E., ed. 1993. *Children's voices: Talk in the classroom.* Newark, DE: International Reading Association.

Cullinan, Bernice E., M. C. Scala, and V. C. Schroder. 1995. *Three voices: An invitation to poetry across the curriculum.* York, ME: Stenhouse Publishers.

Cunningham, Patricia M. 2000. *Phonics they use: Words for reading and writing.* 3rd ed. Boston: Addison Wesley/Longman.

Dahl, Karin L., Patricia L. Scharer, Lora L. Lawson, and Patricia R. Grogan. 2001. *Rethinking phonics: Making the best teaching decisions.* Portsmouth, NH: Heinemann.

Daines, D. 1986. Are teachers asking high-level questions? *Education* 106 (summer): 368–374.

Dakos, K. 2001. Poetry feeds the spirit. *Instructor* 110, no. 7:33–36.

Den Boer, Lloyd, ed. 1996. *Christian pathways for schooling: Language arts handbook.* 2nd ed. Langley, BC: Society of Christian Schools in British Columbia.

Devine, Thomas G. 1982. *Listening skills schoolwide: Activities and programs.* Urbana, IL: ERIC Clearinghouse on Reading and Communication Skills, and the National Council of Teachers of English.

——. 1987. *Teaching study skills: A guide for teachers.* 2nd ed. Boston: Allyn & Bacon.

DeWitt-Brinks, Dawn, and Steven C. Rhodes. 1992. Listening instruction: A qualitative meta-analysis of twenty-four selected studies. Paper presented at the 42nd Annual Meeting of the International Communication Association. Miami, FL, May 20–25. ERIC Document no. ED351721.

Dixon, Neill, Anne Davies, and Colleen Politano. 1996. *Learning with readers theater: Building connections.* Winnipeg, MB: Peguis Publishers.

Doake, David. 1998. *Reading begins at birth.* Richmond Hill, ON: Scholastic–TAB Publications.

Donaldson, Margaret M. 1978. *Children's minds.* Huntington, NY: Fontana/Collins.

Doornenbal, Brian. 1997–2001. *Grade 9 language arts course outline.* Edmonton, AB: West Edmonton Christian School.

Downing, John A. 1964. *How your children are being taught to read with i.t.a.* London: W. & R. Chambers.

——. 1967. *Evaluating the Initial Teaching Alphabet: A study of the influence of English orthography on learning to read and write.* London: Cassell.

——. 1976. The reading instruction register. *Language Arts* 53:962–966, 980.

Durkin, Dolores. 1978–1979. What classroom observations reveal about reading comprehension instruction. *Reading Research Quarterly* 14, no. 4: 481–533.

Edelsky, Carol. 1994. Education for democracy. *Language Arts* 71, no. 4:252–257.

Entwistle, Doris R. 1971. Implications of language socialization for reading models and for learning to read. *Reading Research Quarterly* 7, no. 1:111–167.

Fennema, Jack E. 1980. *Nurturing children in the Lord: A study guide for teachers on developing a biblical approach to discipline.* Phillipsburg, NJ: Presbyterian and Reformed Publishing Co.

Fiderer, Adele. 1998. *35 rubrics and checklists to assess reading and writing: Grades K–2.* New York: Scholastic Professional Books.

——. 1999. *40 rubrics and checklists to assess reading and writing: Grades 3–6.* New York: Scholastic Professional Books.

Flesch, Rudolph F. 1955. *Why Johnny can't read—and what you can do about it.* New York: Harper.

——. 1981. *Why Johnny still can't read: A new look at the scandal of our schools.* New York: Harper & Row.

Fletcher, Ralph, and Joann Portalupi. 1998. *Craft lessons: Teaching writing K–8.* Portland, ME: Stenhouse Publishers.

Flood, James, and Peter H. Salus 1983. *Language and the language arts.* Upper Saddle River, NJ: Prentice Hall.

Fountas, Irene C., Arene C. Fountas, and Gay Su Pinnell 1996. *Guided reading: Good first teaching for all children.* Portsmouth, NH: Heinemann.

——. 1999. *Matching books to readers: Using leveled books in guided reading, K–3.* Portsmouth, NH: Heinemann.

——. 2000. *Guiding readers and writers (Grades 3–6): Teaching comprehension, genre, and content literacy.* Portsmouth, NH: Heinemann.

——. 2001. *The primary literacy video collection: Classroom Management—Video 1: Managing the day* and *Video 2: Planning for effective teaching.* Portsmouth, NH: Heinemann.

Friedman, Paul G. 1978. *Listening processes: Attention, understanding, evaluation.* 2nd ed. Washington, DC: National Education Association.

Fry, Edward B. 1977. Fry's readability graph: Clarifications, validity, and extension to level 17. *Journal of Reading* 21, no. 3:242–252.

Fry, Edward B., Jacqueline E. Kress, and Dona L. Fountoukidis. 2000. *The reading teacher's book of lists.* 4th ed. Paramus, NJ: Prentice Hall.

Gambrell, L. B. 1987. Children's oral language during teacher-directed reading instruction. *Research in literacy: Merging perspectives.* Edited by J. E. Readence and R. S. Baldwin. Thirty-sixth Yearbook of the National Reading Conference.

Gardner, Howard. 1983. *Frames of mind: The theory of multiple intelligences.* New York: Basic Books.

——. 1991. *The unschooled mind: How children think and how schools should teach.* New York: Basic Books.

——. 1999a. *The disciplined mind: What all students should understand.* New York: Simon & Schuster.

——. 1999b. *Intelligence reframed: Multiple intelligences for the twenty-first century.* New York: Basic Books.

Geller, Linda G. 1985. *Word play and language learning for children.* Urbana, IL: National Council of Teachers of English.

Gilbert, L. C. 1940. Effect on silent reading of attempting to follow oral reading. *Elementary School Journal* 40: 614–621.

Gillingham, Anna, and Bessie W. Stillman. 1979. *Remedial training for children with specific disability in reading, spelling, and penmanship.* Cambridge, MA: Educators Publishing Service.

Gleason, Jean B., ed. 2001. *The development of language.* 5th ed. Boston: Allyn & Bacon.

Goodlad, John I. 1984. *A place called school.* New York: McGraw-Hill.

Goodman, Kenneth S. 1986. Basal readers: A call to action. *Language Arts* 63, no. 4:358–363.

——, ed. 1998. *In defense of good teaching: What teachers need to know about the "reading wars."* York, ME: Stenhouse Publishers.

Goodman, Kenneth S., Patrick Shannon, Yvonne S. Freeman, and Sharon Murphy. 1988. *Report card on basal readers.* Katonah, NY: Richard C. Owens Publishers.

Goodman, Yetta, and Kenneth S. Goodman. 1997. To err is human: Learning about language processes by analyzing miscues. *Theoretical models and processes of reading.* Edited by B. Ruddell and H. Singer. 4th ed. Newark, DE: International Reading Association.

Graham, Donovan. 1995. The implications of biblical faith to classroom learning. Paper presented at Council of Christian Colleges and Universities Teacher Education Workshop, August 25–29, Cedar Springs, WA.

——. 2003. *Teaching redemptively: Bringing grace and truth into your classroom.* Colorado Springs, CO: Association of Christian Schools International.

Graves, Donald H. 1983. *Writing: Teachers and children at work.* Portsmouth, NH: Heinemann.

——. 1991. *Build a literate classroom.* Portsmouth, NH: Heinemann.

Greene, Albert E. 1998. *Reclaiming the future of Christian education: A transforming vision.* Colorado Springs, CO: Association of Christian Schools International.

Groome, Thomas. 1980. *Christian religious education: Sharing our story and vision.* San Francisco, CA: Harper & Row.

Gunning, Thomas G. 2001. *Assessing and correcting reading and writing difficulties.* 2nd ed. Boston: Allyn & Bacon.

Halliday, Michael A. 1973. *Explorations in the functions of language.* London: Edward Arnold.

——. 1975. *Learning how to mean: Explorations in the development of language.* London: Edward Arnold.

Harris, Theodore L., and Richard E. Hodges, eds. 1995. *The literacy dictionary: The vocabulary of reading and writing.* Newark, DE: International Reading Association.

Harvey, Stephanie, and Anne Goudvis. 2000. *Strategies that work: Teaching comprehension to enhance understanding.* York, ME: Stenhouse Publishers.

Heaney, Seamus, and Ted Hughes, eds. 1982. *The rattle bag.* London: Faber and Faber.

Heard, Georgia. 1989. *For the good of the earth and the sun: Teaching poetry.* Exeter, NH: Heinemann.

Heath, Shirley B. 1983. *Ways with words: Language, life, and work in communities and classrooms.* Cambridge, MA: Cambridge University Press.

Hill, Susan. 1990. *Reader's theater: Performing the text.* South Yarra, Australia: Eleanor Curtain Publishing.

Hillocks, George, Jr., and Michael W. Smith. 1991. Grammar and usage. *Handbook of research on teaching the English language arts.* edited by James Flood, Julie M. Jensen, Diane Lapp, and James R. Squire. New York: Macmillan.

Hinshelwood, J. 1917. *Congenital word-blindness.* London: Lewis.

Hood, Ida M. 1983. *Is anyone listening? A resource handbook for teachers.* West Vancouver, BC: R. J. Watts and Associates Ltd.

Horn, Ernest. 1927. *The basic writing vocabulary.* Iowa City, IA: University of Iowa.

Hoyt, Linda. 2000. *Snapshots: Literacy minilessons up close.* Portsmouth, NH: Heinemann.

Huey, Edmund B. [1908] 1968. *The psychology and pedagogy of reading: With a review of the history of reading and writing and of methods, texts, and hygiene in reading.* Cambridge, MA: MIT Press.

Hulit, Lloyd M., ed. 1997. *Born to talk: An introduction to speech and language development.* 2nd ed. Boston: Allyn & Bacon.

Hull, John E. 2003. Christian teaching and teaching Christianly. *Christian Scholars Review.* 32 (2): 203–223.

Hull, Marion A., and Barbara J. Fox. 1998. *Phonics for the teacher of reading.* 7th ed. Upper Saddle River, NJ: Prentice Hall.

Hutchins, Pat. 1968. *Rosie's walk.* New York: Scholastic–TAB Publications.

International Dyslexia Association. 1998. *Perspectives Quarterly Newsletter* 4.

Jalongo, Mary R. 1991. *Strategies for developing children's listening skills.* Bloomington, IN: Phi Delta Kappan Educational Foundation.

John-Steiner, Vera, and P. Tatter. 1983. An interactionist model of language development. *The sociogenesis of language and human conduct.* Edited by B. Bain. New York: Plenum.

Johnston, Doris. 1995. Dyslexia. *The literacy dictionary: The vocabulary of reading and writing.* Edited by Theodore L. Harris and Richard E. Hodges. Newark, DE: International Reading Association.

Kjelgaard, Jim. [1945] 1976. *Big Red.* New York: Bantam Books.

Klenk, Laura, and Michael W. Kibby. 2000. Re-mediating reading difficulties: Appraising the past, reconciling the present, constructing the future. *Handbook of reading research.* Edited by M. L. Kamil, P. B. Mosenthal, P. D. Pearson, and R. Barr. Vol. 3. Mahwah, NJ: Lawrence Erlbaum Associates.

L'Engle, Madeleine. 1962. *A wrinkle in time.* New York: Scholastic Books.

Lenski, Susan D., and Jerry L. Johns. 2000. *Improving writing: Resources, strategies, and assessments.* Dubuque, IA: Kendall/Hunt Publishing.

Lensmire, Timothy J. 1994. *When children write: Critical revisions of the writing workshop.* New York: Teachers College Press.

Lewis, C. S. [1952] 1985 On three ways of writing for children. *The riverside anthology of children's literature.* Edited by Judith Saltman. 6th ed. Boston: Houghton Mifflin.

——. 1954. *The horse and his boy.* London: Collins.

Library handbook of the Society of Christian Schools in B.C. 1997. Langley, BC: Society of Christian Schools in British Columbia.

Lindfors, Judith Walls. 1987. *Children's language and learning.* 2nd ed. Englewood Cliffs, NJ: Prentice Hall.

Loban, Walter D. 1963. *The language of elementary school children.* NCTE Research Report Number 1. Urbana, IL: National Council of Teachers of English.

——. 1976. *Language development: Kindergarten through grade twelve.* Urbana, IL: National Council of Teachers of English.

Lucas, Christopher J. 1972. *Our western educational heritage.* New York: Macmillan.

Manguel, Alberto. 1996. *A history of reading.* New York: Viking.

Martin, Bill, Jr. 1982. *Brown bear, brown bear.* Toronto, ON: Holt, Rinehart and Winston Canada.

Matthews, Mitford M. 1966. *Teaching to read: Historically considered.* Chicago: University of Chicago Press.

McCart, William F. 1994. *Learning to listen: A program to improve classroom listening skills in a variety of situations.* Toronto ON: Educators Publishing Service.

McCarthy, Bernice. 1983. *The 4MAT system: Teaching to learning styles with right and left mode techniques.* 2nd ed. Oakbrook, IL: Excel.

McCaslin, Mary M., and Thomas L. Good. 1996. *Listening in classrooms.* New York: Harper Collins.

McCaslin, Nellie. 1990. *Creative drama in the classroom.* 5th ed. White Plains, NY: Longmans.

McClure, A. 1990. *Sunrises and songs: Reading and writing poetry in an elementary classroom.* Exeter, NH: Heinemann.

McGuffey, William H. [1836] 1982. *Eclectic school series.* Milford, MI: Mott Media.

McNeil, John D. 1987. *Reading comprehension: New directions for classroom practice.* 2nd ed. Glenview, IL: Scott Foresman.

Millard, Elaine. 1997. *Differently literate: Boys, girls, and the schooling of literacy.* London: Falmer Press.

Ministry of Education, Victoria. 1988. *English language framework, P–10: Language for living.* Melbourne, Australia: Victoria Ministry of Education.

Moffett, James. 1979. Integrity in the teaching of writing. *Phi Delta Kappan* 61, no. 4:276–279.

Morgan, Michaela 2001. *How to teach poetry writing at key stage 2.* London: David Fulton Publishers.

Morgan, W. P. 1896. A case of congenital word blindness. *British Medical Journal* 2: 1378.

Morrow, Lesley Mandel, ed. 1995. *Family literacy: Connections in schools and communities.* Newark, DE: International Reading Association.

Morrow, Lesley M., Diane H. Tracey, and Caterina M. Maxwell, eds. 1995. *A survey of family literacy in the United States.* Newark, DE: International Reading Association.

Murphy, Sharon M. 1991. The code, connectionism, and basals. *Language Arts* 68, no. 3: 199–205.

Myers, M. P. 1998. Passion for poetry. *Journal of Adolescent and Adult Literacy* 41: 262–271.

Nicholson, Tom. 1999. Literacy in family and society. *Learning to read: Beyond phonics and whole language.* Edited by G. Brian Thompson and Tom Nicholson. New York: Teachers College Press, 1–22.

Perfect, K. 1999. A rhyme and reason: Poetry for the heart and head. *The Reading Teacher* 52: 728–737.

Phenix, Jo, and Doreen Scott-Dunne. 1991. *Spelling instruction that makes sense.* Markham, ON: Pembroke Publishers.

Piaget, Jean. 1971. *Insights and illusions of philosophy.* New York: World Publishing.

Pinnell, Gay Su, and Irene C. Fountas. 1998. *Word matters: Teaching phonics and spelling in the reading/writing classroom.* Portsmouth, NH: Heinemann.

Portalupi, Joann, and Ralph Fletcher. 2001. *Nonfiction craft lessons: Teaching information writing K–8.* Portland, ME: Stenhouse Publishers.

Post, Arden R. 2000. *Celebrating children's choices: 25 years of children's favorite books.* Newark, DE: International Reading Association.

Postman, Neil. 1995. *The end of education: Redefining the value of school.* New York: Knopf.

Prelutsky, Jack, ed. 1983. *The Random House book of poetry for children.* New York: Random House.

Pressley, Michael, and Vera Woloshyn. 1995. *Cognitive strategy instruction that really improves children's academic performance.* 2nd ed. Cambridge, MA: Brookline Books.

Purcell-Gates, V. 1998. Growing successful readers: Homes, communities, and schools. *Literacy for all: Issues in teaching and learning.* Edited by J. Osborn and F. Lehr. New York: Guilford Press.

Pyles, Thomas, and John Algeo. 1993. *The origins and development of the English language.* 4th ed. New York: Harcourt Brace Jovanovich.

Raczuk, Helen, and Marilyn Smith. 1997. *Invitation to readers theatre: A guidebook for using readers theatre to celebrate holidays and special events throughout the year.* Edmonton, AB: U-Otter-Read-It Press.

Read, Charles. 1975. *Children's categorization of speech sounds in English.* Urbana, IL: National Council of Teachers of English.

——. 1986. *Children's creative spelling.* London: Routledge & Kegan Paul.

Rinsland, Henry D. 1945. *A basic writing vocabulary of elementary school education.* New York: Macmillan.

Rog, Lori J., and Wilfrid Burton. 2002. Matching texts and readers: Leveling early reading materials for assessment and instruction. *The Reading Teacher* 55, no. 4: 348–356.

Rosenblatt, Louise M. 1978. *The reader, the text, the poem: The transactional theory of the literary work.* Carbondale, IL: Southern Illinois University Press.

——. 1985. The transactional theory of the literary work: Implications for research. *Researching response to literature and the teaching of literature: Points of departure.* Edited by C. Cooper. Norwood, NJ: Ablex Publ. Corp.

——. 1991. Literature—S.O.S.! *Language Arts* 68, no. 6:444–448.

Routman, R. 2000. *Kids' poems series.* New York: Scholastic.

Rummelhart, David E. 1994. Toward an interactive model of reading. *Theoretical models and processes of reading.* Edited by Robert B. Ruddell, M. R. Ruddell, and Harry Singer. 4th ed. Newark, DE: International Reading Association.

Russell, David H., and Elizabeth F. Russell. 1979. *Listening aids through the grades.* 2nd ed. Enlarged by Dorothy G. Hennings. New York: Teachers College Press.

Russell, David L. 1997. *Literature for children: A short introduction.* 3rd ed. New York: Longman.

Ryken, Leland. 2002. The Bible as literature. *Christian School Education* 5, no. 3:14–16.

Saki [H. H. Munro]. 1980. The storyteller. *The complete works of Saki.* London: Bodley Head.

Schaeffer, Francis. 1968. *The God who is there: Speaking historic Christianity into the twentieth century.* Chicago: InterVarsity Press.

Sedgwick, Fred. 1997. *Read my mind: Young children, poetry, and learning.* London: Routledge.

——. 2000. *Writing to learn: Poetry and literacy across the primary curriculum.* London: Routledge Falmer.

Seidenberg, Michael S., and James L. McClelland. 1989. A distributed, developmental model of word recognition. *Psychological Review* 96:523–568.

Shake, M. C. 1988. Teacher questions: Is there an answer? *Reading Research and Instruction* 27 (winter): 29–39.

Shannon, Patrick, and Kenneth S. Goodman, eds. 1994. *Basal readers: A second look.* Katohnah, NY: Richard C. Owen Publishers, Inc.

Simons, Herbert D., and Sandra Murphy. 1986. Oral and written language differences: Learning to read and write. *Reading – Canada – Lecture* 4(4):229–238.

Singer, Harry. 1970. Research that should have made a difference. *Elementary English* 47, no. 1:27–34.

Skinner, B. F. 1957. *Verbal behavior.* Englewood Cliffs, NJ: Prentice Hall.

Smith, Frank. 1979. The language arts and the learner's mind. *Language Arts* 56, no. 2: 118–125.

——. 1982. *Writing and the writer.* Hillsdale, NJ: Lawrence Erlbaum Assoc.

——. 1988. *Joining the literacy club: Further essays into education.* Portsmouth, NH: Heinemann.

——. 1994. *Understanding reading: A psycholinguistic analysis of reading and learning to read.* 5th ed. Hillsdale, NJ: Lawrence Erlbaum Associates.

——. 1997. *Reading without nonsense.* 3rd ed. New York: Teachers College Press.

Smith, Nila B. [1965] 1986. *American reading instruction.* Newark, DE: International Reading Association.

Smith, Patricia G., ed. 2001. *Talking classrooms: Shaping children's learning through oral language instruction.* Newark, DE: International Reading Association.

Sparks, Dennis. 1992. Merging content knowledge and pedagogy: An interview with Lee Shulman. *Journal of Staff Development* 13, no. 1:14–17.

Spiegel, Dixie Lee. 1991. Materials to introduce children to poetry. *The Reading Teacher* 44:430–448.

Stammer, John. 1977. Target: The basics of listening. *Language Arts* 54 (September): 661–664.

Stanovich, Keith E. 1986. Matthew effects in reading: Some consequences of individual differences in the acquisition of literacy. *Reading Research Quarterly* 21:360–407.

——. 1991. Word recognition: Changing perspectives. *Handbook of reading research.* Edited by R. Barr, M. L. Kamil, P. Mosenthal, and P. D. Pearson. Vol. 12: Hillsdale, NJ: Lawrence Erlbaum Associates.

——, ed. 2000. *Progress in understanding reading: Scientific foundations and new frontiers.* New York: Guilford Press.

Stauffer, Russell G. 1980. *The language experience approach to the teaching of reading.* 2nd ed. New York: Harper & Row.

Sterenberg, Evelyn, and Sharon DeMoor. 1991. *Libraries in the '90s: A handbook for Christian schools.* Edmonton, AB: Christian Schools International. District 11.

Stewig, John W. 1983. *Informal drama in the elementary language arts program.* New York: Teachers College Press.

Strickland, Dorothy S. 1997. Language and literacy: The poetry connection. *Language Arts* 74: 201–205.

——. 1998. *Teaching phonics today: A primer for educators.* Newark, DE: International Reading Association.

Strickland, Dorothy S., and Lesley Mandel Morrow, eds. 2000. *Beginning reading and writing.* Newark, DE: International Reading Assoc.

Stronks, Gloria G. 1990. *The Christian middle school: An ethos of caring.* Grand Rapids, MI: Christian Schools International.

Stronks, Gloria G., and Doug G. Blomberg, eds. 1993. *A vision with a task: Christian schooling for responsive discipleship.* Grand Rapids, MI: Baker Books.

Sulzby, Elizabeth. 1991. The development of the young child and the emergence of literacy. *Handbook of research on teaching the English language arts.* Edited by J. Flood, J. M. Jensen, D. Lapp, and J. R. Squire. New York: Macmillan.

Survey of recommended reading lists: Preschool through grade twelve. 1998. Colorado Springs, CO: Association of Christian Schools International.

Sword, E. H., and V. F. McCarthy, eds. 1997. *A child's anthology of poetry*. New York: Scholastic.

Tarasoff, Mary. 1990. *Spelling strategies you can teach.* Victoria, BC: Pixelart Graphics–Active Learning Institute.

Tarlington, Carole, and Patrick Verriour. 1983. *Offstage: Elementary education through drama.* Toronto, ON: Oxford University Press.

——. 1991. *Role drama.* Markham, Portsmouth, NH: Heinemann.

Taylor, D., and C. Dorsey-Gaines. 1988. *Growing up literate: Learning from inner school families.* Portsmouth, NH: Heinemann.

Teale, William H., and Elizabeth Sulzby, eds. 1986. *Emergent literacy: Writing and reading.* Norwood, NJ: Ablex Publishing Corporation.

Temple, Charles A., and Jean W. Gillet. 1989. *Language arts: Learning processes and teaching practices.* 2nd ed. Glenview, IL: Scott Foresman. [1997. 2nd ed., paperbound. Addison-Wesley]

Temple, Charles A., Ruth Nathan, Frances Temple, and Nancy A. Burris. 1993. *The beginnings of writing.* 3rd ed. Boston: Allyn & Bacon.

Thogmartin, Mark B. 1994. The prevalence of phonics instruction in fundamentalist Christian schools. *Journal of Research on Christian Education* 3, no. 1:103–130.

——. 1996. *Teach a child to read with children's books: Combining story reading, phonics, and writing to promote reading success.* Bloomington, IN: ERIC Clearinghouse on Reading, English, and Communication. The Family Literacy Center: EDINFO Press.

Thomas, Ves. 1979. *Teaching spelling: Canadian word lists and instructional techniques.* 2nd ed. Toronto, ON: Gage.

Thornton, Tamara P. 1996. *Handwriting in America: A cultural history.* New Haven, CT: Yale University Press.

Thurber, Donald N. 1984. *D'Nealian manuscript: A continuous stroke approach to handwriting.* Navato, CA: Academic Therapy Publications.

Tierney, Robert J., Mark A. Carter, and Laura E. Desai. 1991. *Portfolio assessment in the reading-writing classroom.* Norwood, MA: Christopher-Gordon Publishers.

Tierney, Robert J., and John E. Readence. 2000. *Reading strategies and practices: A compendium.* 5th ed. Boston: Allyn & Bacon.

Tizard, Barbara, and Martha Hughes. 1984. *Young children learning.* Cambridge, MA: Harvard University Press.

Tolkien, J.R.R. 1937. *The hobbit: Or there and back again.* London: Allen & Unwin.

——. 1965. *The lord of the rings.* 2nd ed. Boston: Houghton Mifflin.

——. 1938. On fairy stories. Reprinted in *The Tolkien Reader.* 1966. New York: Ballantine Books.

Tompkins, Gail E., and Kenneth Hoskisson. 1995. *Language arts: Content and teaching strategies.* 3rd ed. New York: Merrill.

Tough, Joan. 1976. *Listening to children talking: A guide to the appraisal of children's language use.* Portsmouth, NH: Heinemann.

——. 1977. *The development of meaning: A study of children's use of language.* London: Allen & Unwin.

——. 1979. *Talking and learning: A guide to fostering communication skills in nursery and infant schools.* London: Ward Lock Educational.

Treiman, Rebecca. 1993. *Beginning to spell.* New York: Oxford University Press.

Ur, Penny. 1984. *Teaching listening comprehension.* New York: Cambridge University Press.

Vacca, Richard T., and JoAnne L. Vacca. 2002. *Content area reading: Literacy and learning across the curriculum.* 7th ed. Boston: Allyn & Bacon.

Van Brummelen, Harro W. 1994. *Steppingstones to curriculum: A biblical path.* Seattle: Alta Vista Press.

——. 1998. *Walking with God in the classroom: Christian approaches to learning and teaching.* 2nd ed. Seattle: Alta Vista Press.

Van Dyk, John. 1995. What is distinctive Christian teaching? Paper presented at Council of Christian Colleges and Universities Teacher Education Workshop, August 25–29, Cedar Springs, WA.

——. 2000. *The craft of Christian teaching: A classroom journey.* Sioux Center, IA: Dordt College Press.

Vitz, Paul. 1986. *Censorship: Evidence of bias in our children's textbooks.* Ann Arbor, MI: Servant Books.

Vygotsky, Lev S. 1962. *Thought and language.* Cambridge, MA: MIT Press.

——. 1978. *The development of higher psychological processes.* Edited by M. Cole, V. John-Steiner, S. Scribner, and E. Souberman. Cambridge, MA: Harvard University Press.

Waber, Bernard. 1972. *Ira sleeps over.* Boston: Houghton Mifflin.

Walker, Barbara J. 2000. *Diagnostic teaching of reading: Techniques for instruction and assessment.* 4th ed. Columbus, OH: Merrill/Prentice Hall.

Watts, Irene N. 1990. *Just a minute: Ten short plays and activities for your classroom.* Markham, ON: Pembroke Publishers and Portsmouth, NH: Heinemann.

Weaver, Brenda. 2000. *Leveling books K–6: Matching readers to the text.* Newark, DE: International Reading Association.

Weaver, Constance. 1979. *Grammar for teachers: Perspectives and definitions.* Urbana, IL: National Council of Teachers of English.

——. 1996. *Teaching grammar in context.* Portsmouth, NH: Boynton/Cook Publishers.

Weaver, Constance, ed. 1998a. *Lessons to share on teaching grammar in context.* Portsmouth, NH: Boynton/Cook Publishers.

——. 1998b. *Reconsidering a balanced approach to reading.* Urbana, IL: National Council of Teachers of English.

Weir, Ruth. 1962. *Language in the crib.* The Hague: Mouton.

Wells, Gordon C. 1986. *The meaning makers: Children learning language and using language to learn.* Portsmouth, NH: Heinemann.

Wepman, J. H. 1958. *Auditory discrimination test.* Chicago: University of Chicago Press.

Wiener, Roberta B., and Judith H. Cohen. 1997. *Literacy portfolios: Using assessment to guide instruction.* Upper Saddle River, NJ: Merrill.

Wildman, Daniel, and Martin Kling. 1978–1979. Semantic, syntactic, and spatial anticipation in reading. *Reading Research Quarterly* 14, no. 2: 128–164.

Wolterstorff, Nicholas. 1980. *Educating for responsible action.* Grand Rapids, MI: Christian Schools International/Eerdmans.

Wolvin, Andrew D., and Carolyn G. Coakley. 1979. *Listening instruction.* Urbana, IL: ERIC Clearinghouse on Communication Skills.

Index

Notes to the Index User: A reference containing an "n" (e.g., 83n2) refers to an endnote appearing on that page. Names appearing in **boldface** type are of authors who appear in the reference list.

A

B

F

G

N

O

P

Z